OPEN DEMOCRACY

Open Democracy

Reinventing Popular Rule for the Twenty-First Century

Hélène Landemore

PRINCETON UNIVERSITY PRESS
PRINCETON AND OXFORD

Copyright © 2020 by Princeton University Press

Requests for permission to reproduce material from this work
should be sent to permissions@press.princeton.edu

Published by Princeton University Press
41 William Street, Princeton, New Jersey 08540
6 Oxford Street, Woodstock, Oxfordshire OX20 1TR

press.princeton.edu

All Rights Reserved

Library of Congress Cataloging-in-Publication Data

Names: Landemore, Hélène, 1976– author.
Title: Open democracy : reinventing popular rule for the twenty-first century /
    Hélène Landemore.
Description: Princeton : Princeton University Press, [2020] | Includes bibliographical
    references and index.
Identifiers: LCCN 2020022229 (print) | LCCN 2020022230 (ebook) |
    ISBN 9780691181998 (hardcover) | ISBN 9780691212395 (paperback) |
    ISBN 9780691208725 (ebook)
Subjects: LCSH: Deliberative democracy. | Representative government and
    representation. | Political participation. | Deliberative democracy—Iceland—Case studies.
Classification: LCC JC423 .L3356 2020 (print) | LCC JC423 (ebook) | DDC 321.8–dc23
LC record available at https://lccn.loc.gov/2020022229
LC ebook record available at https://lccn.loc.gov/2020022230

British Library Cataloging-in-Publication Data is available

Editorial: Matt Rohal
Production Editorial: Kathleen Cioffi
Jacket Design: Layla Mac Rory
Production: Erin Suydam
Publicity: Kate Hensley and Kate Farquhar-Thomson
Copyeditor: Karen Verde

This book has been composed in Adobe Text and Gotham

Printed on acid-free paper. ∞

Printed in the United States of America

10 9 8 7 6 5 4 3 2 1

To Sophie and Émilie

CONTENTS

ACKNOWLEDGMENTS

This book took seven years to write, and the acknowledgments I owe are consequently much longer than my memory can keep up with. I apologize in advance if I forgot anyone.

My gratitude goes first to Bernard Manin and Nadia Urbinati, whose respective work has been deeply influential on my views and probed me to question the idea that the historical paradigm of "representative democracy" was the only, let alone best form of democracy we could achieve in the modern age. I realize now that this book is in part an attempt to add my voice to the 2008 conversation that I put them in with each other for the French online magazine *La vie des idées*.[1]

This book also owes a lot to the participants in the Montreal Political Theory Manuscript Workshop that I attended at MacGill University in 2011 to discuss my earlier book, *Democratic Reason*. Someone (I'm very sorry I can't remember who it was) then asked a question that stumped as much as honored me: "What does an ideal Landemorean democracy look like?" This book is, nine years later, an imperfect but more substantial answer to the question than I could deliver then.

I owe many debts of gratitude to the unique nation of Iceland and the generous people in it who have welcomed me and helped me figure out the complexities of Icelandic politics as well as facilitated unforgettable tours of the stunning countryside. I would like in particular to single out Kristinn Már Ársælsson, Thorvaldur Gilfason, Salvör Nordal, Katrín Oddsdóttir, and Jón Ólafsson, as well as Philippe Urfalino, an adoptive Icelander, and his family for kindly hosting me in Reykjavik.

I thank the members of the Great National Debate's randomly selected regional assemblies of Rouen in Normandy and Fort-de-France in Martinique, both of which I was lucky to attend in March 2019. I thank the members of the Citizen Convention on Climate Change in Paris that I followed over the Fall 2019 and Spring 2020. I thank the organizers of these events, specifically Judith Ferrando and Yves Mathieu at Mission Publiques and Sophie Guillain and Gilles-Laurent Rayssac at Res Publica for giving me access and insight into

---

1. Landemore, Manin, and Urbinati 2008.

these processes. I thank Jean-Michel Fourniau et Loïc Blondiaux for their work on the Governance Committee of the Citizen Convention on Climate Change and for helping keep the process documented by and accessible to researchers.

I thank the Yale MacMillan Center for funding most of the field work related to these events.

I thank the participants in four workshops on my book manuscript at various of its stages: one in May 2016 that I convened at Yale University; one organized by Rob Reich at Stanford University in June 2017; a smaller joint workshop I co-organized with Cristina Lafont at Yale University in June 2018; and a larger one organized by Pierre-Etienne Vandamme at the Leuven Center for Public Law, Belgium in October 2019.

I thank the organizers and audiences of countless other workshops, seminars, conferences, and colloquia over the years and in many countries for helping me test, refine, and improve the ideas in this book. In recent months I'm particularly grateful to the audience of the Political Theory Workshop of Nuffield College at Oxford University, which led to a considerable reorganization of what are now chapters 4 and 5. I'm also grateful to a similarly stimulating workshop on chapter 4 at the University of Chicago.

I thank particular individuals, including within these audiences, for help on all or parts of the project, whether in the form of written or oral comments, email exchanges, or enlightening conversations. My gratitude goes in particular to Danielle Allen, Arash Abizadeh, Christopher Achen, Samuel Bagg, Tongdong Bai, Udit Bathia, Camille Bedock, Eric Beerbohm, Deborah Beim, Daniel Bell, Seyla Benhabib, Lucy Bernholz, François Blais, Matteo Bonotti, Julia Cagé, Daniela Cammack, Joseph Carens, Simone Chambers, Elton Chan, Jiwei Ci, Yvonne Chiu, Joshua Cohen, Chiara Cordelli, Hervé Crès, Thomas Cristiano, Zhiyuan Cui, Lisa Disch, Hugo Drochon, John Dunn, Pascaline Dupas, Zachary Elkins, Jon Elster, Eva Erman, Cécile Fabre, Eric Fabri, Andrea Felicetti, Isabelle Ferreras, Jim Fishkin, Bryan Ford, Archon Fung, Jeffrey Friedman, Shterna Friedman, Bryan Garsten, Matthew Gentzkow, Tom Ginsburg, Robert Goodin, Sean Gray, Jürgen Habermas, Jacob Hacker, Clarissa Hayward, Baogang He, Claudia Heiss, Ted Hopf, Donald Bello Hutt, Julien Jeanneney, Huang Jing, Sean Ingham, Demetra Kasimis, John Keane, Joohyung Kim, Alexander Kirshner, Jack Knight, Henrik Kugelberg, Carlo Invernizzi Accetti, Cécile Laborde, Cristina Lafont, Dimitri Landa, Matthew Landauer, Melissa Lane, Youngjae Lee, Dominic Leggett, Ethan Leib, Larry Lessig, Chenyang Li, Mihn Ly, Terry MacDonald, Pia Mancini, Bernard Manin, Karuna Mantena, Jenny Mansbridge, John McCormick, David Miller, Lala Muradova, Patrizia Nanz, Shmuel Nili, Josiah Ober, Martin O'Neill, Zeynep Pamuk, William Partlett, Lex Paulson, Tiaxo Peixoto, James Penner, Tomer Perry, Rick Pildes, Alex Prescott-Crouch, Adam Przeworski, Danny Quah, Rob Reich, Mathias Risse, John Roemer, Geneviève Rousselière, Jennifer Rubinstein, Jay Ruckelhaus,

Javier Gallego Saade, Rahul Sagar, Emma Saunders-Hastings, Thomas Scanlon, Hans Schattle, Claudia Schwalisz, Melissa Schwartzberg, Maija Setälä, Yves Sintomer, Santiago Siri, Steven Smith, Jiewuh Song, Sarah Song, Nicolas Southwood, Céline Spector, Amia Srinivasan, Jürg Steiner, Ana Stilz, Nenad Stojanovic, Susan Stokes, Peter Stone, Milan Svolik, Kudzai Takavarasha, Sor Hoon Tan, John Tasoulias, Nora Timmermans, Richard Tuck, Mark Tushnet, Nadia Urbinati, Laura Valentini, Chiara Valsangia, Ronald Van Crombrugge, Els Van Dongen, Sixtine Van Outryve d'Ydewalle, Cyril Velikanov, Camila Vergara, Daniel Viehoff, Mark Warren, Stuart White, Bryan Wong, Yongnian Zheng, and Linda Zerilli.

Several people deserve special thank yous for extensive, sometimes line-by-line comments on the whole manuscript: Lisa Disch, Giulia Oskian, Pierre-Etienne Vandamme, and David Wiens.

I am grateful to the whip-smart graduate students at Yale University (some of whom have long graduated), who have helped along the way with excellent research and editorial assistance. They include Joshua Braver, David Froomkin, Samantha Godwin, Mie Inouye, Maximilian Krahé, Vatsal Naresh, Erin Pineda, Naomi Scheinerman, and Alexander Trubowitz.

Thank you to my Princeton University Press editors, Rob Tempio and Matt Rohal, for their enthusiastic support and for shepherding this project to completion. Thank you to the two anonymous reviewers for excellent comments and for making this publication process much less painful than the previous one.

Finally, my gratitude goes to my empowering, true-blue husband, Darko Jelaca, who was renovating our house and keeping our two girls fed and entertained while, at various times, I was traveling the world to research chapters or present my ideas. This book would not have been possible without his love, support, and many sacrifices.

I dedicate this book to our fun, energetic, and endlessly amazing daughters, Sophie and Émilie. Thank you for keeping me honest, inspired, and loved "bluer than the ocean" and "bigger than the universe."

PROLOGUE

Democracy is in crisis, or so we are incessantly told. The 2016 US presidential elections and the Brexit referendum are just the most striking illustrations of a larger phenomenon observable across the Western world. Everywhere, there is widespread backlash against established electoral elites, a backlash that can in turn empower authoritarian or populist rulers and ultimately threaten democracy's foundations. Democracy is on the defensive beyond the Western world, too. After the spectacular failure of democratic nation-building attempts in Iraq and Libya, some started to speak of a global "democratic recession" (Diamond 2008). The bitter end of the Arab Spring, with the stunning but fragile exception of Tunisia, only seems to confirm the trend. Meanwhile, some voices are emboldened to reject democracy altogether (Brennan 2016) while others tout China and Singapore—so-called meritocratic systems—as the new path forward (e.g., Bai 2020; Bell 2013; Chan 2013; Khanna 2017). As the century of Chinese superpower unfolds, democracy thus seems to be on the wane. This decline is taking place even as new global threats, such as climate change or, as I am finishing this book, the first of what are probaby many pandemics to come, present new challenges to any local regime forms and seemingly call for coordinated global solutions that the current international order is ill-equipped to offer.

Inverting the negative interpretation of recent events, however, one could argue that the crisis of democracy as we know it—which has come to be symbolized for many by Trump or Brexit—is a sign of its vitality as a normative ideal. People throughout the Western world (and beyond as well) resent and distrust their political personnel and institutions precisely because they fail to deliver the promise of democracy: *demokratia*—people's power. The silver lining of otherwise disenchanting events is that they tap into an obvious desire to gain or regain control and wrest power from runaway elites, seen as no longer, not sufficiently, or not at all responsive to the wishes of the population. The crisis of democracy could be, in other words, a case of frustrated, perhaps even rising, democratic expectations coming to terms with the limitations of an existing paradigm.

The flaws of this existing paradigm of democracy are well-known. "Representative democracy," as we call it, is historically dated and tied to eighteenth-century epistemologies and technologies. It is arguably a liberal-republican rather than democratic construct, primarily oriented toward the protection of certain individual rights rather than the empowerment of citizens per se and congenitally tied to the ideal of the mixed regime known as "representative government." This regime form has historically consisted in privileging the idea of people's *consent* to power over that of people's *exercise* of power. On such a skewed understanding of democracy, the decisions of elected elites are equated with the people's choice. But this equivalence, long taken for granted, is now being questioned. Because representative democracy is clearly not democratic enough—some would say it has become explicitly oligarchic and, more specifically, plutocratic in recent decades—the people then turn their only direct access to power in this regime form, namely voting in national elections or the occasional referendum, into an opportunity for exercising their voice against the system rather than for the common good. (Although these two sometimes overlap, we have no guarantee that this will be the case.)

Yet not all the news is bad. Democracy remains a cherished ideal and an aspiration for populations the world over. Democracy is the official regime form of more than half the countries in the world, where it is institutionalized not just in perfectible electoral politics at the national level but also in deeply rooted and long-standing participatory practices at the local level, from the town hall meetings of New England in the United States to the constitutionally mandated *gram sabas* of Indian villages,[1] and even in practices that scale all the way from the local to the national, as in the National Public Policy Conferences in Brazil.[2] Furthermore, there are signs that, where troubled countries are not succumbing to the temptation of antidemocratic populism and/or straightforward authoritarianism, they seek to deepen democracy in deliberative and participatory ways. In 2012, in Finland, for example, a Citizens' Initiative resulted in the passing of a law on marriage equality.[3] In 2017, in South Korea, a Citizens' Assembly gave recommendations on energy policies that were implemented over the executive's preferred choice.[4] In 2017, Mongolia passed a law requiring that a Deliberative Poll (a body of randomly selected citizens gathered for a few days to deliberate about political issues) be held prior to constitutional amendments.[5] In May 2018, in Ireland, a popular referendum

---

1. See, e.g., Sanyal and Rao 2018.

2. See, e.g., Pogrebinschi 2013.

3. Six years before, Ireland had already used a mixed assembly (two-thirds random, one-third officials) to pass a law decriminalizing homosexuality. See https://blogs.oii.ox.ac.uk/policy/finnish-decision-to-allow-same-sex-marriage-shows-the-power-of-citizen-initiatives/.

4. https://thediplomat.com/2017/10/south-koreas-nuclear-energy-debate/.

5. https://news.stanford.edu/2017/05/02/collaboration-stanford-leads-mongolian-parliament-passing-law-public-opinion-polling/. Last accessed July 23, 2018.

validated the recommendations of a specially convened Citizens' Assembly of ninety-nine randomly selected citizens to decriminalize abortion.[6] Taiwan is now involving citizens in government decisions via crowdsourcing techniques, which have allowed for successful negotiations among the Taiwanese authorities, citizens, and companies like Uber and Airbnb.[7] In 2019, in Belgium, the Parliament of the German-speaking community voted to establish a randomly chosen Citizens' Council to help the elected parliament chamber formulate legislation. That same year, my native country of France engaged in its largest deliberative experiment to date with a two-month-long Great National Debate involving around 1.5 million participants and immediately followed it with a months-long Citizen Convention on Climate Change, a national-level Assembly of 150 randomly selected people tasked with making socially fair policy recommendations on how to tackle climate change. According to a recent OECD report, a "deliberative wave" of experiments has washed over the Western world in the last ten years.[8] All over the world, meanwhile, countless experiments in so-called democratic innovation[9] have been proving for several decades, at least, that politics can be conducted both more democratically and successfully.

Among all these examples, three experiences specifically account for this book's relative optimism in these times of democratic despair. In 2012, I became involved in the study of the then ongoing process of constitutional redrafting in Iceland, which quietly revolutionized for me, and seemingly many people around the world, the meaning and scope of democratic politics. Instead of the usual appointed officials writing a text behind closed doors and submitting it much later to a popular referendum, Icelanders chose a radically new format, involving a randomly selected forum of 950 citizens, an elected assembly of twenty-five citizens, and the use of crowdsourcing techniques that allowed the public to participate in the drafting of the new constitution.[10] The process resulted in a document that compares favorably with constitutional proposals written by Icelandic experts at about the same time. That document was approved in a 2012 referendum by two-thirds of the voting population. It is one of the most inclusive constitutions in history and touts some radically new ideas, such as the nationalization of previously unowned natural resources, the right to Internet access, and the principles of citizens' initiative (the right

---

6. https://www.irishtimes.com/news/ireland/irish-news/the-citizens-assembly-a-canny-move-on-the-road-to-repeal-1.3510373.

7. https://blog.pol.is/uber-responds-to-vtaiwans-coherent-blended-volition-3e9b75102b9b.

8. See OECD 2020.

9. See Smith 2009.

10. All these novel practices, incidentally, are perfectly scalable (a point I return to in the chapter on Iceland).

for citizens to propose a law) and right of referral (the right for citizens to initiate a referendum on an existing law).

Studying the Icelandic process over the last few years has been eye-opening. First, that the institutional features of the Icelandic process could come as such a surprise, not just to me but to many international observers around the world, said something about the limitations of the dominant conceptual framework we use to think about democracy. It opened the possibility that representative democracy, the model of democracy with which we are so familiar, may not be the only possible institutionalization of the ideal of people's power, including at scale and even within familiar liberal constitutional frameworks.

Second, if a constitutional process—the process meant to generate the fundamental law of the land—could be reinvented in such innovative and inclusive ways, why could processes for ordinary law-making not be reinvented as well? What contemporary Icelanders did for constitution-making appeared to me as an inspiration for democracy more generally. The Icelandic case is therefore fundamental to the argument made in this book. The Icelandic example also emboldened me to conclude that the limits of our current systems, as well as the changes brought about by globalization and the digital revolution, call for a radically different approach to the question of the best regime—one that interrogates the very institutional principles of democracy as we practice it today.

Another source of inspiration was a crowdsourced policy process in Finland in which I was involved between 2012 and 2013.[11] The focus was the reform of a law on off-road regulation (snowmobile regulation, for the most part), which the Finnish government had until then failed to put in place and for which they were willing to try innovative participatory methods. The design involved the public at three distinct stages: problem identification, idea-gathering, and solution evaluations. I learned from the experiment and, more specifically, from reading and sifting through the comments that had to be synthesized and organized between these three stages that, when properly incentivized and mobilized, citizens can be remarkable sources of arguments, information, and even solutions. Like the Icelandic one, the Finnish experiment allowed me to verify empirically, to a degree, a hypothesis I had formulated in earlier work on the basis of an idealized model of democracy and some limited amount of macro-evidence about democracies' comparative success.[12]

11. I arrived at this project through an encounter with Tanja Aitamurto, the principal instigator on this project, who was then a PhD student from Finland researching crowdsourcing methods for her dissertation and a Visiting Scholar at Stanford University, where I was on sabbatical. Two additional collaborators—Ashish Goel (Professor of Engineering at Stanford University) and his then PhD student David Lee—were brought onboard later on, to provide an algorithm called "CrowdConsensus" that allowed us to rank and evaluate the crowd's input as per the crowd's preferences.

12. See Landemore 2012 and 2013a.

Finally, just as I was putting what I thought were the final touches to this book in the Fall 2018, France engaged in an unprecedented experience of large-scale deliberation: the Great National Debate, followed a few months later by the French Citizen Convention on Climate Change. I spent much of 2019 and the first half of 2020 traveling back and forth between the United States and France to study these experiments.[13] The French Great National Debate, though flawed in many respects, had the virtue of falsifying the claim that ambitious deliberative experiments can effectively take place only in small and homogenous countries like Iceland, or Estonia, or even Ireland (a common objection to my use of the Icelandic case study until then). The French Great National Debate also falsified the claim that such large-scale experiments can never amount to anything, since one direct result of it was the national Citizen Convention on Climate Change.[14] I did my best to integrate France as a shadow case in this book, to illustrate the fact that a country that is both large (67 million people) and multiculturally diverse can experiment, somewhat successfully, with greater inclusion, deliberation, and participation. Whether the Great Debate and the French Convention on Climate Change point the way toward the possibility of "a Republic of permanent deliberation,"[15] as in French President Macron's arresting formula, is still very much an open question at this moment in time. But these measures provide, to my mind, reasons for optimism.

This book builds on my previous work on epistemic democracy, the intuitions I developed in the context of a close study of these three experiments, and on all else I know about other democratic innovations. It aims to change minds, develop intuitions, and expand our imaginations by introducing into our conceptual toolbox a new paradigm of democracy and a new metaphor: open democracy. Open democracy is the ideal of a regime in which actual exercise of power is accessible to ordinary citizens via novel forms of democratic representation. Avoiding the pitfalls of both electoral democracy and direct democracy (as the wrong cure for the problems of electoral democracy), the institutional paradigm of popular rule offered here is primarily non-electoral yet (more) democratically representative than any existing regime form. This paradigm of open democracy can be summarized as "representing and being represented in turn."

13. At problematic costs to the environment, as the members of the Convention on Climate Change I became friendly with did not shy away from frequently pointing out.

14. *Pace* some French critics who implausibly claim that the two experiments have nothing to do with each other and that in most important aspects, the Convention on Climate Change is "the anti-Grand Débat."

15. President Macron used this phrase to describe his intentions for the country on January 15, 2019, at the end of a heavily mediatized, 7-hour-long debate with regional mayors in the city of Bourgtheroulde in Normandy.

The book recasts today's "crisis of democracy" in a sunnier light—as the historic moment when it becomes obvious that democracy's meaning and potential are much greater than the sum of electoral moments to which democracy is currently reduced. It therefore reaffirms the value and meaning of *people's power*. Perhaps now we may finally break free from old paradigms and threadbare institutions to reinvent popular rule for the twenty-first century. Against some significant trends today, this book resists the temptation to give up on democracy. It pursues instead the constructive strategy of offering an alternative normative conception of popular rule, one true to the democratic values of inclusiveness and equality, and one we can use to imagine and design more participatory, responsive, and effective institutions. Practically speaking, this book aims to nudge along efforts to put people's power back at the center of the institutions by which societies rule and organize themselves.

OPEN DEMOCRACY

1

Introduction

> The vast and wonderful knowledge of this universe is locked in the bosoms
> of its individual souls. To tap this mighty reservoir of experience, knowledge,
> beauty, love, and deed we must appeal not to the few, not to some souls, but
> to all. [. . .] The real argument for democracy is, then, that in the people we
> have the source of that endless life and unbounded wisdom which the rulers of
> men must have.
>
> —W.E.B. DU BOIS, "ON THE RULING OF MEN" (1999: 84)

Democracy means, etymologically, "people's power." As a regime form, it
means rule in which all can share equally. But what does popular rule mean,
practically?

To the ancient Greeks who invented democracy, it meant gathering in a
public space—the agora in the fifth century BC, the larger Pnyx in the fourth—
and making laws on the basis of an agenda set by a randomly selected assembly of five hundred other citizens.[1] To the Icelandic Vikings, who invented
a different form of it in Northern Europe a few centuries later, democracy
meant gathering every summer in a large field south of Reykjavik known as
Thingvellir, the place of their annual parliament, and talking things through
until they reached decisions about their common fate. To the members of

---

1. Around the same time, India was also practicing forms of deliberative institutions (*sabhas,
kathas, panchayats,* and *samajs*) which, even though they were not a pure form of democracy
since not everyone in them was equal, were nonetheless open to "different qualities of people and
opinions" rather than "the scene of a pronunciamento by caste elders" (Bayly 2006: 187, cited in
Sanyal and Rao 2018: 7) and democratic to that extent. It appears as if similar institutions grew
up from completely separate roots all over the world.

the Swiss confederacy a few centuries later, democracy meant participating in open-air assemblies—the famous *Landsgemeinde* that could gather up to 10,000 male adults—to vote on the laws of their respective cantons. To New England Puritans who fled Europe in the seventeenth century to found their own self-ruling communities in the New World, it meant determining their common fate at regular town hall meetings. To some of the Native American tribes, it had all along meant talking things over and making decisions among equals.

Democracy, in these older, perhaps simpler times, was "open." In theory, any individual qualifying as a member of the political community (admittedly defined in exclusionary ways) could access the center of power and participate in the various stages of decision-making. Citizens could literally walk into the public space to be given a chance to speak and be heard. Once you were counted as a member of the demos, or a citizen, in other words, you were *in*.

Our modern representative democracies are very different. The franchise is, admittedly, much broader. It is indeed "universal" with respect to a given demos, in that it extends to all native-born or naturalized adults of that demos. Modern democracies have extended political rights and citizenship to a number of people who would have been excluded under the premodern arrangements. Similarly, restrictions on who can run for elections and hold political offices have been progressively eliminated, except for some remaining age limitations. Yet many have the feeling in modern representative democracies that even among the legal demos ordinary citizens are left out of the most important sites of political power, while the political personnel form an elite separate from them. Modern parliaments themselves are intimidating buildings that are hard to access for the vast majority of citizens. They are typically gated and guarded. It also feels to many as if only certain types of people—those with the right suit, the right accent, bank account, connections, or even last names[2]—are welcome to enter them. To top it all off, the legislation that comes out of such places is largely incomprehensible, written by and for lawyers.[3] Something has thus arguably been lost between ancient democracies and modern ones: accessibility or, in other words, openness to the ordinary person. It is as if the

2. On the dynastic nature of American politics, see for example E. Dal Bó, P. Dal Bó, and Snyder 2009, who show that "political power is self-perpetuating: legislators who hold power for longer become more likely to have relatives entering Congress in the future." I don't have evidence for other countries, but I suspect the same holds true in many, perhaps most advanced democracies.

3. Pia Mancini, political scientist and public speaker, has made this point powerfully in her presentations about the need to, in her words, "upgrade" democracy for the twenty-first century. She often starts her lectures by reading a piece of legislation and then asking the audience who among them understood it, with predictable and edifying results.

eighteenth-century move to "representative democracy," a mediated form of democracy seen as unavoidable in mass, commercial societies, had been, at the same time—despite greater enfranchisement—a move toward what I will call the "enclosure of power."[4] But does the necessary restriction of the ruler class to a manageable number of people have to entail such an enclosure of power?

This entailment seems doubtful. For one thing, the enclosure of power in the eighteenth century was less a practical necessity than the product of an ideology. The representative systems we now call "democracies" were indeed initially intended as anything but democratic. Instead, they were initially the product of a liberal-republican, rather than strictly democratic, value system. By "liberal," I mean here deriving from an ideology primarily concerned with protecting the inalienable rights of individuals against the encroachment of governments, including popular governments.[5] By "republican," I mean an ideology where the ideal of non-domination of the individual trumps the ideal of popular rule (though those two ideals can perhaps be reconciled).[6] This priority of liberal-republican commitments and goals over purely democratic ones was compatible with giving the people some say over the choice of rulers, but not as clearly compatible with the ideal of popular rule per se.

The American Founders, for example, famously claimed to want to create a "republic," as opposed to a democracy, which they associated with mob rule. James Madison, in particular, feared the tyranny of the majority as much as he disliked and rejected the old monarchical orders.[7] He wanted to create a mixed regime that would protect individuals not only from powerful minorities but also from oppressive majorities. Against oppressive majorities, Madison's solution had several prongs: representation by elected elites, with representation serving to filter and refine the raw judgments of the people; a large size

4. Another form of closure, which this book does not address, comes from the progressive transfer of power from political institutions to national and suprational administrations and bureaucracies (in Europe in particular). Further research will be needed to figure out how to resist this tendency or implement the principles of open democracy there as well.

5. For a critical take on this common understanding of the word "liberal," see Rosenblatt (2018), who emphasizes the Cold War origins of this interpretation, specifically the fear of totalitarianism, and points out to an older meaning of liberalism as referring to "a giving and a civic-minded citizen; it meant understanding one's connectedness to other citizens and acting in ways conducive to the common good" (Rosenblatt 2018: 4). Although I take this historical point, I do not consider it far-fetched to see in the motivations of the eighteenth century advocates of representative government elements of liberalism as we define it today, including a fear of both tyrannical majorities and direct democracy as they understood it.

6. See the excellent volume by Elazar and Rousselière (2019) for an exploration of the complex historical and conceptual relationships between republicanism and democracy.

7. For arguments to the contrary, see de Djinn (2019) to the effect that Madison, far from being a mere liberal or a liberal-republican, was in fact an authentically democratic republican with the utmost respect for the majoritarian principle. See also Tuck 2016.

to the polity, which would multiply and consequently neutralize large factions; and also a cluster of counter-majoritarian mechanisms and institutions, including federalism, bicameralism, the presidential veto, and judicial review. Most important for Madison, the American republic would be characterized, in contrast to ancient democracies, by "the total exclusion of the people in its collective capacity from any share in [the government of the republic]" (Hamilton, Madison, and Jay 2003, 63). The founders thus explicitly presented as a superior feature of their intended republic the fact that it was not meant to rest on *demos-kratos*, or people's power, but instead on the power of elected elites, itself properly limited by the separation of powers and a complex system of checks and balances.

Representative "democracy" was originally intended as a form of elite rule in contrast with rule by ordinary citizens. Yet the authors of the Federalists Papers and their fellows unsurprisingly did not describe the central distinguishing feature of their system as elected oligarchy versus democracy, but rather as "representative" versus "direct" rule.[8] The effect of this emphasis was to suggest that elite rule was a necessary solution to a problem of size as well as to entrench the notion that representation implied elections (rather than, for example, the use of the lot, as in ancient Athens or the Italian republics). It could be presented as a simple fact that, because ordinary citizens could not all rule at once together, they had to delegate power to an elected elite. This subtle semantic slide has blinded subsequent generations to another conceptual possibility: that of representative (indirect) rule by ordinary citizens.

While paying lip service to the ideal of popular sovereignty, the resulting liberal-republican ideal of representative government arguably marked a different enclosure of power from previous orders, one that, while in some ways expanding the rights of the governed, arguably still contradicted possible interpretations of this form as a "democracy."

This eighteenth-century enclosure of power continues to emerge today in the metaphors that have dominated our best political theories since the end of World War II. Consider the two most prominent political theorists of the postwar period: John Rawls and Jürgen Habermas. If there is one institution that best captures the concept of public reason—the reason of the public—in Rawls's famous writings, it is that of the Supreme Court (Rawls 1993: 231). For Rawls, the Supreme Court is more than an institution. It embodies the rational ideal of public deliberation—deliberation of the public about matters of the

---

8. Even as Madison himself recognized that "the principle of representation was neither unknown to the ancients nor wholly overlooked in their political constitutions" (Hamilton, Madison, and Jay 2008, 63). But he may here have been referring only to the small elected component in the Athenian constitution, not to its much larger component of what I will call later "lottocratic representation." I thank Jenny Mansbrige for this point.

public good. A Supreme Court is a group of nine superior minds supposedly immune to partisan political pressure, able to stand above the fray, speaking in dispassionate terms and issuing decisions often counter-majoritarian in spirit.

Meanwhile, an important metaphor at the heart of Habermas's influential theory of deliberative democracy is that of the sluice—a system of water channels controlled at their heads by a gate. The sluice captures the appropriate relation between the two communicative tracks of the public sphere, namely the space of informal public deliberation where public opinion is formed and the space of formal decision-making (the Parliament, the Courts, the administrative agencies) (Habermas 1996: 556, following in part Peters 1993; see also Peters 2008).[9] In Habermas's usage, the metaphorical sluice is meant both to ensure transmission of information from the outer periphery of diffuse public opinion to the center where decision-making takes place, and, critically, to properly filter that information. The metaphor is meant to capture the ways in which the two tracks—ordinary citizens on the one hand and their representatives on the other—are connected in constructive ways. But it also emphasizes subtly the ways in which the track of public opinion has flaws.

It is not a criticism of the analytic power of Rawls's and Habermas's respective theories to point out that these metaphors are a product of their times and out of sync with contemporary democratic expectations. The Supreme Court's connotations are visibly elitist and exclusionary. The sluice's connotations, while less obviously exclusionary, are mechanical, rigid, slow, and explicitly, although in some ways hardly noticeably, hierarchical. In most democratic interpretations of representative democracy that have been offered since Rawls and Habermas, the democratic credentials of public decisions still come principally from their having been made by elected elites, albeit elites who are supposed to be engaged in a circular, reflexive, and dialogical exchange with the public, via intermediaries such as the media, political parties, and the pressure of an informal public opinion formed in part through these institutions and civil associations.

What is so wrong with this enclosure of power, one might ask? And conversely, what is so desirable about the openness of power to all on an egalitarian basis? In an age increasingly skeptical of democracy, this question deserves an answer. This book intends to provide that answer. It will do so in part by analyzing what has been lost in the move to representative democracy.

Democracy has historically been associated with various ideals, such as popular sovereignty, self-rule (or autonomy), and equality (Kloppenberg 2016: 16).

---

9. According to Habermas, "binding decisions, to be legitimate, must be steered by communication flows that start at the periphery and *pass through the sluices of democratic and constitutional procedures situated at the entrance of the parliamentarian complex or the courts*" (Habermas 1996: 356, my emphasis).

Popular sovereignty is a principle of legitimacy whereby the will of the people is the sole source of legitimate authority. This ideal is both sublime and somewhat vague, so much so that it has been embraced by various regimes to legitimize non-democratic practices, as long as the authority in question can invoke the fiction of some unanimous moment of consent in a state of nature or the practice of plebiscitarian moments of popular consultation.[10] Augmented with the ideals of self-rule and equality, however, popular sovereignty conjures up a more demanding type of rule. Self-rule means that individuals are entitled to participate in making the laws that bind them. Equality means that they should be able to do so on equal terms.

A minimal definition of democracy as popular rule is the one proposed by political scientist Robert Dahl. Democracy, he wrote, is a system in which "all the members are equally entitled to participate in the association's decision about its policies" (Dahl 1989: 37).[11] "Participate in," however, admits of extremely minimal participation. In my understanding, popular rule requires that the people be involved not only in the moment of voting, but *in the process leading up to it as well*, especially and crucially in the deliberation through which an agenda is set and options and arguments are debated. This book deliberately anchors the definition of democracy in "deliberative democracy," the theory of political legitimacy according to which laws and policies are legitimate only to the extent that they are the result of a deliberation among free and equals (e.g., Cohen 1989; Habermas 1996; Gutmann and Thompson 1996). Deliberative democracy is a relatively recent paradigm in democratic theory that can help us usefully specify the ideal of popular sovereignty by making it clear that final say, in the moment of a vote, is not enough to render a decision legitimate. For deliberative democrats, legitimacy also requires the possibility for citizens to speak and be heard in the process leading up to a vote.

What is so valuable about democracy thus defined? Arguments for democracy tend to be of two types: intrinsic and instrumental. On the first view, democracy is valuable because it treats, and respects, citizens as equals. On the second view, democracy is valuable because it delivers good outcomes, where the goodness is defined in absolute terms (e.g., levels of welfare) and relative

10. As we will see in chapter 3, Rousseau himself could argue, via a clever distinction between government and administration, that rule by aristocrats was perfectly compatible with popular sovereignty.

11. An alternative definition has recently been advanced by Sean Ingham: democracy is a regime of popular control, in which popular control is defined with reference to multiple majorities rather than a unified "people" and, specifically, by the possibility for each of these majorities to have the final say over any two options at any point in time, should they care enough about the outcome (Ingham 2019). I take it that this definition is compatible with the deliberative notion of democracy used here, as long as agenda-setting (the choice of the two options), presumably done in a deliberative fashion, is internalized into the idea of "control."

to the citizens' preferences themselves. The intrinsic defense is vulnerable to the extent that it depends on a priori "democratic faith" in the equality of all citizens, an ideal in which non-democrats have no difficulty poking holes.[12] The instrumental defense is vulnerable to the extent that, and if, other regimes can be shown to be more able than, or at least as able as, democracies to deliver good governance and satisfy citizens' preferences, then we would have no reason to privilege democracy over those other regimes.

It is possible, however, to treat these two arguments as integral to each other: by showing that the (broad) responsiveness of democratic decision-making to citizens' preferences, as well as, more generally, its ability to track something like the common good, stem *from the very fact* that democracy lets *all and every single one of its citizens* enter the decision process and lets them enter it *on equal standing*. One of the key aspects of epistemic arguments for democracy is to tie together, in an essential way, the intrinsic and instrumental properties of democracy. I have argued in other work for democracy as a regime of political equals on the basis of its "epistemic" properties, namely its ability to generate and aggregate the knowledge necessary to the pursuit of the common good as well as, in some sense, to track the factual and moral truth about the world (Landemore 2012, 2013). Specifically, I have argued that it is *inclusive deliberation of all on equal terms followed by inclusive voting on equal terms* that offers us the safest epistemic bet in the face of political uncertainty (Landemore 2012, 2013a, and 2014a). On this view, positing political equality is a necessary precondition for the generation of common good-tracking properties. One cannot compromise political equality without compromising the instrumental (specifically epistemic) properties of the decision process.[13] This is arguably the gist of sociologist, political philosopher, and early epistemic democrat W.E.B. Du Bois's argument for democracy in the quotation used as an epigraph for this chapter. Du Bois poetically captured the idea that each of us can uniquely contribute to the human quest for knowledge about our common world (the universe), where knowledge is understood as a broad category with scientific, esthetic, moral, as well as political dimensions. Societies that silence or shut off some voices (women, Blacks) condemn themselves not only to injustice, but also to ignorance.

---

12. See Landemore 2014b: 192–196 for this point.

13. Contrary to what critics have sometimes mistakenly suggested (e.g., Urbinati 2014 or Lafont 2020), an epistemic democrat is never tempted to sacrifice equality for the sake of outcomes, since on their theory desirable outcomes can only be produced on the basis of genuine political equality, that is, a process that gives equal voice and vote to the members of the demos. This empirical prediction is tied to an assumption about the fundamental uncertainty of politics (e.g., Landemore 2014a). Unless the world could be made a lot more predictable than is currently the case, there is no scenario under which an epistemic democrat would be in a position to consider a trade-off between the principle of political equality and desirable outcomes.

I stand by the conclusion that, in a complex and uncertain world, empowering all members of the demos equally, and in particular giving them all an equal right of access to the deliberation shaping the laws and policies that govern us all, is overall the best method we have to figure out solutions to common problems.[14] This is where I assume much of the value of popular rule comes from, though readers should feel free to anchor that value elsewhere as well.[15] The advantage of this position is that it easily explains what is lost in a system that is less inclusive of voices and points of view. Such a system will not deliver as many good outcomes as it could.

One problem (among many) with closed regimes, therefore, is that they blind themselves to a wide range of useful perspectives, heuristics, and interpretations. Our electoral systems suffer from such blind spots. It is worth acknowledging that wider perspectives sometimes burst out onto the scene anyway, empowered by external factors like the digital revolution. But social movements like "Black Lives Matter" and "Me Too" were made possible, one might argue, in spite of our representative institutions (in the larger context of a liberal society entrenching freedom of speech among others), not thanks to them. Similarly, in recent years the most radical and ultimately sustainable changes to have come for gay rights and abortion rights were forced on parties and electoral assemblies by ad hoc citizens' assemblies (Ireland) and the pressure of citizens' initiatives (Finland).[16] Representative democracy, in short, is often not as smart and capable as the sum of its citizens. Even if the pressure of civil society can make some long overdue reckonings happen anyway outside the representative system, it seems like an unnecessarily costly and haphazard way to let those voices in. A more sensible solution, it would seem, would be to rethink what we mean by democratic representation and, more generally, to rethink democratic institutions as a whole so they are more genuinely inclusive, egalitarian, and empowering—in other words, more open. This is what this book aims to accomplish.

I still have one formidable objection to address. Even if I am right that our institutions do not do justice to the ideal of popular rule and may even underperform epistemically compared to how a true democracy would, so what? Isn't the protection of individual rights a higher ideal? To the extent that representative democracies are able to secure such rights, and as long as they

---

14. I also share the "democratic faith" that treating individuals as political equals is the right thing to do.

15. For purely procedural arguments for democracy see, e.g., Waldron 1999; Christiano 1996; Pettit 2012; or Urbinati 2016.

16. Compared to liberal court decisions imposed on a reluctant public, with the potential for backfiring that we now observe in the United States. See also Rosenberg 1991 for a critique of the "hollow hope" that courts are the best agents of social change.

perform decently enough on collective metrics of good governance (welfare gains and a broad distribution of those, say), why should we risk it all for a romanticized and seemingly antiquated notion of democracy? Isn't representative democracy the only viable form of (howsoever attenuated) popular rule at scale and for commercial societies of busy individuals? And when it comes to the current crisis of our democracies, shouldn't we be much more concerned with the erosion of their liberal and constitutional elements (via the reinforcement of the executive, the politicization of courts, or generally the corruptive role of money in politics) rather than the erosion, or the preexisting deficit, of people's power per se?[17]

I take these objections very seriously and do my best to answer them in chapter 7. Ultimately, though, the comparative question of whether electoral democracies of the kind we are familiar with provide a better combination of individual rights' protection and welfare gains, say, than a genuinely open and as yet unrealized democracy of the kind I am theorizing in this book cannot be resolved a priori.

Let me nonetheless preemptively poke some holes in three common misconceptions. The first is that "representative democracy," as a historical regime form, is the only viable system of democratic rule at scale. The second is that ordinary citizens in modern commercial societies do not have the time or desire to participate in government. The third is that any involvement of ordinary citizens in government would entail the risk of tyrannical majorities and be a threat to individual rights or even, god forbid, the rule of law.

To the first point—that the sheer size of modern nation-states necessitates representation—one can reply that representation need not be electoral and tasked to those able to garner enough votes in a competitive election. A large part of the provocation of this book will be to argue for non-electoral forms of democratic representation, including those based on sortition and self-selection. Additionally, one can also question the status of the nation-state, or even any form of physical territory, as the only legitimate locus of popular sovereignty and thus popular rule. Though I take the territorial premise of the nation-state for granted in much of the book, chapter 8 begins questioning this premise and argues for decentralizing decision power to the infra-level of smaller communities, like cities and municipalities; transferring it where pertinent to the supra-level of international communities, whether regional organizations like the European Union or, at the limit, that of a global cosmopolitan order; and de-territorializing it altogether in order to allow for the self-regulation of communities of interests.

The second point is that citizens in market economies where slave labor has been abolished do not have as much time for politics as the Ancients did, nor

17. See for example Ginsburg and Huq 2018.

would they necessarily want to spend much time at all on politics were they to have that time. The freedom of the moderns, the argument goes, demands a division of labor between the vast majority of private citizens and a few professional leaders endorsing public functions. This argument fails to acknowledge that the time constraints on citizens are partly endogenous to the political systems we build (market-based economies like Sweden and Denmark leave more leisure time to their citizens than, say, the United States). Additionally, technological change may free up considerable time for political activities as well as rendering these activities much less time-consuming to begin with, if only by making it possible to deliberate online and vote electronically. Regarding the willingness of citizens to participate in politics beyond the time commitments we observe in contemporary societies, that is certainly a big unknown, though it will likely depend on the ease, attractiveness, and perceived efficiency of such political participation. But more importantly, this objection wrongly assumes that the only alternative to rule by elected professionals has to be rule by all citizens at all times. On the contrary, a proper division of labor can be organized between different subsets of citizens, some going on about their private lives and economic affairs and others temporarily willing to put in the time and effort to be at the helm. In keeping with Aristotle's definition of democracy as "ruling and being ruled in turn," or, as I prefer to put it, "representing and being represented in turn," this book actually assumes that involving citizens does not have to mean involving them all at once and all the time. Far from being a defense of direct democracy as a viable or desirable regime form, this book is about alternative, more democratic forms of political representation. Like electoral democracy, open democracy aims to be economical of citizens' time and to avoid taking "too many evenings."[18]

As to the third and last point about the instrumental value of representation in achieving the liberal goal of securing individual rights, it is empirically plausible yet probably overstated. I postpone a proper treatment of this objection to chapter 7, where I will argue that recent theoretical and empirical developments suggest that there may be an opportunity to recover some of the accessibility of older, pre-liberal, or more participatory democracies (such as classical Athens, the Viking parliamentary regime, or modern-day Switzerland) without necessarily endangering the individual and minority rights we moderns care so deeply about, especially in societies as large and diverse as ours.

The full scalability of an open democracy is, of course, also a central question.[19] But before assuming that size requires closure and scalability implies delegation of power to elected elites, we should first spend time asking the

18. Unlike socialism, according to the famous Oscar Wilde's quip, which is sometimes applied to proposals for direct democracy.

19. Though it is less so, I would argue, since the French case of the Great National Debate.

following questions: What are the core institutional principles of democracy, at any scale? And is there a way we could recover the openness of ancient democracies in today's world and modern, plural mass societies? Can we, in other words, imagine a large-scale democracy that would put ordinary citizens back at the center, as opposed to the periphery, of power? And what would be the metaphor of popular rule that such a democracy would take inspiration from?

A New Paradigm

Insofar as we think that "more democracy" is at least worth exploring as a solution to the ills and indeed "crisis" of modern electoral democracy, one needs to think carefully about the kinds of democratic innovations that should be implemented and tested (perhaps in lab or field experiments; perhaps at the level of neighborhood, city, or state; perhaps at a large scale but for a limited time or limited jurisdiction). At present, however, democratic innovations take direct democracy as their model. My ambition is to provide an alternative model for democratic innovators, one that includes novel democratic forms of representation through which power is made open to all on equal terms.

Openness is an umbrella concept for general accessibility of power to ordinary citizens. Whereas representation, especially of the electoral kind, always creates the risk of robbing the people of the right to participate in law-making, an open system guarantees that citizens can make their voices generally heard at any point in time and initiate laws when they are not satisfied with the agenda set by representative authorities. Openness prevents the closure and entrenchment of the divide between represented and representatives that inevitably accompany representation. Openness means that power flows through the body politic, as opposed to stagnates with a few people.

The central contribution of this book is to rethink democratic representation in a manner that opens it up to ordinary citizens. Doing so, I argue, would both increase the expected performance and the political legitimacy of the system (since on my view the latter is at a minimum constrained by the former). I theorize two kinds of authentically "democratic" representation, namely, lottocratic and self-selected. I also consider the possibility of democratizing electoral representation by turning it into what I call "liquid" representation (though I ultimately remain cautious about its democratic potential). Lottocratic representatives are selected by lot and frequently rotated. The combination of sortition and rotation ensures that lottocratic assemblies are accessible and "open" to all, not spatially speaking, since those not selected are excluded, but over time. Self-selected assemblies, by contrast, are spatially accessible and open at any point in time since anyone able and willing can in theory join. In both cases, citizens have equal chances of accessing the status of representatives. "Liquid" representation, finally, is a kind of electoral representation based on vote delegation. While it is not as fully democratic as the other two (because it still relies, like electoral representation, on an aristocratic principle of distinction), it maximally lowers the barriers to entry to the status of elected representative. Under the modern circumstances of mass democracies, I argue that we probably need a combination of these various forms of democratic representation, used to various ends, to maximize participation by ordinary citizens.

Building on this reconceptualization of democratic representation, the book is also, more broadly and speculatively, about theorizing a set of core institutional principles that a genuine democracy would seek to implement and live by in the twenty-first century. There are five principles in total:

1. Participation rights
2. Deliberation
3. Majoritarian principle
4. Democratic representation (as introduced above)
5. Transparency[20]

At first glance, these principles and conditions may seem utterly familiar. It may come as a surprise that they do not already form the pillars or regulative ideals of our existing governments. As I will argue, however, their combination contrasts starkly with the more closed off (electoral), not all that deliberative, and mostly liberal principles of representative democracy, while improving on some features of ancient democracy. As a result, I offer this combination of principles as a new paradigm of democracy, one that should inform our mental schema about what to expect from democracy and guide institutional reforms going forward. I intend this new paradigm both as a critical lens through which to look at our existing institutions and a set of relatively abstract but not completely impractical guidelines for envisaging new or at least reformed ones.

With regard to specific institutional arrangements, the book considers various possibilities inspired in particular by the Icelandic and French experiments but offers neither country's design choice as the ultimate blueprint. There is no single best way to implement open democracy and the related set of principles. The most appropriate institutional arrangement for any given political context is likely to reveal itself via trial and error and local experimentation rather than

---

20. This list is somewhat different from the list put forth in Landemore 2017c. I have replaced the clumsy and unstranslatable term "empowered rights" with the conceptually simpler and more accurate term "participation rights." I now recognize that I did not need a neologism to express the radical potential of giving people participation rights, even as the familiarity of the term may lure us into thinking that we already enjoy such rights. I also changed "open representation" to "democratic representation"—again realizing that the key issue is what we mean by "democratic." Finally, for simplification purposes, I now subsume the rotation principle under "democratic representation."

either induction on the basis of one or a few cases or sheer deduction. Nonetheless, at an ideal level, a central leitmotif of this book will be what I propose to call the "open mini-public": a large, all-purpose, randomly selected assembly of between 150 and a thousand people or so, gathered for an extended period of time (from at least a few days to a few years) for the purpose of agenda-setting and law-making of some kind, and connected via crowdsourcing platforms and deliberative forums (including other mini-publics) to the larger population.

One might think of the open mini-public as a supersized version of the criminal jury in the American system or the jury d'assise in the French system. The jury is one of the few authentically democratic institutions of (some of) our representative democracies and celebrated as such by historians, political scientists, legal scholars, and even playwrights and filmmakers. Jury service has even recently been held as the answer to some of our contemporary problems (Chakravarti 2019). Yet it has limitations of its own. Its size is too small to offer a descriptively accurate sample of the larger population. Its selection method, while supposedly random, cannot entirely avoid self-selection and can even be manipulated to favor certain outcomes or at least avoid others. Finally, while juries have a great deal of power in the United States,[21] they are also "routinely conceptualized as 'mere' fact-finders" (Leib and Ponet 2012: 276) and explicitly "tasked to adjudicate *factual* rather than *legal* or *value* questions" (Leib and Ponet 2012: 282, emphasis in the original). As such, it would not be accurate to describe the jury as a legislative institution in its own right. By contrast, the open mini-public is meant to be to the criminal jury what a full-grown tree is to a bonzai: a much larger, less constrained, and more empowered entity, fully expressing the democratic potential of trusting a larger, descriptively representative group of ordinary citizens.

I name open democracy by what I take to be the main resulting feature of this combination of institutional principles, that is, openness to ordinary citizens. What does openness mean?

Openness is, first, the opposite of closure, in both a spatial and temporal sense. In a spatial sense, openness can mean various things, depending on the context, from degrees of porosity to accessibility, participation, and inclusion. Openness is to both voice and gaze. This openness is inclusive and receptive— of people and ideas. This openness characterizes a system that lets ordinary

---

21. As commentators put it, the criminal jury "can bankrupt multinational conglomerates, sentence individuals to their deaths, and decide that the law is to be ignored in particular circumstances [in case of 'nullification'], letting guilty persons go unpunished" (Leib and Ponet 2012: 275–276). Additionally, juries "provide input, albeit indirectly, into how we govern ourselves" (282) through the value judgments they "cannot help but generate" (ibid.), for example by excusing defendants because they are being subjected to unpopular laws or have been subjected to enough punishment.

citizens in, whether the spatial openness is facilitated by architectural design or technological tools. In a temporal sense, openness means open-endedness and, therefore, adaptability and revisability. It means, concretely, that democratic institutions must change as the people they are meant to serve change. An open-ended system is more likely to adjust to the rapid changes in complex, large-scale, connected societies. Open democracy, finally, is also a system that aims to cultivate and nurture open-mindedness in its citizens, as opposed to narrow-mindedness (or its close cousin, partisanship).[22]

In keeping with this broad idea of openness, one of the main distinguishing features of open democracy is that legislative agenda-setting power becomes accessible to ordinary citizens at any point in time when it comes to the deliberative phase and is equalized over time when it comes to the decision phase (via rotation of the open mini-public members). Contrary to what we have historically been led to believe, elections and referendums are not the be-all and end-all of democracy. Democracy also implies the possibility to shape, and deliberate about, the political agenda. Democracy, in other words, is not just about having the choice of one's representatives or the final say on some specific issues. It is *also* about, among other things, having the first say, and indeed a say anytime we want. Democracy, then, must begin at the start and never cease. It must be open.

Open democracy shares common features with what is commonly known as "participatory democracy" and can be considered a variety of it. But it is not premised on mass participation at all times. Participation as such, in the sense of mass participation, is not, in particular, one of the five institutional principles of open democracy (though participation rights are). This is so because, on my model, mass participation of the public is not a requirement so much as an opportunity and a possible but not necessary implication of the implementation of the five institutional principles. People may or may not choose to activate their participation rights. In times of "normal" or quiet politics, citizens may be happy to mostly delegate the task of decision-making to their democratic representatives (lottocratic or otherwise), whereas in times of rapid change or turmoil, they would decide to participate much more frequently, for example by launching new social movements, reactivating old ones, initiating referendums, calling for a greater number of mini-publics on various issues, and generally investing en masse the spaces open to them in the system. Yet mass participation is not an actual requirement of the model. Instead, the model leaves it up to citizens to determine how much and how often they are willing to participate in politics at any point in time. In open

22. One of the probably controversial claims I make is that to the extent that representative democracy thrives or even just depends on partisanship, this is one more reason to want to move beyond it.

democracy, even if mini-publics were generalized to all levels of the polity and participation in them made mandatory, these mini-publics would only formally mobilize at any point in time a small percentage of the entire population (even as the rest would probably be informally more civically "activated" by more or less direct contact with the latter). The vast majority of citizens would be free to pursue their private lives unburdened by the tasks of attending meetings and making decisions.

In many ways the concept of openness is already pervasive in the vocabulary of activists, grassroots associations,[23] and even the jargon of government officials. US President Barack Obama's administration famously launched an *Open* Government Initiative (my emphasis), whose motivation was the catchphrase of "transparency, public participation, and collaboration."[24] As to its implementation, the Open Government concept in the end leaned toward the more limited goal of "open data"[25] and improved efficiency of government service delivery.[26] It did not aim at expanding people's power per se and really involving them in decision-making. In terms of transparency, we now know that the Obama administration proved as, if not more, opaque and secretive as any administration prior to it. Given the use and abuse of the concept of "openness" in the world of existing practices and government marketing strategies, more rigorous work must be done to establish the principles of what a truly open democracy would look like.

The concept of openness also owes a lot to the world of coders and advocates for self-organization and freedom on the Internet. The open-source movement promotes so-called open-source software, which is software with source code that anyone can inspect, modify, and enhance.[27] Open-source software is best known for some of the co-created public goods it has generated, for example, the operating system Linux and the generalist online encyclopedia

23. E.g., the phrase "open democracy" is also the name of a UK-based political website that seeks to encourage democratic debate around the world.

24. From a 2009 White House memorandum: "transparency, public participation, and collaboration." See https://obamawhitehouse.archives.gov/realitycheck/the_press_office/Transparency_and_Open_Government.

25. Initiated by the Freedom of Information Act of the 60s, Open Data is a movement that requires all taxpayer-funded government data to be made easily available online for free. The type of data open to the public ranges from public officials' salaries to the more mundane agency budget figures and public transit maps.

26. This has been explicitly acknowledged by Beth Noveck (2012), for whom the goal of Open Government was never transparency but increased efficiency. See http://crookedtimber.org/2012/07/05/open-data-the-democratic-imperative/.

27. In other words, it is software that is accessible to all at all times, not just in terms of being visible but in terms of being usable, shareable, manipulable, and modifiable by all. By contrast, so-called closed-source or "proprietary" software is software that only one person, team, or organization has control over and can modify.

Wikipedia. The image of open-source software is applicable and relevant to democracy because if, as some have argued, "code is law" (Lessig 2000), one could argue, conversely, that democratic law should be more like code, or at least code of the kind made available in Linux or other open-source communities. In other words, instead of being something created and guarded by small groups of insiders or experts, in a democracy the law should be something to which all have access and on which all can make an impact. Everyone should be able to write and claim authorship over the law. Democratic authorship is exactly what the Icelanders tried to achieve with their revolutionary constitutional process. It is also the idea behind experiments in participatory budgeting, crowdsourced law reforms, or the most recently forged, all-encompassing concept of "crowdlaw."[28]

The movement of open-source software certainly contains democratic aspects of the kind this book is interested in.[29] Yet, despite the role of new technologies in enabling certain aspects of open democracy, the book is not centrally about the role of the Internet and new technologies in enhancing the possibilities for democracy in the twenty-first century. The digital revolution has brought humanity unprecedented ways of advancing democracy, in part by democratizing access to information, facilitating coordination of individuals at scale, and suggesting new ways to distribute power widely. Unsurprisingly, therefore, many of the experiments reported on in this book make use of technological solutions (such as crowdsourcing platforms) that were not available even a decade ago. That said, the digital revolution has also created unprecedented potential for mass surveillance and the spread of false information and propaganda. The question of the ways in which digital technologies can empower democracy is a separate object of study.[30] In any case this book is about democracy's principles, rather than the technological tools that may or may not help to implement them. As a result, the book remains, at a fundamental level, one of political theory and philosophy, more concerned with traditional concepts from democratic theory (central power, legitimacy, and representation) and less with technological issues.[31]

---

28. Beth Noveck 2018.

29. Additionally, the openness of open-source software is aligned with the mediations built into my concept of open democracy. Contrary to some misperceptions, open-source software is not anarchy and radical immediacy. In open-source software design, there are hierarchies of reputation and certain established or evolved protocols and norms that ensure that open entry does not turn into destructive intrusion. But these mediating layers are managed while maintaining the principle of accessibility to all and preventing anyone from appropriating or controlling the code.

30. As a separate endeavor, I have addressed the question of digital technology in relation to democracy in a collaborative editorial adventure with Rob Reich and Lucy Bernholz from Stanford University (Bernholz, Landemore, and Reich 2020).

31. This is why I chose the title "Open Democracy" rather than, say, "Open Source Democracy," which I think would have demanded a greater foray into technological questions.

Open democracy, finally, is also indebted, with a nod, to the liberal Popperian tradition of the "open society" (Popper 2013 [1945]). Building on a contrast between closed and static traditional societies and modern open ones, Popper defined the open society as a dynamic society, in which government is expected to be responsive, tolerant, and relatively transparent, and citizens are free to use their critical skills to criticize laws and traditions. Open democracy can be interpreted as a subset category of an open society, in which the government is not just liberal but genuinely democratic and, furthermore, democratic in an "open" manner that facilitates participation of ordinary citizens. Open democracy is the democratic answer, and in many ways a complement, to the essentially liberal concept of the open society. Unlike in the liberal tradition, the object of openness is the space of political power itself, the place from which power is exercised, not just the society ruled or structured by it.

As I hope will become clear, open democracy is not premised on a repudiation of the principle of representation as delegation of political authority per se, as in "direct" or "unrepresentative" democracy. Though it comes after the historical paradigm of "representative democracy" and is meant to supplant it, open democracy is not "post-representative." It simply acknowledges that democracy is always representative in some form and that the real question is whether representation allows ordinary citizens to be in charge. Open democracy means to be a broader, richer, more complex, and more authentically democratic paradigm than the dominant paradigm of representative democracy, in part because it has integrated the lessons of institutional successes and failures in humanity's 2,500-year-long effort to get democracy right. Consequently, in open democracy, representation is no longer the regime's defining or essential feature, but, at best, one feature among many.

This conception of open democracy is therefore not a return to an antiquated and largely impractical ideal of direct democracy. The fix for the constitutive democratic deficit of representative democracy as we know it is not to eliminate representation altogether, but instead to rethink it.

But isn't calling for more citizen participation and a lesser role for elected institutions a form of populism, the reader might wonder? The debate over the meaning and valence of populism has been raging in recent years, so I should probably comment on it. Contrary to many theorists of populism (e.g., Werner-Mueller 2016), I do not think that populism is bad by definition and must always be associated with anti-pluralism and the tendency of a fraction of the people to claim the authority of the whole. In my view, not only is the meaning of the term irreducibly polysemic (Elster 2020), but even when it comes to one specific meaning relative to claims made on behalf of the people I would argue that there can be a good and a bad populism, the good version an effort to speak on behalf of the ordinary citizen in a context where power is captured by elites (see also Schmitter 2019). By this more modest definition, I am, perhaps, a populist. However, my aim in this book is not to take a political stance in current debates over our oligarchized post-democracies. It is instead the scholarly one of offering, or perhaps uncovering, a more meaningful institutional understanding of popular rule.

On Vocabulary

Let me justify, on that point, my use of the vocabulary of "ordinary citizens" as opposed to "elites." This dichotomy may seem to cast in the wrong light the professional and knowledgeable political class any regime needs. But I all take these words in a descriptive rather than evaluative sense. Ordinary citizens for me are groups of citizens that could be plucked at random from the larger population. They would include nurses, students, retired people, Walmart employees, and every minority in proportion to their demographics; about half of this group, like the rest of the population, would consist of women. They would also, rarely, include the odd billionaire and the occasional Nobel Prize winner. "Ordinary citizens" is for me a statistical category. By contrast, I use the term "elites" to refer to a socioeconomic group of privileged people who would not likely be selected at random. While a billionaire or a Nobel Prize winner might turn out to be selected in a mini-public of five hundred people, it is highly unlikely that such a group would include a majority of them. In that sense I see most elected assemblies, paradigmatically the House of Representatives in the United States (where most people are, for example, wealthy), but also most Parliaments around the world, as elite groups.

There is another sense of "elite" that is occasionally used and that I try to avoid: people put in a position of power, regardless of the way they are selected and regardless of whether the resulting assembly is composed of ordinary citizens or sociological elites. It is in this sense that one could call "elites" the members of mini-publics who are able to influence policymaking in recent democratic innovations. As soon as they are given power over others, one could argue, even ordinary citizens become "elites"—political ones, that is. I have no problem recognizing the necessity of creating and empowering political "elites" in this more restricted, political sense. I am not convinced, however, that using the word "elite" to refer to ordinary people in a position of democratic and temporary power is the best choice as opposed to, say, "rulers"—in part because of the sociological and usually suspicion-filled connotations attached to the term "elites." Either way, the point is to avoid drawing the necessary political "elite" only from the sociological elite or turning it into one. I think democracy is compatible with the existence of temporary political elites, as long as they are not drawn only from sociological elites.

On Method

Let me now say a word about the kind of political theory I engage in with this book. I do not see it as ideal theory of the type that critics argue is ultimately irrelevant to politics—what David Estlund has provocatively defended as "hopeless" utopian political theory (Estlund 2020) and Gerald Gaus would call mere "dreaming" (Gaus 2016). This kind of hopelessly utopian ideal political theory orients us toward an ideal regime that has no likelihood of being brought into being or cannot specify a feasible path from where we are to where we should go. Critics will probably argue that offering a paradigm of democracy in which elections are optional is too radical a move and puts me squarely in the camp of such utopian and hopeless dreamers.

I do not expect politicians or even most citizens in the West to embrace open democracy as a viable political platform any time soon. The exercise I engage in with this book is not primarily, or at least not immediately, prescriptive in the sense of telling us where we should go and along what path. I see it instead first as an exercise in concept clarification and "measurement calibration" (Ragin 2008), allowing us to have a better understanding of what democracy means and what regime forms can legitimately count as such.[32] The book is primarily an attempt to capture what popular rule should mean institutionally in light of the definition of the concept, the various forms of democracy that have existed in the world, the alternative paths that could have been taken at various points in the history of such regimes, actual empirical evidence about feasible democratic innovations, and, yes, some speculation as to what could be done to push such innovations further.

An implication of such conceptual clarification, however, could be radical. If I am right, many of the regimes we call representative democracies are hardly democracies in the genuine sense of the term and are de facto usurping the term. Instead, these regimes should be seen for what they are, elected oligarchies of sorts, where the popular component is highly constrained and does not translate into adequate rule by, of, and for the people. In this sense, I side with political scientist Robert Dahl, who long ago coined the term "polyarchy" to refer to this liberal electoral regime that falls too short of democratic criteria to deserve the name democracy per se (Dahl 1971) and with political philosopher John Dunn, who claims that the liberals usurped the term democracy as early as the eighteenth century (Dunn 2019). My original contribution is to specify the institutional principles that a genuine democracy would instantiate if it were to qualify as genuine popular rule.

---

32. I'm grateful to David Wiens's very helpful suggestions here in helping me formulate the exact nature of the project.

While the primary goal of this book should thus be seen as an effort to clarify the meaning of the concept of democracy, I also believe that the institutional principles I am putting forward herein could serve to orient and guide political reform, if not at the nation-state level directly, at least at the level of cities and municipalities; if not in the United States, in other countries; and if not in the "real" world of physical democracies, in the virtual world of online communities. I say more about this in the last chapter.

The theoretical exercise conducted in this book is also not one in pure deductive theory, in the sense of a modeling exercise such as I have engaged in previously—specifically in my book *Democratic Reason*. Many of the ideas that I advance under the umbrella of open democracy actually come from fundamentally direct empirical observation of so-called democratic innovations (Smith 2009) that are occurring now, on the ground, across the world, one of which I was directly involved in designing.[33] In this sense I see this project as, in large part, "inductive political theory"—a form of political theory that builds on the generalization, refinement, and deeper exploration of collective intuitions already widely shared in the public as well as those tested on the ground by activists. In some cases this took place with the help of visionary politicians and the support of bold governments, the intuitions of particular individuals engaged in democratic innovations and reflecting upon their role in the larger system, as teased out in interviews and informal conversation, and of course my own personal intuitions, developed through the direct observation of specific experiments and in dialogue with various actors. The idea with this book was to start by looking at what is going on in actual democracies, among circles of citizens, activists, and officials trying to fix the system by calling for and experimenting with new democratic methods and procedures, and inferring principles that are both true to the ideal of democracy and have some likelihood of being supported and embraced. This is why a central chapter of this book is about Iceland, the case study that did the most to influence my new and enlarged understanding of democracy and a country that perhaps more than most has been willing to experiment with the concept and practice of democracy. The role of Iceland in my larger defense of open democracy is both generative and illustrative. It was Iceland that spurred me to rethink what we mean by democracy, and the evidential richness of this case study is rhetorically necessary to my defense of a new democratic paradigm. Among crucial ideas that are directly indebted to the Icelandic design is the idea that mini-publics need to be "open," that is, connected to the rest of the citizenry,

33. While I was essentially an observer of the Icelandic experiment, I was part of the team of researchers involved in the design and implementation of the Finnish experiment of crowd-sourced policymaking. I even got initiated to the joys of coding for the purpose of analyzing the results of this latter experiment.

for example through crowdsourcing platforms, referendums, or other means.[34] Iceland, in other words, plays the part of the "myth" in relation to my argument for open democracy. It is meant to equip the reader with a set of intuitions that philosophical analysis can then help itself to and build on. By contrast, the shadow case of France—with the Great National Debate and the Convention on Climate Change—is meant to illustrate the possibility of open democracy at scale, even as the ambition of the Great National Debate was ultimately less impressive than its scale (since at no point was it envisaged to give participants any actual decision power) and there are still question marks, as of this writing, as to whether the Convention on Climate Change will have any real impact. Several ideas came uniquely from my observations of the French experiments. One is the idea that what citizens mostly bring to political decision-making is the ability to open or re-open questions closed or seen as closed by professional politicians and experts. Another is the view that the openness of mini-publics to the larger public need not be imposed from the top down by organizers, as it is in fact relatively organic and endogenous to their composition and the desires of most of its members.[35]

Although this book is anchored in the empirical study of actual democratic experiments, it is not primarily US-centric. For various reasons I became involved in the study of experiments taking place in Northern Europe more than experiments in innovative governance taking place in the United States, though the latter do exist and are very much worthy of attention (mostly on a sub-federal level, under the radar of most mass media it would appear).[36] Moving away from the United States, however, is also a deliberate choice. Despite the universal attraction people around the world feel toward a 250-year-old model of liberal democracy (and despite the self-aggrandizing mythology that Americans themselves like to cultivate and export to the rest of the world), American democracy is in rather bad shape at the moment. It is no surprise that people who spend too much time examining the American model exclusively

34. In contrast with the more "closed" vision of representation my previous book still implicitly assumed (as correctly suspected by Lafont 2020, though contra her criticism I never made this a point of argument).

35. In the Convention on Climate Change, citizens were aware that their legitimacy depended in part on the degree of outreach and connection they managed to develop with the larger public, and they did all they could to create such connections, including by overriding the protections put in place by the organizers (on the fearful model of what had been put in place during the Great National Debate) to preserve their anonymity and the privacy of some of their deliberations. One of their genius strokes was to invite the French president to their meeting, an invitation that he accepted and that led to massive media buzz.

36. See for example the multiple participatory budgeting experiments taking place in New York, Chicago, Boston, San Valejo, etc., or the way San Francisco is leading in innovative use of digital technologies in the service of democratic ends (Newsom 2014).

would only see cause for despair. I therefore look elsewhere for hope and creative thinking.

In a globalized age, this will, I hope, appear both appropriate and healthy. Additionally, change is most likely not going to come from big ocean liners like the United States, or the European Union for that matter, or any other large political entity too entrenched in its ways and at a scale at which it is extremely costly to try new things. Instead, as is often the case, change is likely to emerge at the margins, in small countries, or at the level of cities and regions without much global visibility and with less to lose. This is why the tiny and agile vessel of Iceland, in my story, plays such an oversized role—though other countries, some of them considerably larger, such as Switzerland, Ireland, Finland, Belgium, India, and Brazil make an appearance. I also carve out some additional space for my native country of France, partly because I know it best and partly because of the really interesting democratic developments it has experienced in just the last few years.

I would like to conclude this chapter with the following thought, which is partly an avowal of the limits of this book. In today's world there is no question that the way we do political theory needs to be less insular, more empirically engaged, more interdisciplinary, more racially (e.g., Rogers and Turner 2020) and globally aware, including of African-American and non-Western traditions of political thought, and generally "deparochialized" (Williams 2020).[37] As things stand, I am part of a generation of theorists exclusively trained in the Western tradition and I was not able to integrate the wisdom of other philosophical traditions in this book.[38] My references are borrowed almost exclusively from Anglo-Saxon and European political theory and history. My focus on Northern European case studies—countries that are predominantly white and Christian—might also strike some readers as unduly narrow. I plead guilty on all counts.[39] It is still my hope that open democracy as I conceptualize it can be of universal appeal and become part of a global conversation about what democracy could and should mean today, above and beyond the appeal of the historical, Western paradigm of representative democracy.

The rest of the book is structured as follows. Chapter 2 turns to the crisis of democracy. The chapter argues that while this crisis can be attributed in part to specific empirical corruptions (e.g., the role of money in politics, a public sphere captured by corporations, etc.), which are themselves likely the result

37. As Melissa Williams pointedly puts it in the introduction to this edited volume and as she tries to answer in her own contribution to it, "How can a theory of democracy in the global era claim global validity if it draws exclusively on Western political experience?" (Williams 2020: 1).

38. The closest I got to engaging with Eastern thinkers, for example, is in Landemore 2014b.

39. I would look forward, however, to opportunities to team up with specialists of other traditions and geographic areas to enrich the account of open democracy offered in this book with insights and examples from non-Western political theory, cultures, and contexts.

of contingent external shocks (e.g., globalization, technological change), the crisis of democracy can also be traced, more fundamentally, to an original design flaw: the restriction of democratic representation to "electoral" representation. This restrictive understanding of democratic representation has by construction exclusionary effects in terms of who gains access to power. These exclusionary effects are not contingent and cannot be fixed a posteriori.

Chapter 3 turns to the alternative to representative democracy sometimes defended by its democratic critics: direct (or unmediated) democracy. The chapter argues that direct democracy is a false alternative, one that is credible only if one accepts the mistaken Rousseauvian view of sovereignty as limited to having the final say—and a non-deliberative one at that. In the end, direct democracy is parasitic on non-democratic forms of agenda-setting and deliberation, or else must turn representative—i.e., involve a delegation of authority—to some degree. Even Classical Athens, the chapter further argues, was not the paragon of "direct" democracy as it is often portrayed and functioned along broadly representative or proto-representative (though non-electoral) lines.

Chapters 4 and 5, the central theoretical chapters, jointly conceptualize new forms of democratic representation in addition to the electoral one, namely "lottocratic," "self-selected," and "liquid" representation. These chapters also disentangle various concepts, such as representativeness, democraticity, and legitimacy. I found it necessary to distribute a long reflection over two chapters rather than one but, as their common title indicates, they are both dealing with the same question of rethinking "legitimacy and representation beyond elections."

Chapter 6 builds on the previous chapters to sketch the alternative paradigm of "open democracy." This chapter first draws on a stylized contrast between Classical Athens and modern representative democracy. The chapter then theorizes a new model of democracy—open democracy—which layers new principles on top of the most normatively appealing ones found in the previous models, expanding the scope of some principles and occasionally replacing or reformulating others entirely. This chapter goes on to offer a list of five core institutional principles: (1) participation rights, (2) deliberation, (3) the majoritarian principle, (4) democratic representation, and (5) transparency.

Chapter 7 turns to the real-life case study of Iceland to illustrate some of the principles of open democracy. The chapter closely examines the 2010–2013 Icelandic constitutional process from which many of the ideas behind this book originally stem. Despite its apparent failure—the constitutional proposal has yet to be turned into law—the Icelandic constitutional process created a precedent for both new ways of writing a constitution *and* envisioning democracy. The process departed from representative, electoral democracy as we know it in the way it allowed citizens to set the agenda upstream of the process, write the constitutional proposal or at least causally affect it via online comments, and observe most of the steps involved. The chapter also shows that the procedure was not simply inclusive and democratic but also successful in one crucial respect—it produced a good constitutional proposal. This democratically written proposal indeed compares favorably to both the 1944 constitution it was meant to replace and competing proposals written by experts at about the same time.

Chapter 8, intended for the skeptical reader, addresses some understandable worries about the feasibility and desirability of open democracy, including issues of competence of ordinary citizens, the danger of capture by bureaucracies and interest groups, the possible illiberalism of a more majoritarian system, and the problem of the transition from our current systems to more open ones.

In brief conclusion, chapter 9 explores the thought that in a globalized world we need to expand the *scope* of democracy both upward (toward global democratic institutions) and laterally (into the "economic" or "private" sphere of firms). The chapter tentatively puts forward two additional principles, which cannot be fully argued for but pave the way for more research, namely "dynamic inclusiveness" and "substantive equality." These principles point in the direction of cosmopolitan democracy and workplace democracy, respectively. The chapter also considers the need to disseminate democratic principles to the local level while also creating the tools for running dematerialized, non-territorial democratic communities.

2

The Crisis of Representative Democracy

Is democracy, today, in crisis? Judging solely by the number of books, articles, and conferences on the topic, the answer should be a resounding yes.[1] And indeed this book's premise it that democracy is sufficiently "in crisis" to justify rethinking it at the institutional level.

My main point in this chapter will be to trace a certain understanding of the "crisis" of contemporary democracy not so much to contingent external factors (though they obviously play a role) but, rather, to more fundamental democratic flaws in representative democracy's original design. The main problem, I will argue, is that representative democracy was designed on the basis of electoral premises that prevent even its best, most democratized contemporary versions from reaching the full potential of genuine "popular rule," that is, a rule that empowers all equally. If democracy, when properly conceived, can be seen as an engine for the production of what I have called elsewhere "democratic reason" (Landemore 2013a), then this same design mistake, which fails to empower all equally, necessarily limits the epistemic potential of today's democracies and may well partly explain their crisis. Even under the best circumstances, democracies as we know them would be likely

---

1. To cite just a few books, see for example Przeworski, *The Crises of Democracy* (2019); Levitsky and Ziblatt, *How Democracies Die* (2018); Mounk, *The People Versus Democracy* (2018); Galston, *Antipluralism* (2018); Runciman, *How Democracy Ends* (2018). Similar alarm bells were rung earlier by Hayward, *The Crisis of Representation in Europe* (1996); Crouch, *Post-Democracy* (2004); Norris, *Democratic Deficit* (2011); della Porta, *Can Democracy Be Saved* (2013); Papadopoulos, *Democracy in Crisis* (2013); and Tormey, *The End of Representative Politics* (2015).

to perform suboptimally. Aditionally, the cognitive dissonance between the reality of the regimes we live in and the democratic expectations people attach to them can only grow over time.

The first section briefly addresses the claim of a crisis of democracy at the empirical level. Though not the focus of my argument, it is important to take stock of the reasons some people fear democratic deconsolidation and to measure how alarmed we should be by the alleged crisis of democracies as we know them. The main point will be that while the situation may not be as dire as some may fear, there are indeed reasons for concern, reasons that plausibly point to internal problems with representative democracy.

The second section traces these internal problems to a core principle of representative government: the principle of elections, which is baked, historically and conceptually, into the definition of representative democracy (Manin 1997). Elections introduce systematic discriminatory effects in terms of who has access to power, specifically agenda-setting power. By so doing, elections skew the type of perspectives and input that shape law-making, likely resulting in suboptimal results. Second, elections entail a type of party politics that is itself not all that conducive to deliberation or its prerequisite virtues, such as open-mindedness, rather than partisanship.

The third section takes a historical detour to the eighteenth century. I discuss an alternative to the Federalists' preferred "filter" vision of democratic representation and explore the reasons why the Anti-Federalists' favored "mirror" theory of representation never led to an embrace of sortition as an alternative selection method for democratic representatives.

The fourth section, finally, addresses the "realists'" objections that there is no crisis of democracy since representative democracy is working as intended and that the current muddling through is the best we can hope for. It is my aim that by the end of this chapter, the reader will be convinced that, whether or not actual democracies are in trouble, representative democracy does not and indeed never could fully do justice to the ideal of popular rule and that, if only for that reason, we are in need of an alternative paradigm.

The Crisis of Representative Democracy: Empirical

A crisis is the turning point of a disease, when an important change takes place, indicating either recovery or death. Etymologically, the Greek word κρίσις means "judgment" or "trial" or the "moment of decision." A crisis refers to a time of intense difficulty, trouble, or danger, when a difficult or important decision must be made. What are the signs that democracy has reached such an acute state of illness? The symptoms vary from country to country, but some have been widely noted. A first symptom that things are not right is the decline in voter turnout all over the Western world over the last seventy years or so.[2] A second symptom is the concomitant decline of parties as vehicles for mass participation, a decline that can be traced to both ordinary citizens' abandonment of mass parties and their own withdrawal from traditional political activities in favor of merely rent-seeking ones (securing funding and positions of power for their top members) (Mair 2013).[3] Other worrying symptoms are, among others, the general polarization of the political landscape, as well as the rise of extremism and populism.[4] In a number of countries, like Poland, Hungary, and Turkey, the trends are even more worrying, with the triumph of nationalistic and authoritarian leaders openly embracing a form of "illiberal democracy." In terms of absolute numbers, the number of democracies seems to have slightly regressed since the early 1990s, the high mark of democratic triumphalism when Francis Fukuyama famously proclaimed the end of history (Fukuyama 1989). For some, it is now time to talk of a democratic "recession" (Diamond 2016; Rachman 2016), "deconsolidation" (Foa and Mounk 2016), or "decay" (Zakaria 2018).

The empirical evidence about such lethal threats to democracy is contested and leads to different interpretations (e.g., against Foa and Mounk's alarmism, Alexander and Welzel 2017; Bermeo 2016; Norris 2017; Voeten 2017). Some authors also emphasize that, in historical perspective, democracies are doing better than they ever have. As political scientist Treisman argues, for example, the proportions of democracies in the world, on most (arguably rather minimal) definitions of a democracy used by political scientists (Polity, Freedom House, etc.), "turn out to be at or very close to an all-time high" (Treisman 2018: 1).

Democracy, the facts would seem to indicate, is not an endangered regime.

How do we explain, then, the looming sense of crisis among, if not the academics studying the phenomenon with some detachment and a view to the *longue durée*, at least democratic citizens themselves? To an extent, perception is reality and it is a fact that citizens in democratic societies experience a sense of loss and disenchantment well-captured by sociologist Colin Crouch's concept of "post-democracy" (Crouch 2004). In post-democratic societies,

---

2. The 1960s saw the high-water mark of voting participation, but it has since dwindled in most Western countries, the United States being the lone exception, attributable perhaps to its already low levels of participation.

3. For Mair, the health of mass parties is essential to meaningful popular sovereignty. Therefore, the decline of parties has dramatic implications, marking the retreat from popular to constitutional democracy and the concomitant downgrading of politics and of electoral processes.

4. In the United States, Donald Trump and Bernie Sanders arguably marked the two extremes of populism, while the white supremacist movement grew in visibility; in France, Marine Le Pen—the heiress of a movement once mostly known for its xenophobic and anti-Semitic views—made it to the second round of the 2017 presidential elections, garnering 35 percent of the popular vote.

as Crouch sees it, all the elements of representative democracy are present: periodic free and fair elections, separation of powers, free press, even alternation of parties in power. Yet the democratic functioning of these institutions has been hollowed out, with what he sees as a growing disconnect between policies and majorities' preferences and de facto control by economic elites, often global ones. So, while measurements of formal features (such as those captured by empirical political scientists) may not be able to detect a democratic crisis, it is nonetheless the case that democratic citizens experience a growing alienation from their system and indeed a form of "democratic dissonance." It is also possible that what citizens mean by democracy has changed and is no longer captured by the formal measurement of Freedom House or Polity. It could be a case of mostly elevated democratic expectations that are no longer met by the status quo.

Indeed, citizens in most advanced democratic countries have grown disaffected with their institutions. Parliamentary assemblies struggle to obtain the approval of the very people they are meant to serve. This is particularly striking in the United States where, after being on a downward trend since at least 2001 and hovering on average below the 30 percent mark since such polls were conducted for the first time in 1971, the approval rating of the US Congress reached an absolute low of 9 percent in November 2013.[5] Widespread dissatisfaction may be less dramatic in other countries (or even absent in outlier countries like Switzerland or Denmark) yet it seems to hold across a large number of Western democracies.

For some observers (e.g., Crouch 2004; Mounk 2018), systematic dissatisfaction suggests that despite all formal evidence (of elections, free press, etc.) to the contrary, existing "democracies" suffer from fundamental democratic deficits. In the United States, the suspicion is now that the regime hardly deserves the title of democracy to begin with. Martin Gilens and Benjamin Page (2014) argue that there is no correlation, in the United States, between majority preferences and policy outcomes once one controls for the preferences of the richest 10 percent.[6] This should be alarming for any democrat if, as Andrew Rehfeld puts it, "the presumption of democracy is that there be a close correspondence between the laws of a nation and the preferences of citizens who are ruled by them" (Rehfeld 2009: 214). More fundamentally, we expect the majority of citizens' preferences to be *causal* in the way laws and

5. A clear sign of distrust in either its competence or its trustworthiness, or perhaps both.

6. Over the forty years of data they have looked at (up to 2005), there is only a correlation when the majority's preferences happen to map onto those of the preferences of the 10 richest percent of the population, which do drive policy and law-making. In the authors' own words, "mass-based interest groups and average citizens have little or no independent influence" on U.S. government policy (Gilens and Page 2014). In simpler terms, representative democracy as we know it, at least in the United States, is more akin to rule by economic elites—plutocracy some might say—than to rule of the people.

policies are determined. But in the United States, some time between 1981 and 2002, neither correspondence nor causation seems to have obtained (and it seems hard to believe that things were better before 1981 or have improved significantly since 2002). Combined with the growing global inequalities documented by economists Emmanuel Saez, Thomas Piketty, and others, whereby the richest 10 percent in most societies are growing further and further apart in wealth from the rest of the population, these results suggest that the gulf between majoritarian preferences and actual laws and policy outcomes is here to stay. There is no reason to think that European democracies, though they seem to fare better in terms of absolute inequalities, face fewer worrying trends. The suspicion becomes this: representative democracies are no longer able, if they ever were, to satisfy majoritarian preferences—except during the brief golden age of 1950–1970, now seen as exceptional historically (Piketty 2013), and this is only becoming apparent as we now have the tools and data to measure the gap more precisely. To the extent that some correlation between majoritarian preferences and public policies is a sign of democratic health, it is reasonable to talk of a crisis of democracy, if only in terms of disappointed expectations.

Surely, the inevitable objection will rise: all such claims are too alarmist. What you call the "crisis" of democracy can also be read as the growing pains of a system trying to adjust to the constraints of a globalized economy, an interconnected world, and rising democratic expectations. Democracy may be experiencing some turbulence and may even be sick, but it is not terminally ill. After all, this question of a crisis of representative democracy is one that recurs periodically, every time there is high abstention, a corruption scandal, a demonstration, etc. One could in fact point out that this question is as old as representative democracy, whose history is but a history of crises (Runciman 2013). The fact that representative democracy has successfully negotiated various historical transitions confirms that it remains a viable, resilient regime form.

This is the answer given by, for example, Bernard Manin.[7] According to Manin, it is an overstatement to talk of a crisis. What we have been witnessing in the last twenty years, more markedly so perhaps since the 2008 Great Recession, is just a metamorphosis stage in an evolutionary path—a moment of transition between two equilibrium stages. We progressed similarly from parliamentary democracy to party democracy, a transition in which parties that used to be considered factions ultimately came to be seen as essential to the functioning of democracy. We then went from party democracy to what Manin calls "audience democracy," or "democracy of the publics," a form of democracy in which partisan loyalties are arguably weakened to the benefit of candidates who cultivate direct, personal ties with their public (Manin 1997).

7. See also Landemore, Manin, and Urbinati (2008).

The election of a Trump, on this more optimistic view, presumably signals the entry into a new kind of democracy, not a crisis or retreat of democracy. According to Manin, the only reasons to worry about the stability and viability of representative democracy would be if people lost interest in politics, which he does not think is the case despite the rise of abstention and party abandonment, or if the principles of representative government could be shown to be challenged.

So, which is it? Crisis or no crisis? My interpretation is that, while democracy may still be doing fine on a sufficiently minimalist definition of it (as typically measured by political scientists), it is blatantly failing to measure up to the idea of a regime that includes all equally in policy decisions. As a result, it also fails to deliver the goods, namely, navigate the world successfully and, in a time of globalization that amplifies the constraints on governments, satisfy the preferences of the vast majority of its citizens. I will say more about this possibility in the next section.

For now, we should also ask: is the driver of what we observe, whether "mere" problems or a genuine "crisis," internal or external to democratic regimes? In other words, is the crisis of democracy the result of an unfortunate historical conjuncture, which democracies may or may not be able to overcome but does not indict them as a regime form as such? Or is it that, while the conjunctural elements surely amplify the problems, they do not cause them to begin with and that there is something deficient about democracy as institutionally designed?

Let me consider briefly the first perspective. What if all of the contemporary problems of democracy were due to external shocks? What if democracy wasn't suffering from some internal disease but was stifled by exogenous factors? Indeed, many blame the contemporary problems of democracy not on democratic institutions per se but, instead, on external shocks to the system that would destabilize any regime. These external factors have various names: globalization; technological change; rising economic inequalities; or, sometimes, the "crisis of capitalism."

The problem with globalization is that it weakens local (national) governments, and this is especially true the smaller the country. To the extent that representative democracy is attached to the boundaries of the nation-state, and governments remain committed to the principles of free trade and economic integration, democracy is limited in its ability to control economic forces that transcend those boundaries. Democracy, as a result, will always be susceptible to co-optation by mobile global economic and financial elites.[8] It is entirely possible that democracies' problems currently are just a by-product

---

8. This is the problem captured by economist Dani Rodrik's famous trilemma. One can only have two of these three things at once: democracy (or sovereignty), deep economic integration, and the nation-state (Rodrik 2007).

of globalization, not the result of their own internal flaws. One solution would then be a return to protectionism and nationalist politics (the temptation at play in the Brexit and Trump votes). Another solution would be accepting that democracy is a game that can now only be played meaningfully at the larger scale of supranational organizations, where political sovereignty, including over giant international corporations, can be reconquered.

The second external reason representative democracy now seems weak and out of touch to so many is technological change. Technological change is usually invoked in relation to globalization as one of the factors that are causing rising inequalities in the Western world. Technological change, on one story at least, is supposed to have so vastly outpaced education levels that it has created disproportionate rewards, in a globalized economy, for the sliver of people with the relevant competence (Goldin and Katz 2007; Mankiw 2013).[9] These inequalities, in turn, harm democratic political processes, when the few people with money are allowed to buy politicians and elections, which in turn generates a populist backlash, further harming the stability of democratic institutions.

Technological change has probably also impacted democratic expectations. The Internet revolution, together with the more recent rise of digital technologies, social media, and the now ubiquitous use of smartphones, have changed the relation of citizens to political action in ways that previous technological revolutions—print, radio, or TV—did not. They have changed citizens' expectations in terms of the ease and speed of feedback they can expect from their interactions with the world and have generated growing frustration with the archaic nature and slow pace of election cycles, especially compared to that of the marketplace.[10] Digital technologies have also allowed for multidirectional communication, in ways that challenge the still mostly unilateral, top-down, vertical, distant, and generally opaque exercise of power in representative democracy.[11] The age of de facto post-democracy means there is a growing gap between the ideal of democracy and representative democracy as we know it.[12]

9. The standard counter-argument is that even though inequality has increased nearly everywhere in the economies that are technologically cutting edge, the increase in inequality is small in some countries (e.g., France) and quite vast elsewhere (e.g., US/UK). Given widely differing effects, it is unlikely that a singular cause explains them all (see Piketty 2013: 330–335).

10. While individuals have grown accustomed, as consumers, to rating movies, products, and Airbnb rentals in a few seconds, the only way to give feedback to politicians about the merits of implemented policies and their general performance is still through a vote every few years.

11. Rosanvallon notes that citizens now want representatives who "are accessible, receptive and *open*" and who "react to what they hear and are willing to explain their decisions" (Rosanvallon 2011b: 171, my emphasis).

12. This is also probably one of the many reasons why Trump won the 2016 election. He used a social media platform, Twitter, in a way that many people responded to, the same way Kennedy before him used the TV.

Another external cause might be the nature of the economic system in which our democracies are embedded. Capitalism, a system combining free markets and private ownership of the means of production, is the only game in town in most of the world, including supposedly socialist China. Yet doubts that capitalism is a system fully compatible with democratic principles are mounting. One of the simplest reasons for this suspected incompatibility is the rise of economic inequalities that capitalism, except during rare historical phases (the twentieth-century interwar and postwar parenthesis for example), seems to generate. Thomas Piketty's *Capital in the Twenty-First Century* (2013) argues that the norm in capitalism is for the rate of return to capital to outpace that of labor, a dynamic that has returned with a vengeance in the West since the late 1970s, creating a growing divergence in wealth between capital owners and laborers in all advanced democracies (see also Saez and Zucman 2014). These economic inequalities ultimately leak into the political system and affect it. In the United States, for example, the rise of economic inequalities tracks almost perfectly the rise in political polarization that fuels a sense of democratic crisis (McCarthy, Poole, and Rosenthal 2006). In France, the problem of increasing inequalities affecting the political process can be measured through the increasing role played by money in politics (Cagé 2020).

These problems, all probably related in complex ways, are not intrinsic to democracy. They are external factors that make it vulnerable and in need of adaptation. But that would be true of any regime exposed to similar threats. It is thus entirely possible that at least some of these external shocks—of globalization and technological change, among other things—could eventually be absorbed. Representative democracies may be able to keep muddling through for a long time.

Another explanation worth exploring, however, is that the external problems democracy faces today only amplify one or even several fundamental design flaws.[13]

Worse, some of these problems, like globalization and the rise of economic inequalities, might themselves result from these original design flaws. For example, perhaps globalization does not simply "happen" to democracies, an external factor they have no power over, but is a goal pursued by the representative elites at the helm of representative democracies, if necessary, against

---

13. I should say that I do not have the ambition (or the ability) in this book to *prove* the causal impact of this design flaw on democracy's current woes. My point is simply this: if we agree that democracies are not completely powerless in the face of economic and technological forces (after all, we see that different policies lead to different outcomes in different countries, indicating that politics still has some room for maneuvering at least in large political entities like the United States or Europe), then the fact that democracies systematically fail to meet their citizens' expectations anyway must have to do with something more fundamental.

the interests and desires of their populations (see Slobodian 2018). From this perspective, globalization, as well as its resulting economic inequalities in many democracies, is closer to an internal problem than an exogenous one. It should be addressed via a reflection about political and legal institutions and the ideologies that undergird them (see also Piketty 2019).[14]

To understand what is wrong with representative democracy on that reading, we need to turn from empirical political science to history and normative political theory. Let us therefore take a closer look at what representative democracy means, both historically and conceptually.

The Crisis of Representative Democracy: Conceptual

The form of democracy that re-emerged in the eighteenth century (after a more than 2,000-year eclipse since the Greeks) at the time of the French and American revolutions is the historical paradigm known as representative democracy. There are various reasons to think that even the most democratized version of such a system—with full enfranchisement and no restriction on who can run for office—cannot fully measure up to the ideal of popular rule, which we defined earlier, as a regime in which "all the members are equally entitled to participate in the association's decision [including deliberation] about its policies" (after Dahl 1989). The problem with democracy today might thus be the price we pay for conceptual mistakes committed at the inception of this regime form, which no amount of marginal institutional reform (e.g., banning money from politics) can properly fix. According to Dahl himself, most existing democracies fail one or more of the five procedural criteria he associated with his definition of democracy (see also Landemore 2017c). In Dahl's view, existing "democracies" would be more accurately called "polyarchies," in reference to the multiplicity of actors that have power in it, as opposed to just "the people."

Here, however, I am more interested in measuring the gap between the best possible *normative* reconstructions of representative democracy and the ideal of popular rule. I turn first to the historian of ideas Bernard Manin, who, in his seminal analysis of representative government, identifies four central principles underlying this regime form. These four principles are not ideal criteria but generalizations of established historical practices. Though they have essentially descriptive value in Manin's account,[15] I want to evaluate them as normative institutional guidelines. The four principles of representative government are, for Manin:

14. I thank Max Krahé for this point.
15. Manin himself claims to have done only the "descriptive" work of characterizing stable institutional arrangements in place since the eighteenth century.

1. Periodic elections
2. Independence of the representatives
3. Freedom of opinion
4. Trial by discussion

The first principle, periodic elections, is the most central and indeed the one that most people the world over associate with democracy. It is a principle of authorization of representatives, which is renewed at periodic intervals. The periodicity is crucial in that it is supposed to ensure, beyond renewed consent and thus authorization, accountability and responsiveness of the representatives as well. The second principle of representative government, the relative independence of elites from their constituents, ensures that there exists a meaningful space for maneuvering and deliberation among representatives, who can depart from their constituents' preferences as needed. The third principle—freedom of opinion—counterbalances the second one by ensuring that representatives, despite their freedom, can be criticized for their decisions and choices in the public sphere. Popular pressure does not jeopardize representatives' independence but supposedly ensures, like periodic election, a form of accountability and responsiveness, including, crucially, between elections. The last feature of representative government is that public decisions are subject to trial by discussion, a method meant to test the validity of a proposal rather than yield decisions per se.

For Manin, whereas the direct democracy of the Ancients used to mean the ability for all citizens to hold offices, representative government thus means instead the ability to consent to power exercised by an elected subset and put some sort of discursive pressure on it between elections (Manin 1997: 79). While radical in comparison to regimes in the eighteenth century, such a system is far from entitling all equally to participation in the polity's decision. Barring even the question of non-universal enfranchisement, which would only be solved in the late twentieth century, Manin himself describes representative government as a mixed regime, which borrows both from oligarchy and democracy. The oligarchic aspect comes from the use of elections, which by nature select for extraordinary—however this notion is defined—rather than ordinary individuals for office and from the principle of independence of the representatives, who once in office are mostly free to do what they want. The first two principles—elections and independence of the representatives— entail unequal power between those who have a chance of being elected and all the others. The democratic aspects of the regime, however, come from the periodic renewal of consent to and authorization of the choice of rulers themselves that regular elections ensure. It also comes, though to a much lesser degree, from the freedom to express one's view and the possibility of putting laws and policies to the trial of public debate.

We need to turn to explicitly normative theorists, however, to find an attempt at bridging the gap between representative democracy as the institutions we have historically evolved from representative government, and the normative ideal of popular rule per se, which supposedly undergirds them. I turn here to two prominent political philosophers, Nadia Urbinati and Jürgen Habermas.

For Nadia Urbinati, representative democracy should be conceived of as democratic through and through, rather than as a mixed regime. To this end, Urbinati invites us to reinterpret representation as a form of *participation*, de-emphasizing consent and delegation of power in favor of the mediated and reflexive presence of the people. For Urbinati, it is thus possible to understand representation as "a mode of political *participation* that can activate a variety of forms of citizen control and oversight" (2006: 4, my emphasis).

On Urbinati's account, the principles of representative democracy thus reinterpreted include all of Manin's, embraced as normatively desirable in their own right rather than merely recognized as de facto practices,[16] but crucially augmented with the following two additions to the list:

5. "Advocacy"
6. "Representativity"

For Urbinati, advocacy is a principle meant to ensure the democratic credentials of a regime based on delegation of authority by turning elected representatives into the "advocates" of their constituents. Representation in representative democracy is not just acting on behalf of someone else and making them indirectly present when they are absent, it is "giving them a voice in the intermediary time between elections" (Landemore et al. 2008). But reporting on the constituents' needs, interests, and worries is not sufficient per se. Beyond their roles as advocates, representatives have an additional responsibility of ensuring some form of "representativity," which is a principle meant to ensure that the views, perspectives, and interests of the population are not just reported on but made present in the political sphere. Representativity guarantees that there is some minimal amount of identification and similarity between represented and representatives.

Urbinati's picture of the representative democracy is more democratic than representative government as theorized by Manin. As a result, Urbinati's picture of representative democracy is more appealing, normatively speaking, if only because it seems to entail a greater correlation between what civil society wants, as partly expressed through political associations, the media, etc., and actual policy outcomes.

---

16. Though she does not list them explicitly in the book, Urbinati mentioned that she accepts all of Manin's principles in Landemore, Manin, and Urbinati 2008.

On such a reconstruction of representative democracy, can we say that all citizens are equally entitled to participate in law-making? I would argue, *pace* Urbinati, that they are not. First, Urbinati's theory retains the two crucial principles of elections and independence of representatives as central to her model. As a result, she accepts as a given the premise that democratic representation must be *electoral* and, despite the promise of a participatory model of representation, seemingly limits citizens' possibility for action to judgment and criticism. Additionally, because of her central distinction between "judgment" and "will"—respectively the sphere of public opinion where citizens operate and formal politics, where elected politicians operate, the sort of judgments and criticism open to citizens is largely decoupled from actual decision-making. In the end, Urbinati's understanding of electoral representation as a form of vicarious citizens' participation turns the ideal of participation into a rather metaphorical affair, where "presence through ideas and speeches" is seen as equivalent, indeed superior, to participation as an immediate and physical presence (2006: 3). If we question this equivalence of presence through ideas and speeches and actual participation, let alone the superiority of virtual presence over actual participation, then Urbinati's model cannot do justice to an ideal of popular rule where all citizens are supposed to have equal opportunity of access to power.[17]

Let me finally consider here what I deem to be the most normatively attractive account of representative democracy to date, namely "deliberative democracy." This account is attached to prominent figures such as Joshua Cohen, Jürgen Habermas, and many others. In Habermas, the normative picture of representative democracy is presented as a sociologically induced ideal-type, meant to capture the true spirit of our institutions by pinpointing the sort of presuppositions necessary to its functioning at all. Of all existing theories of democracy, it is the most demanding and, arguably, the most democratic. However, I want to show that it too runs into certain predictable limits.

Deliberative democracy, in a nutshell, posits that only laws and policies passed through the filter of a public exchange of arguments among free and equal citizens are legitimate. On deliberative democrats' view, policies and

---

17. In fairness, and unlike other authors who favor an aphasic model of citizenship (e.g., Green 2010), Urbinati maintains the centrality of citizens' voice to representative democracy. But she seems to limit the expression of that voice to places outside the sites of real power. As in Manin's representative government, in Urbinati's representative democracy citizens can protest and criticize all they want, but they are not meant to have any form of direct access to the formal decision-making process of agenda-setting, deliberation, and most decision-making, which is still confined on her model to elected elites. Similarly, even final say about the agenda is missing from Urbinati's model, where citizens can only hope to influence the representatives' agenda through the overly blunt mechanism of party platforms and elections and the indirect and ultimately insufficient pressure of public opinion.

laws are supposed to result from processes yielding to the "unforced force of the better argument" in Habermas's famous phrase, rather than the result of compromises, bargaining, coercion, or a by-product of elite competition.

Deliberation is valued by deliberative democrats for a number of reasons, among which are:

1. It allows laws and policies resulting from it to be supported by public reasons and justifications, rather than mere numbers.
2. It gives all citizens a chance to exercise their voices and be heard.
3. It has beneficial side effects, such as educating citizens, building a sense of community, and promoting civic engagement.
4. It generalizes interests (Habermas).
5. It increases the chance of the group successfully solving collective problems (a dimension more specifically emphasized by so-called epistemic democrats).[18]

This book embraces all the above reasons for putting deliberation front and center of a theory of democracy.

Deliberative democracy is an ideal that is supposed to apply to both direct and representative democracy. Early proponents of the theory assumed direct democracy as their base model, but very little was supposed to change, normatively speaking, when deliberation took place among elected representatives rather than the people themselves. The legitimacy was simply transferred to the outcomes of the deliberation among representatives, as if it played out as a perfect substitute for deliberation among all citizens.[19] This fits quite neatly within Habermas's famous model of a two-track deliberative democracy.

In Habermas's model, there are two kinds of deliberation, one taking place "in the wild," i.e., the larger public sphere, and the other in a formal sphere oriented toward decision-making. The first kind of deliberation is unregulated, decentralized, distributed, and diffuse. The second type of deliberation takes place within the formal political process, which includes elections, legislative decision-making, and the work of agencies and courts. For Habermas, the two tracks are connected by a metaphorical sluice, allowing for mediated exchange and interaction between the two spheres. This "sluice" presumably corresponds to the intermediary bodies—parties, civil associations,

18. See for the relation of epistemic democracy to deliberative democracy, Landemore 2017c and Chambers 2017. Argument 5 may or may not subsume argument 4, depending on the way one partitions the space of epistemic political discourses (whether, in other words, "epistemic" is—as I believe—a category that cuts across both factual and moral questions).

19. To ensure a seamless translation of democratic legitimacy from the direct to the representative context, most people resorted to the then-dominant theory of representation formulated by political scientist Hannah Pitkin in 1967. At an abstract level, representation is, for Pitkin, the conceptual solution to the problem of "making present" that which is absent.

procedures—that ensure the proper transmission, filtering, and processing of information between the two tracks. On the one hand, track 2 is supposed to translate the opinions formed in track 1 into legislation and policies. From that perspective, track 1 sets the agenda for the deliberations taking place in track 2. On the other hand, track 1 is supposed to monitor and maintain pressure on this translation and, down the road, the execution of the resulting decisions by administrative bodies. Track 2 in turn is supposed to provide regular justifications back to track 1 for the decisions, laws, and policies ultimately passed.

This picture of representative democracy is enormously attractive, essentially because of the centrality of deliberation in it and the circular and reciprocal relation between the two tracks.

Yet I would argue that the picture of representative democracy as a system of juxtaposed tracks connected by a sluice still suffers from the problems observed in Manin and Urbinati's model—namely the separation of a ruling elite of elected officials, appointed courts, and administrative bodies on the one hand and the mass of ordinary citizens on the other. To the extent that the two tracks are conceptualized as imbricated in each other in concentric circles rather than juxtaposed in parallel stripes, the metaphor even suggests that ordinary citizens are on the outside of the circles, while professional politicians and administrators are at its center, closest to power. Additionally, and as already mentioned in the introduction, the very metaphor of a sluice (or even a multiplicity of sluices) connecting the two tracks suggests slow, rigid, and mechanical forms of communicative exchanges (watercrafts move only one at a time and not very fast in such a system), based on the slow temporality of dated technologies.[20] Finally, the idea that the decentralized deliberations of citizens "in the wild" add up to a meaningful way of setting the agenda for the formal decision-making sphere is not convincing. There are many reasons to think that the larger public sphere is itself shaped by the formal deliberative track in a way that is not reciprocal. The collective action problems faced by "the public" are enormous compared to those faced by the powers that be. Moreover, even in the best-case scenario of a fully functional public sphere, why should we expect a series of haphazard, unregulated, and decentralized deliberations among groups of different sizes and compositions, which are not intentionally oriented toward this outcome, to be the proper way of setting up the agenda for the formal deliberative track? Does such "deliberation in the wild" even amount to proper deliberation? Habermas himself acknowledges

20. One could of course imagine the relationship as made more porous, fluid, and speedy in the age of digital technologies, where some elected representatives are now connected 24/7 to their constituencies on Twitter or Facebook. But the problem might run deeper, in that this fluidification wouldn't really challenge the dualism of the metaphor.

the limitations of such an "anarchic structure," which renders "the general public sphere [. . .] more vulnerable to the repressive and exclusionary effects of unequally distributed social power, structural violence, and systematically distorted communication than are the institutionalized public spheres of parliamentary bodies" (1996: 307). Habermas goes on to note that "on the other hand, it has the advantage of a medium of unrestricted communication" (ibid.). Yet somehow, the unrestrictedness of communication does not seem to be nearly worth the trade-off of immense power asymmetries inherent to an anarchical system.

There are reasons to believe, further, that representative democracy is not all that conducive to the deliberation deliberative democrats have in mind or the virtues and dispositions on which it depends. Because of the central principle of periodic elections, representative democracy depends on parties to structure the public debate as a competition between policy platforms backed up by partisan justifications. Parties are thus essential intermediary bodies between individual citizens and the institutions of the state, in that they bundle issues and aggregate views, perspectives, solutions, and information into coherent policy proposals and a cognitively manageable quantity of bullet points, value statements, and other ideological shortcuts. To the extent that parties are necessary, so is the virtue of partisanship that sustains them.

Yet we know from empirical evidence that parties and partisanship do not go well with deliberation. Diana Mutz's empirical work on the relation between participation and deliberation strongly suggests that we cannot have it both ways: Either people will be willing to engage with dissenting others and enjoy the epistemic benefits of exposure to diverse, or even conflicting, views; or they will be willing to vote, campaign for candidates, and generally be engaged as partisans in the political arena (Mutz 2006). But they cannot be deliberatively minded and politically engaged at the same time. This is so, she argues, because most people, when faced with even minimal disagreement in the political realm—what she calls "cross-cutting perspectives"—recoil from engaging and prefer to retreat to the sphere of their like-minded peers and political friends. In other words, Mutz finds that partisan political participation and deliberation do not go together. To the extent that exposure to diversity and disagreement through political discourse threaten interpersonal harmony, people will tend to avoid entering into political territory at all. They will apply the etiquette of the polite guest—let's not talk about politics—or they will seek the company of like-minded people (see also Landemore 2014a: 210). Mutz's work thus raises interesting questions about the compatibility between the ideal of deliberative democracy and the reality of partisan politics.

All in all, it appears that representative democracy, on its best normative reconstruction, is neither sufficiently democratic nor intrinsically or at least obviously conducive to deliberation. But was there ever any other choice? What other path than representative democracy, with all its problems, was ever available to us in the modern age?

The Road Not Taken

In this section, I question the historical inevitability of representative democracy as we know it in order to open the reader's imagination to other institutional paths. I also want to suggest that the selection mechanism for representatives chosen in the eighteenth century was premised on a poor understanding of what it takes to create assemblies with good deliberative potential.[21]

It is puzzling to consider why, in the eighteenth century, the original non-electoral model of Classical Athens was not taken up again when democracy was reinvented in the eighteenth century in the West, especially given the concerns over "factions" held by theorists like Jean-Jacques Rousseau in France or the American Founding Fathers. If we go back to the debates among the Federalists and the Anti-Federalists in the United States, notable for their particular historical salience and, I believe, representativeness, we get a glimpse of the road not taken.

The Federalists—history's victors—favored the idea of a "republic" where individual competence and virtue of the leaders were central. They aimed to staff representative assemblies with people of talent and wisdom capable of enlarging and refining common people's views (Hamilton, Madison, Jay 2008: article 10). They privileged a vision of representation as a "filter" primarily seeking to maximize the average competence of the representatives while accepting the costs of reducing their group to a sociologically and economically homogeneous group of people (the "natural aristocracy" denounced by critics).

By contrast, the Anti-Federalists (Melancton Smith in particular, taking up ideas put forth by John Adams) favored an ideal regime closer to the direct democracy so scorned by their opponents and which they saw successfully implemented in the contemporary Swiss confederacy, of comparable size, population, and wealth to the United States. Short of directly democratic institutions, they envisaged as a second-best an ideal of representation as "mirror" or "miniature portrait of the people" (Adams [1776] 1856: 193). They argued that only people with at least a number of similar traits and lived experience could properly speak on behalf of common people and, indeed, have the relevant political knowledge. Whether they realized it or not, their model privileged the reproduction on a small scale of the diversity of the entire citizenry and was much less concerned with the competence of individual representatives.

---

21. The following draws on Landemore 2018.

Why did the Anti-Federalists, who anticipated some of the contemporary ideas about the factors of collective intelligence and the benefits of cognitive diversity, lose the battle of ideas in the eighteenth century? French historian Yves Sintomer offers one possible explanation. For Sintomer, advocates of the mirror model of representation simply lacked the conceptual tools to support their otherwise correct intuition about the merits of a descriptively representative assembly (Sintomer 2018). In particular, the idea of a "random sample" was not available just yet (it would become available only in the late nineteenth century, with the rise of statistics as a science) and, as a result, the polling techniques that would have rendered selection based on sortition feasible were also unavailable.

Additional hurdles, beyond the epistemological and technological, stood in the path of the advocates of representation as mirror image. One of them was the ideological dominance of elections as the marker and carrier of political legitimacy. As Manin describes it, elections in the eighteenth century "triumphed" over any other alternative selection method (including the obvious democratic alternative of lotteries) because of the theory of political legitimacy that was dominant at the time, which linked legitimacy to consent (since the seventeenth-century social contract theory) and, specifically, consent at the ballot box (Manin 1997: 67–93). As a result, the Anti-Federalists could only imagine selecting representatives by election, which is not a method suited to produce a "mirror image" of the nation. The Anti-Federalists' solution to this problem was to plead for smaller constituencies and a larger number of representatives, hoping that these conditions would generate assemblies at least representative of the middle class rather than just the "natural aristocracy" of the country. But of course, this second-best solution, which had other problems of its own, failed to convince. By contrast, the idea of representation as a filter and the practice of elections as selecting the more competent from among the citizenry were a perfect conceptual and ideological fit.

The next historical step in the evolution of representative governments was to go from parliamentary democracy—where the legislative assembly is seen as a place of deliberation among individually superior minds—to party democracy. Now, the entire public sphere, including the formal one, became a competition between policy platforms that individual citizens or their representatives adjudicate between via voting.

Representative government, from its early elitist beginnings to today's partisan version, thus corresponds to a dated understanding of what makes groups smart and the civic virtues one should cultivate in both leaders and citizens to foster collective intelligence in politics. Today, however, social-scientific tools and evidence suggest where the advocates of the filter idea of representation went wrong and the advocates of the mirror image went right. One important insight, I would argue, is about the benefits of a cognitively diverse group for decision-making. Under certain conditions, cognitive diversity turns out to be more crucial to the problem-solving abilities of a group than does the average competence of its individual members (Hong and Page 2004; Page 2007: 163).[22] This surprising result turns on its head the past received wisdom that group competence is merely a function of individual competence, or that, in other words, the more we staff our decision-making group with "the best and brightest," the smarter the group will be.[23] It turns out that such a strategy will often be less successful, specifically when the best and brightest are too homogeneous in their way of thinking, than a strategy that consists in simply aiming for a high enough level of individual competence but maximizing the cognitive diversity of the group along the relevant lines. If the goal is to compose an all-purpose assembly of democratic representatives, for which there is ex ante uncertainty as to what the relevant diversity should be, and assuming that, on average, citizens are at least competent enough to address most political questions, a good strategy is to take a random sample of the larger population and form a statistically representative mini-public (Landemore 2012, 2013a).[24] In light of this contemporary understanding of what makes groups smart, one way forward in dealing with the crisis of democracy could thus be, instead of rationalizing away the electoral democracy we have inherited from the eighteenth century, to start imagining different institutions, which would aim to maximize cognitive diversity of the law- and policymakers and whose attendant civic virtue would be open-mindedness rather than partisanship.

Initially considered a great tool for democratization, periodic elections present several problems from a democratic point of view: they are by nature

22. This insight is likely as old as humanity and dating back at the very least to the Greek Sophists. It is first captured in writing in Aristotle's idea that "many heads are better than one" (Politics III, 11). In recent years, however, it has been more rigorously captured and formalized in Hong and Page's "Diversity Trumps Ability Theorem" as first elaborated in Hong and Page 2004: 16 and Page 2007: 163.

23. For a discussion of the theorem and its application to political science (and the real world more generally), see critics such as Quirk 2014; Thompson 2014; Brennan 2016: 182. For the defenders, see Landemore 2014b; Page 2015; Kuehn 2017; Singer 2018.

24. Working with a random group of sufficiently smart people rather than a relatively similar-thinking group of very bright people has several benefits, which can be summarized via the topographic metaphor commonly used in the literature on diversity (Page 2007; Weisberg and Muldoon 2009; Landemore 2013a; Gaus 2016): it allows the group to explore more of a given epistemic landscape and increases its chances of reaching its highest peak. A view from someone who thinks differently, in this context, jolts other people out of their cognitive comfort zone and helps them enlarge and refine their understanding of a question by opening up vistas they would not have contemplated otherwise. Deliberating with diverse-thinking individuals takes people places, metaphorically speaking, that they would not have been able to reach on their own. By contrast, a more homogeneous group of smarter people might well end up stuck on a familiar and high but ultimately suboptimal peak of the landscape.

an ambiguously democratic selection mechanism, creating and thriving from inequalities between people; they do not mesh well with the seemingly valuable ideals of deliberation and open-mindedness put forward by deliberative democrats in the last thirty years; and they do not produce enough of the diversity needed for good decision-making. As such, elections may legitimately be seen as preventing rather than facilitating genuine rule by the people.

It seems to me that these democratic flaws at the heart of representative democracy are sufficiently serious to account for at least some of its current institutional crisis. Perhaps globalization and technology, as well as the economic inequalities they entail, made things worse, but the fragility was in the initial design.[25] *Pace* Manin's claim that the principles of representative democracy are not in question in the current crisis of democracy, I would argue that at least two of the principles of representative democracy—periodic elections and independence of the representatives—are now being challenged in ways that are rather new and profound. We can see challenges to the first principle of periodic elections in the rise of social movements and parties calling for direct forms of democracy that bypass elections altogether, as well as movement that calls for their replacement with direct referendums and randomly selected mini-publics (more on this in chapter 3). A book like Van Reybrouk's *Against Elections* (2016), for example, which combines a call for abolishing elections and running the polity via mini-publics of randomly selected citizens would not have been taken seriously even a decade ago.

We can see challenges to the second principle of independence of the representatives in the rise of "monitory democracy" (Keane 2009), in which citizens keep a much closer watch on their representatives' actions between electoral cycles, as well as the symptomatic emergence of forms of "delegative" or "liquid" democracy (Ford 2002, 2014)—used for example by European Pirate parties—where individuals can delegate a vote on the basis of more or less strict mandates (for certain issues, for a certain time) and can recall their vote at any time. The concept of liquid democracy questions not just the definition of who can count as a representative but also the freedom and independence

---

25. An even stronger claim, which is not strictly needed here but is quite plausible and worth mentioning, is that representative democracy, as a combination of oligarchy and democracy (Manin 1997), is *bound* to exhibit a drift toward oligarchy over time. While the current trend we observe today may seem like a contingent drift caused by external "shocks" like globalization and technology, it is perhaps more fundamentally due to the nature of the regime itself. Thus, globalization and technological change may well be tools that parts of the elites in representative democracies have actively pushed (or done nothing to slow down or redirect) *precisely in order to undermine the more democratic elements* of representative democracy (see Max Krahé for a bold political economy argument to that effect: "What is wrong with capitalism?" [2019]).

such representatives have in relation to the represented, increasing the agency and control of the latter at the expense of the former (I say more about liquid democracy in chapter 5).

The Realists' Objections

Before I turn to a false solution to the limits of representative democracy in the next chapter, let me now turn to a likely objection to everything that has been said so far—the "realists'" objection. In their recent book, *Democracy for Realists: Why Elections Do Not Produce Responsive Government*, Christopher Achen and Larry Bartels suggest an alternative answer to the apparent problems of contemporary democracies. From their perspectives, there is no crisis, and democracy is simply working as intended: poorly. In their view, the problem is not with reality, but with the inflated normative expectations they call "the folk theory of democracy," whereby democratic procedures are supposed to track a phantasmagorical general will and express popular sovereignty.

Against such an idealized picture, Achen and Bartels set out to do two things: one is to offer an accurate portrait of the voter's psychology; the other is to curb our normative expectations about democracy. The main positive contribution of Achen and Bartels's book is thus to disabuse us of any romantic idea about voters' behaviors and motivations. Far from voting based on self-interest, ideological preferences, or any other seemingly rational basis, people mostly vote based on their group identity, quite regardless of the actual performance of political candidates. If this is true, they argue, then the rational choice theory literature, which assumes rational and informed voters, fails; the literature on cues and heuristics meant to rescue it fails; and the normative literature in deliberative or participatory democracy, which assumes truth-oriented and reasonable voters, fails as well. On the basis of such devastating conclusions, Achens and Bartels then plead for swapping our lofty ideas about popular sovereignty for a more "realist" picture of how democracy works and what it should be about.

This, of course, seems a perfectly reasonable thing to ask, and parts of the book stay within that more reasonable demand of questioning the descriptive picture we have of democracy in the United States and other Western countries.

Nonetheless, Achen and Bartels go one step too far into normative theory. They pull the classic "realist" move of deriving the undesirability of an ideal from the shortcoming of its attempted implementations in the real world. To the extent that their argument becomes normative, it is morally and politically problematic: since "democracy" as rule of, by, and for the people is unachievable, let us reconcile ourselves with the reality of what we have in the United States and much of the West, which is more or less elite rule with electoral moments that amount to a random shock to the system.

Achen and Bartels's normative realism is a particularly pernicious denial of the crisis of democracy because it consists in asking us to resign ourselves to the fact that chronic dissatisfaction is all we will ever get from politics. In the sober tone of scientists with their feet firmly planted on the ground, Achen and Bartels gently ask us dreamers (the archetype of whom are deliberative democrats, barely worth a paragraph or two in the whole book) to grow up and close the gap permanently between practical reality and normative ideal. If the reality cannot match the ideal, then the ideal must be wrong.

But there is a big difference between correcting a description of the psychology of voters in twentieth-century "democracies" on the one hand and refuting the possibility of implementing a distinct normative ideal on the other. Even if Achen and Bartels are right about the psychology and behavioral characteristics of voters in most Western democracies, they do not prove as much as they think they do.

Indeed, they fall prey to two classic mistakes. The first mistake is, as already mentioned, the naturalistic fallacy of deriving an ought from an is, or rather, in their case, an "ought not" from an "is not." Because voters *are not* informed or rational decision-makers, they argue, we *ought not* pursue democracy as deliberative, participatory, and oriented toward the common good. The second mistake they make is to essentialize the behavior of voters under existing electoral democracies into a fixed "nature," as if voters were not largely responding to incentives. Just because citizens do not behave as we would like in existing systems does not mean that we should not pursue an ideal of democracy that is more demanding of them. Such demands might be met in a rather different-looking system that sets up different incentives.

What Achen and Bartels would reply, presumably, is that all they do is point out that "ought implies can." And if voters *cannot* reason and engage in political debates on the basis of reasons, then there is no point in telling them they ought to. From that point of view, they do strike a blow to the possibility of improving our electoral democracies through more education or more deliberation among citizens as mere voters.[26] But, precisely, and here is a possible point of agreement between my views and Achen and Bartels's:

---

26. Though to be fair, there are very few normative theorists who would recognize themselves as disagreeing with Achen and Bartels here. They hardly mention any normative theorists of any stature in their book, so it is hard to tell who they have in mind. For most normative theorists today (say, Jürgen Habermas, Nadia Urbinati, etc.), the aggregative conception of democracy Achens and Bartels reason about is not the model of democracy they have in mind and within which they make demands on citizens. It is thus hard to see who the "folk theory of democracy" is supposed to refer to, except perhaps the usual Rikerian interpretation of Rousseau and rational choice theory. This view of democracy as a normative ideal is not so much a "folk theory" as a strawman.

maybe the problem is with the current institutional translation of democracy as merely electoral and the reduction of citizenship to voting. Isn't it possible that in a different institutionalization of the democratic ideal, citizens could be as informed, rational, engaged, and generous with their time as they can be when they shop smartly, contribute to Wikipedia, participate in citizens' assemblies or deliberative polls, or spend hours marching against a president they do not like? In other words, an implication of Achen and Bartels's findings is *not* that we have the wrong ideal of democracy. Instead it is that we have the wrong institutional translation of it. If that is the case, we need, more than ever, the leverage of normative criteria that Achen and Bartels want to deprive us of, precisely in order to allow us to imagine new institutional principles that would better satisfy these criteria. By dismissing normative criteria such as Robert Dahl's or deliberative democrats' as too unrealistic, Achen and Bartels fail to recognize that they are tying themselves to what is and making themselves powerless to imagine anything other than the system they rightly criticize. In other words, by diminishing the normative value of democracy, they make it impossible to escape the shortcomings of democratic realities.

For all their self-proclaimed "realism," Achens and Bartels are nevertheless intent on fixing democracy as we know it by, among other things, pursuing campaign finance reform and social and economic equality. It is not clear where these prescriptive injunctions come from in the book, nor is it at all obvious how campaign finance reform and equalizing social and economic policies are supposed to solve the problem of voters' ignorance and irrationality. By contrast, one set of reforms they vehemently oppose is the agenda of involving ordinary citizens more directly in policymaking. It is incompatible with their view of voter competence and, they argue, it has proved a fool's game in the past. Achen and Bartels thus have very harsh words for people like the Populists and the Progressives, who in their view promoted more direct citizen participation to no good effect, only facilitating capture of the system by powerful interest groups (a point also made at length by Shapiro 2016).

In order to show that we cannot ask citizens to reason and engage on the basis of arguments, however, one would have to show that citizens cannot do so in *any* democratic context, not just the context of electoral democracies where their participation is limited to voting once every four years. Unsurprisingly, Achen and Bartels hardly consider the multiple examples of democratic innovations that display these abilities in ordinary citizens. They made short work of citizens' assemblies[27] and do not consider any of the other successful

---

27. They give what is widely considered by deliberative democrats a successful example of citizen participation the faintest of praise by calling it a "seemingly worthwhile Canadian initiative" before condemning it as "an expensive, dramatic failure" because the recommendations of the mini-public failed to pass a referendum with a rather high threshold (66%) (Achen and

examples of mini-publics that are widely documented today. Can such counter-examples be rationalized away so easily when they are so much closer to the meaning of democracy that normative theorists have in mind than the profoundly flawed American system? They never mention Ancient Greece; they never consider Switzerland. Would their conclusions about citizen incompetence apply to these other democracies?

Second, the fact that popular participation has often been captured by private interests in past democratization attempts is no proof that it cannot be deployed in a smarter way under different circumstances. The examples of direct initiatives and referendums in California form only one data point (and even a contested one, see Matsusaka 2005). How about, again, Switzerland, where popular participation is deeply entrenched and is usually acknowledged to serve the common good? What about Citizens' Initiatives in Finland? Zooming out of the American case, which is in many ways an outlier, might diminish their skepticism.

While Achen and Bartel's findings are dispiriting, they simply demonstrate that we have gotten the psychology of voters in electoral democracies wrong. Their demanded correction—that we recognize that voting has more to do with in-group preference than ideology or reason—does not amount to a normative argument against the idea of people's rule, including in its more demanding version, such as the one advanced by deliberative democrats.

Contemporary Solutions and Their Limits

Let us assume, then, that there is a crisis of existing democracies as both empirical realities and the abstract set of institutional principles underlying such regimes. What about the solutions and the remedies? In particular, is there any alternative theory of democracy on offer that would help us overcome the problems with representative democracy as such? In the last chapter of their book, Achen and Bartels throw up their hands: "Unfortunately, we are not prepared to supply, in this concluding chapter, a well-worked out, new theory of democracy" (2016: 298).

Let me now briefly review the most promising existing attempts by normative political theorists at "saving democracy" and show why, in the end, they still fall short of the mark. To preempt my conclusion, the main choice seems to be between, on the one hand, various rationalizations of the status quo in the form of repackaged defenses of elitist democracy and, on the other, participatory variations on deliberative democracy. None of these solutions

---

Bartels 2016: 302). They never pause to consider that making an impact is not the only measure of success. By that standard alone, elections are indeed very successful, despite the fact that they often yield terrible results.

offer the cure we need because none of them fundamentally question electoral representation.

Among the rationalizations, the most spectacular, quite literally, is Jeffrey Green's defense of a revamped Schumpeterian democracy, in which the people are encouraged to give up on the ideal of the voice and embrace instead the "power of the gaze" (Green 2010). The gaze is, for Green, citizens' ability to put "ocular" pressure on the leaders, forcing them into a position of "candor" that is supposed to ensure greater democratic accountability. Since people cannot really exercise any meaningful direct decision-making power, Green reasons, let us celebrate spectatorship instead, as this is, realistically, the only thing that is left.[28]

In a very different, more hopeful vein, the philosopher and historian John Keane converges toward surprisingly similar conclusions (2009). Surveying the history of democracy since the dawn of time, Keane shows that our democratic societies have been steadily evolving toward what he calls a "brand-new historical form of democracy." He characterizes this new paradigm in passing as "post-representative" (also post-Westminsterian), but his favorite label for it is "monitory democracy." By labeling it monitory democracy, Keane means to emphasize the ways in which the powers that be are today watched, made accountable to, and generally kept on their toes by various new forms of popular power other than elected representatives, including civil associations, Non-Governmental Organizations, and the like. Monitory democracy, to the extent that it has a normative component, is evocative of Green's ideal of a system where the "power of the gaze" keeps political elites on their toes.[29]

Keane's trichotomy—assembly democracy, representative democracy, and monitory democracy—is formally close to the distinctions I draw in this book between direct, representative, and open democracy. However, unlike Keane, my approach is more purely normative than historical, prescriptive rather than descriptive. Open democracy is meant to be desirable in ways that monitory democracy is only ambiguously so. Additionally, monitoring power, and keeping it accountable, is not quite the same as exercising it. To the extent that it is normative, a theory of monitory democracy (just as the theory of the

---

28. To its credit, Green's theory captures the spirit of American democracy at the moment. In the age of Kardashian binge-watching and growing political apathy, celebrating spectatorship is a philosophy for the times. In his latest book, Green even doubles down on his theorizing in a sour-grapes mode by celebrating envy for the rich as the appropriate virtue in an age of growing inequalities (Green 2010).

29. Keane's view is also somewhat similar to the central concept of Pierre Rosanvallon's *Counter-Democracy* (2008), which refers to the set of institutions supporting as well as opposing formal democratic power. The difference between Kean's monitory democracy and Rosanvallon's counter-democracy, it seems to me, is that Keane's monitory democracy expands above and beyond strictly political and national institutions.

gaze in Green) remains too wedded to the status quo and the framework of representative democracy.[30]

I worry that such philosophical postures and conclusions, of ostensible realism and acceptance of the limits of what is feasible, are also dangerous. Even if we interpret them charitably as a defense of transparency and openness in government (and of empowering the gaze of the people), these theories of democratic power overestimate the imbalance between the gaze of the people and that of Leviathan in the age of the global Panopticon. The amount of watching that can be done by the people will never match state capabilities, in part because the model depends on the willingness of government to open itself up to people's scrutiny. "Monitory" democracy is always at risk of turning into "monitored" democracy.

Second, the danger of overestimating what "the gaze" can do alone is that it downplays the centrality of voice in the ideal of democracy. At worst, a philosophy of monitoring and spectatorship as the ideal of democratic citizenship in the twenty-first century paves the way for the kinds of conclusion one gets in recent defenses of epistocracy (e.g., Brennan 2016): we should take away the voice of the least literate—literally disenfranchise them—because, after all, it wouldn't make much of a difference to them and would marginally improve political decision-making.

Solutions building on rationalizations of the status quo are not a promising path to saving democracy. Meanwhile, on the republican side, which aim for the more ambitious goal of minimizing domination, we find an interesting diversity of proposals that range from amendments to electoral democracy to radically populist proposals. Philipp Pettit conservatively supports a classic mixed constitution pitting various branches of government against each other, combined with the existence of independent bodies countering dangerous majoritarian features and some new participatory elements (2016). Ian Shapiro (2016), in contrast, favors more majoritarianism and party competition, criticizing Pettit's favored institutional schemes for creating too many veto points and empowering powerful minorities rather than protecting vulnerable ones. Both Pettit and Shapiro agree on the necessity of various forms of intervention to limit the role of money in politics, the practice of gerrymandering, and other corruptions of voting electoral mechanisms. None of them, however, in the name of feasibility and realism, venture very far from electoral democracy as we know it. At most, Pettit seems willing to advocate

---

30. This status quo bias is exemplified in Keane's interpretation of the role of new technologies in monitory democracy. Keane sees new technologies merely as means for greater and non-electoral control of representatives. To me, new technologies are more fundamentally about empowering ordinary citizens, in the sense of returning to them actual power to affect the outcome, not just power to influence and control the representatives.

for mandatory voting, Australian-style. As to Shapiro, his model looks to a romanticized past where strong bipartisanism constrained the possibility of political debate.

John McCormick, a self-avowed populist republican, does break from the mold with his proposal of a "Machiavellian democracy" exposing and building on class distinctions. The central institution of his model is an assembly on the model of the Roman Tribunate whose function would be to fight the oligarchic tendencies of our electoral regimes by empowering randomly selected ordinary citizens to veto one piece of legislation per year, call one referendum per year, and impeach one official from each branch of government per year (McCormick 2011: 178–188). While the theoretical boldness is to be commended, there is something unattractive and indeed undemocratic about a scheme that pits representatives of the wealthy against representatives of the poor, reifying class conflict and, as a result, problematically denying the fundamental political equality that should be at the heart of an authentic democracy.

Other strategies for rescuing democracy consist in rethinking representation rather than democracy itself. For example, Michael Saward's novel theory of representation as claim-making, which focuses on claims to represent by various actors, including non-elected ones, rather than on existing electoral institutions per se, opens the possibility of elevating representative democracy from a historical reality to the status of perfectible ideal: "If we can succeed in making representative democracy *strange*, it becomes less a 'thing,' more a complex aspiration; and less a political compromise and more of a political ideal" (Saward 2010: 168). Saward usefully complicated our understanding of representation, exploring the relation between bearers of claims, the constituencies they make claims for, and the audiences that may or may not recognize those claims as legitimate. He calls for greater empowerment of citizens via a novel understanding of representation. Saward's is thus an attempt to reclaim the concept of representation and build into it new, more democratic meanings. However, he too remains mostly within the parameters of electoral representation and keenly admits the limits of his ambition: "[I]t has not been my task to provide a new blueprint for representative democracy [. . .]. My intention has been to enhance recognition of the complex ecology of representation as a practice, avoiding the pitfalls of overly stipulative or moralized approaches, and indeed approaches that do not question orthodox views enough" (2010: 168).

More subversively, a number of democratic theorists have started advocating for non-electoral forms of representation that blur the line between direct and representative democracy. Such non-electoral forms of representation involve randomly selected bodies (e.g., Gastil and Wright 2019; Guerrero 2014; Abizadeh 2020) or self-authorized representatives (e.g., Castiglione and Warren 2006; Urbinati and Warren 2008). Jim Fishkin has also defended an ambitious vision of democracy, making greater use of his own preferred model of mini-publics (deliberative polls)—yet inscribing it within the paradigm of representative democracy rather than offering it as an alternative to it (Fishkin 2018). Others have additionally applied representative democracy, of a deliberative kind, to the international or global scale (Benhabib 2006; Macdonald 2008), thus breaking with the mapping of democratic sovereignty over the pre-defined, territorial boundaries of nation-states and recognizing the legitimacy of geographically more complex and even non-territorial claims and constituencies (an important issue, to which I turn briefly in the conclusion). In a less academic, more militant style, David Van Reybrouck and Brett Hennig, among others, have been making the radical case "against elections" and for "the end of politicians" respectively with a model of democracy entirely run by mini-publics (Van Reybrouck 2016; Hennig 2017; see also Bouricius 2013). In many ways these new proposals aim to fundamentally alter the meaning of "representative democracy."

In theory, nothing precludes us from changing the meaning of the term "representation" and consequently "representative democracy" and recovering the latter to mean a more truly democratic system. In the following chapters I pursue, like many of these latter authors, such a strategy of de-familiarization to defend new ways of understanding and institutionalizing democratic representation. My sense, however, is that this is not enough to make the term "representative democracy" appealing again. There are limits to a strategy consisting of renovating an old paradigm. We are better off starting fresh, for at least four reasons.

The first, and perhaps most important reason, is that calling democracy "representative" is not a helpful way of characterizing it to begin with. If "representation is democracy," as Plotke (1997) puts it, and as many democratic theorists seem to concur, then we are not saying much by saying "representative democracy." If democracy always involves some form of representation, the expression "representative democracy" is largely redundant and unhelpful.

The second reason is the fundamentally elitist origins of representative democracy, which are hard, if not impossible, to ignore. As we saw in this chapter, representative democracy was born as an alternative to democracy—the mixed regime known as "representative government." It was only slowly and painfully democratized over the last two centuries. Despite theorists' best efforts, there is only so much one can do to revamp a fundamentally elitist construct into one in which power is returned to ordinary citizens. The expression "representative democracy" is not only redundant, it is tainted.

The third, related reason is pragmatic: it is simply too difficult at this point to clear the name of a paradigm that is, the world over, associated with electoral (and thus elitist) democracy. Consider the Freedom House definition of democracy as a political system "whose leaders are elected in competitive multi-party and multi-candidate processes in which opposition parties have a legitimate chance of attaining power or participating in power" (2000: 2).

How do we recover the non-electoral forms and meanings of representation when representative democracy is defined, for most people, by elections? It might simply be too late for a strategy of de-familiarization. The stakes are too high and the need too pressing to bet on the impact of an intellectual reconceptualization of something that has been so shaped by oligarchical principles.

A fourth reason, finally, has to do with the de facto association of representative democracy with the territorial nation-state and a narrow understanding of what counts as "political." In today's global age one can argue that our understanding of democracy should be more ambitious, expanding both laterally (to the economic sphere) and vertically (to the international level), and perhaps becoming dematerialized or at least de-territorialized altogether.

Our task should be, therefore, to offer the blueprint for democracy that Saward and others do not. Instead of refurbishing the paradigm of "representative democracy," let us take for granted that some form of representation will remain needed and desirable in any modern system of governance and proceed to offer a substantively different paradigm of democracy, one that would take us past and beyond representative democracy rather than offer a few friendly amendments to it. Such a model would take representation for granted, with no assumption that it should necessarily translate into electoral mechanisms, and the emphasis would be placed instead on other things, including the openness of the entire decision process to ordinary citizens. This emphasis is a radical departure from the principles of representative democracy as a historical construct, which is built on the exclusion of ordinary citizens from most of the spaces where real power is exercised. Ideally, this new paradigm would also make deliberation central to its institutional design.

Before I begin developing this new paradigm of democracy, let me consider another, in my view wrongheaded though intuitively attractive solution, which consists in returning to a direct form of popular rule, in which all citizens directly make decisions on all issues, without the mediation of representatives. While perhaps tempting at first, this solution proves both practically unfeasible and normatively undesirable.

3

The Myth of Direct Democracy

While some would have us turn to non-democratic regime forms in reaction to the crisis of democracy (an option I will not entertain in this book[1]), many instead seek salvation in a return to direct democracy as truer to the ideals of popular power, popular sovereignty, self-rule, and genuine political equality. Direct democracy advocates often claim to find illustrations of such an ideal of direct democracy in Ancient Greece, certain aspects of the Roman Republic, or the Swiss system.

A first group of direct democracy advocates thus comprises social movements and political experiments as diverse as Occupy Wall Street, the Zapatistas in Mexico, the Indignados in Spain, the Kurdish experiment in "democratic confederalism" in Northern Syria, the social groups that started the Arab Spring, the social protests against Erdogan in Turkey, and the Yellow Vests in France. These groups tend to reject delegation of power or hierarchy within their midst. What they mean by direct democracy is leaderless, self-organized, face-to-face assembly-democracy, typically implemented in rather small settings, with the possibility of federating such small settings in order to cover a larger community without losing any "directness."

A second group argues that new technologies, the Internet in particular, have now made direct democracy feasible even for mass societies. They aim to bypass representation at scale by developing models of digitally enabled inclusive deliberation and voting among all citizens (e.g., Fuller 2015; Tormey

---

1. See instead my forthcoming book with Jason Brennan, where he defends the epistocratic alternative to democracy and I defend the opposite view (Brennan and Landemore forthcoming).

2015[2]). A growing literature in cyber-utopianism and e-democracy thus assumes that all the advantages of small-scale direct democracy supposedly found in the past can be made available again because of the new technologies that have turned the globe into a village and will allow millions of us to do electronically what could only be done face-to-face among small numbers (see, e.g., Bohman 2004; Coleman 2005; Dahlgren 2005; Hindman 2010; Velikanov 2012). In the concluding chapter of his book, *The End of Representative Politics*, Simon Tormey calls his model "post-representative democracy" (Tormey 2015: 144). While high on promises, these proposals are low on concrete specifications.[3]

A third group of direct democracy advocates includes movements and parties like Syriza in Greece, Podemos in Spain (which was itself born from the Indignados movement), or the Pirate Parties of Northern Europe. Though these movements are the products of elections and are classically structured as parties, they nonetheless claim to function along anti-representative principles and to preserve a more direct connection to their electorate. Their practice of democracy appeals to a theory of "liquid" or "delegative" democracy (Ford 2002, 2014), whereby the party base has direct influence on the party platform and its decisions both internally and while in power. In liquid democracy models, members can choose either to vote directly on issues or to delegate their votes to anyone they choose.[4] Once in power, the goal of such parties is, in part, to reinvigorate public institutions by making referendums much more frequently and introducing massive online direct democracy participation mechanisms. What these movements mean by direct democracy is, in Rousseauvian fashion, multiplying voting opportunities and referenda-like moments of final say by the whole people.

Finally, some authors use the vocabulary of "direct" and "anti-representative" democracy to defend what are in fact better characterized as populist institutions and measures (e.g., McCormick 2011), whereby the lower social classes (i.e., the poor) are given special representative institutions and mechanisms

2. Tormey, however, does not quite flesh out what he means by post-representative democracy, beyond gesturing toward a much more direct form of democracy.

3. For more details, one can turn to the conceptualizations of engineers, such as Cyril Velikanov's theorized "mass online deliberation" (Velikanov 2012), which lays out the principles of an online platform allowing a community of individuals to self-organize through the help of algorithms. "Mass online deliberation" would allow individuals to deliberate online with each other in unlimited numbers and promises us the possibility of a return to the Ancient Greek ideal, only on a scale and with a fluidity previously unthinkable.

4. This mode of decision-making has so far been used mostly in the internal context of parties, but its advocates sometimes envision liquid democracy as a viable system at the large scale of nation-states and federations of states, substituting for parliaments and other classically representative institutions. See chapter 5 for more on this.

(only accessible to them) allowing them to push back against the tyranny of the rich.

The ideal of self-governing citizens that do away with the mediation of elected representatives or, at the very least, the mediation of representatives as independent trustees rather than as delegates is undeniably attractive. This chapter, however, argues that for all its appeal, direct democracy, whether face-to-face or enabled by new technologies, is not a viable solution to the problems of representative democracy because it is either feasible but normatively undesirable or, if it is defined in normatively desirable terms, entirely unfeasible.

In doing so I push back against three common beliefs (common in the sense that they undergird our own representative democracies: (1) the Rousseauvian (originally Hobbesian) idea that sovereignty is essentially about having the final say; (2) the historical claim that representation was rendered necessary by the size of mass societies; and (3) the view of Classical Athens as the archetype of a direct democracy. By contrast I argue, first, that sovereignty, contra Rousseau, must include control over two additional dimensions of power beyond the final say, namely agenda-setting and deliberation. Second, I argue that representation is necessary not because of the particular size constraint under which mass societies operate but because of the centrality of deliberation to democratic legitimacy and because of the need, at any scale, to construct and identify interests. Finally, I argue that even Ancient Athens's governance system included representative (though non-electoral) elements. Ultimately, I conclude that since democracy must always be representative, the new forms of citizen participation advocated by direct democracy advocates are best conceptualized as forms of "citizen representation" (Warren 2013), or, in my vocabulary, "democratic representation" (see chapter 4), meant to rival, if not supplant, classical electoral representation.

Before I start making my case, let me pause and offer the definition of representation I will operate with. Definitions of representation are plentiful and sometimes contradictory. Here I want to use a simple one, which I borrow from Andrew Rehfeld's general theory of representation (2006). By representation, I thus mean the act of standing for someone else (individual or group) that is recognized and accepted as such by a relevant audience. The relevant audience that validates the act of representation may be distinct from the represented entity and can express this acceptance / validation / authorization through various mechanisms or decision-procedures. On this descriptive definition, representation need not be good, legitimate, or democratic. The definition of representation I use here is thus compatible with non-democratic and non-normatively legitimate representation, as in the "virtual representation" of yesteryear, which did not require the authorization or even the enfranchisement of the represented. *Democratic* representation is thus a subset of political representation, the main characteristic of which is that access to the position of representatives is open to all, that is, accessible to all on an equal basis.

The chapter proceeds as follows. The first section turns to the foremost advocate of direct democracy, namely Jean-Jacques Rousseau. This section shows that not only is Rousseau's understanding of direct democracy very different from what contemporary participatory democrats have in mind, but also it should be normatively unappealing, at least on the reconstruction attempted here, to anyone who thinks that democratic sovereignty on a large scale must mean more than having the final say once in a while. The second section challenges the received *doxa* on direct versus representative democracy by questioning the common assumption that representation is a modern solution to the problem of the size of democracies in mass societies, as opposed to a problem of size in any polity, whether ancient or modern. The third section then turns to the example of Ancient Athens. I argue that its constitution was not as straightforwardly directly democratic as is often thought. Despite the absence of a proper conceptual and legal framework for representation, Ancient Athens is better seen as a proto-representative democracy, including in its most famous practice—deliberation and voting in the People's Assembly. The fourth section suggests that we need to go beyond the misleading dichotomy of direct and representative democracy and conceptualize instead varieties of more or less democratic forms of representation. Proper conceptualization would help those social movements pushing for greater participation of ordinary citizens in politics avoid the twin dangers of paralysis and undemocratic populism.

Rousseau's Mistake

For Rousseau, democracy was direct or it wasn't. As he famously put it, "the instant a people gives itself Representatives, it ceases to be free; it ceases to be" (*Rousseau 1997, 115*). In other words, representative democracy is no democracy at all. Instead, in the *Social Contract*, Rousseau famously put forward a democratic ideal involving a small republic of free and equal citizens characterized by little social and economic inequality and a great deal of value homogeneity. In this model, the people gather at certain times to vote about laws and policies. They do not deliberate with each other but only within themselves (with "no communication among themselves") in order to vote and thus express what the general will is supposed to clearly require (Rousseau 1997: 60). There is to be no mediation between the people's will and the general will, even as, sometimes, the popular will can miss its target. For Rousseau, indeed, "[a]ny law which the People has not ratified in person is null; it is not a law. The English people thinks it is free; it is greatly mistaken, it is free only during the election of Members of Parliament; as soon as they are elected, it is enslaved, it is nothing" (Rousseau 1997: 114).

As a result of his radical hostility to representation, Rousseau also thought that democracy in the purest sense was only achievable in smaller states (Rousseau 1997: 90), if at all. Despite his avowed preference for direct democracy, however, Rousseau's model was not Ancient Athens. In keeping with his distrust of deliberation, Rousseau thought Athens not so much a democracy as "a very tyrannical aristocracy governed by learned men and orators" (Rousseau 1964: 246,[5] my translation). His model was instead the equally small-sized Swiss cantons and, specifically, his native city-state of Geneva (Miller 1984: 14–25), in which the votation system allowed for the kind of public gathering and independent voting of all citizens at once that Rousseau seems to have had in mind.

At the eve of modernity, the consistently anti-modern Rousseau thus seemed to foreclose the very possibility of mass democracy and seemingly endorsed instead an ideal of small-scale, direct, and participatory democracy. This common reading of Rousseau, however, though influential and often used in support of "strong" democracy models (Barber 1984), does not square well with his later writings on Corsica or Poland, which, instead, defend what looks like elected aristocracies as the best implementation of popular sovereignty at the scale of nations (as opposed to the scale of cities like Geneva). One puzzle is whether these later views form a revision of his earlier views on the unrepresentability of the sovereign or, on the contrary, merely specify them. Recent interpretations lean on the side of confirmation rather than revision.

Thus, on Richard Tuck's view, "Rousseauian democracy was not an idyll of an ancient city-state transported to the present day, but a serious attempt at working out how a modern commercial state might genuinely deserve the title of a democracy" (Tuck 2016: 142). On Tuck's view, it is precisely because nation-states were too big and modern citizens too bourgeois that Rousseau had to move away from the Ancient Athenian model. Bourgeois citizens in large nation-states simply do not have the space or time to gather frequently, as a people, to make the laws themselves. Rousseau's peculiar solution to the problems of size and time constraints was the distinction between sovereignty and government. Like Hobbes, from whom he most likely inherited the distinction, Rousseau envisaged democracy as "a sleeping sovereign" (Tuck 2016). On this reading, a regime can be said to be democratic, even as the tasks of ordinary law-making and policymaking are delegated to a "government" of aristocrats, now understood as an essentially bureaucratic body in charge of implementing and executing the general will.

---

5. "[. . .] *Athènes n'était point une démocratie, mais une aristocratie très tyrannique, gouvernée par des savants et des orateurs*" ("*Sur l'Economie Politique*").

Why, one might ask, shouldn't this body of delegates be conceptualized as "representatives"? Drawing on another of Rousseau's distinctions, that between will and judgment, Nadia Urbinati points out that the "delegates" of the people, whether appointed or elected, are merely in charge of the part of ruling that pertains to judgment, whereas the will remains exclusively and always the prerogative of the people as a whole. This is why

> [w]hen Rousseau writes of the delegates who vote in the assembly that they are not really voting but opining (*"ce n'est pas voter . . . c'est opiner"*) he is saying two things: first, the delegates do not make authoritative decisions; and second, the delegates exercise only the faculty of judgment, not the will. Judgment, because it is parasitical on laws or rules it does not itself create, is a weak power; this makes it transferable without risking the violation of liberty and equality (Urbinati 2006: 73).

What seems to be doing most of the work in allowing for the possibility of popular sovereignty on a large scale is thus a peculiar conception of sovereignty, which for Rousseau is the real, strong power of having the final say over a decision, including one shaped by others, in contrast to the "weak" power of reflecting about or formulating the choice itself. The final decision power seems to refer exclusively to a vote in a plebiscite or referendum (the common institutional translation of Rousseau's more abstract ideas). On this definition, whatever delegates do prior to this final say, including voting on laws, is not an act of sovereignty. Despite all the delegation that actually takes place in Rousseau's governmental designs, these schemes can still claim the label of "direct" or at least unrepresentative democracy because the final ratification moment remains the people's prerogative.

Interpretations differ, however, in terms of what "final say" or sovereignty ultimately means. For Urbinati, it seems to imply a ratification or veto right on any law formulated or even voted on by the "delegates" in charge of deliberating on behalf of the sovereign. What Rousseau must have had in mind, on her view, is thus more or less what we call representative government, but supplemented by frequent ratification procedures involving all the people, so that *all* the laws voted on in Parliament are signed off on and thus authorized by the people themselves. In such a directly democratic model, the "participation" required of citizens is extremely thin, reduced to a mere act of voting, but it is presumably quite frequent.

Richard Tuck makes the case for an even more minimalistic interpretation of democratic sovereignty, which reduces the frequency of such a thin form of direct participation, ostensibly to just a few occurrences a year. What is crucial for determining the nature of the regime, on Tuck's reading of Rousseau, is that the entirety of the people remain somehow directly involved at the level of fundamental law-making. Ordinary legislatures, however, are just part of the government and thus do not require the active interference of the sovereign. We are thus led to believe that democratic sovereignty, for Rousseau, is really only to be sought and found at the level of the constitution, not in the organization and practices of the actual government, including in its ordinary legislative functions (Tuck 2016: 135).

Both interpretations neatly reconcile the dramatic anti-representative views expressed in the *Social Contract* and Rousseau's later, seemingly contradictory embrace of what looks to us moderns like representative institutions in his *Letters from the Mountain*, or his writings on a constitutional project for Corsica or on the government of Poland. While Rousseau rejects the idea of representation where *sovereignty* is involved, he fully accepts it at the level of government. These readings also make sense of Rousseau's otherwise strange preference for aristocracy. Aristocratic governments are compatible with the existence of a democratic regime to the extent that they do not claim to hold or represent popular sovereignty, but are simply in charge of implementing and putting into practice what the democratic sovereign dictates in the abstract, in the form of the general will. The only remaining question is whether democratic sovereignty, for Rousseau, exists mostly in a dormant state, intermittently activated during constitutional moments (that would be Tuck's reading) or is frequently activated, albeit to the minimal act of ratification (that would be Urbinati's reading). To the extent that contemporary representative democracies are indebted to Rousseau's theories, Tuck's minimalistic interpretation might be closer to the mark. It matches well our contemporary electoral democracies' eery resemblance to de facto oligarchies (e.g., Crouch 2004; Gilens and Page 2014) as well as our modern understanding of referendums (outside Switzerland) as rare moments of popular sovereignty (Tuck 2016: 144–180).

But if these interpretations are correct, they also bring into relief the fundamental mistake at the heart of Rousseau's theory as well as its contemporary legacy. This mistake is not so much the distinctions between sovereignty and government, or representation and delegation, or will and judgment, even though these distinctions allow for a problematic accommodation of what we would, or should, consider undemocratic schemes of governance. The deeper mistake is in the idea that democratic sovereignty is merely about having the final power of ratification. On this view, agenda-setting and deliberation, the tasks that come before the actual moment of decision and can be subsumed under the Rousseauvian category of "judgment," are tasks that are not central to democratic sovereignty and can thus be easily taken away from the people and delegated to government administrators, bureaucrats, experts, or elected oligarchies. Rousseau's mistake is thus in seeing judgment as "a weak power," unessential to democratic sovereignty and thus citizens' liberty and equality (Urbinati 2006: 73).

Rousseau's theory of democratic sovereignty, indeed, runs against central contemporary insights from both political science and normative political philosophy. One insight from the political sciences is that agenda-setting and agenda control are where most, if not all, the political decision-making power is to be found. Agenda-setting power—or "non-decision-making power," as it is also called—is the less visible "second face" of power so compellingly painted by Peter Bachrach and Morton Baratz (1962; see also Lukes 1974). Agenda-setting power is as essential to power, if not more so, as casting the final vote—the first, most visible face of power, which most people focus on. Given that issues or options to be voted on cannot formulate themselves, someone needs to be in charge of doing just that and, in the process, is bound to exercise an enormous amount of power. Yet the paradox of Rousseau's democracy is that "delegated power plays the greatest role in the life of the state and is kept out of citizens' sight and control" (Urbinati 2006: 70). By allowing this enormous power to lie elsewhere than with, and indeed hidden from, the people, Rousseau's views result in a considerable weakening of democratic sovereignty.

Another insight, this time coming from normative political philophy, runs directly against Rousseau's views. It is the view that public deliberation among free and equal citizens *is* the main source of political legitimacy (e.g., Cohen 1989; Habermas 1996; Gutmann and Thompson 1996). It is not conceivable, on such a view, that a decision could be democratically legitimate if it merely happened to have been voted on by a majority of citizens. The required prior step is to have citizens deliberate on it, whether directly or indirectly (through legitimate democratic representatives). For deliberative democrats, therefore, Rousseau's vision of a democracy in which the crucial deliberative step is delegated to appointed bureaucrats or aristocrats is hardly democratic at all.

Joshua Cohen has tried to rescue Rousseau from such antidemocratic implications by arguing that he intended to keep some degree of agenda-setting in the hands of the people by allowing them to input and condition the content of the deliberation among government officials through the mechanism of citizens' initiatives (Cohen 2011: 172–173, contra Fralin 1978). Cohen also points out that in his *Letters from the Mountain*, Rousseau defended the possibility for the direct legislative assemblies of Geneva to both set their own agenda and deliberate about it (Cohen 2011: 171). This interpretation of Rousseau as a "deliberative" democrat, however, is hard to reconcile with the generally anti-deliberative stance of the *Social Contract*. It seems to apply only to the small-scale deliberative assemblies of Geneva. However, if we accept (following Tuck) that Rousseau's theory of democracy in the *Social Contract* is a non-representative answer to the problem of size in mass commercial societies, then assemblies where deliberation is feasible (and indeed desirable) can only be the assemblies of delegates of the people, not assemblies of the people themselves (because there are simply too many of them). For the people as a whole, at scale, the sovereign act can only be the silent act of voting.

But on the deliberative theory of political legitimacy embraced by many contemporary democratic theorists, for laws and policies to truly reflect the will of the people, as Rousseau himself requires, the people themselves—or else their democratic representatives—have to be *in the room*. They have to be active participants of the deliberation, from beginning to end. Since, in Rousseau's model, popular sovereignty at the large scale requires delegation of power, and those delegates are not representatives, they should be seen for what they are: a non-democratic subset of the nation wielding most of the political power. Rousseau thus cannot inaccurately be described as embracing at scale "a regime in which [. . .] a largely self-sustaining political elite [. . .] monopolizes the legislative process in all but its final stage" (Cohen 2011: 132, summarizing critics' view of Rousseau as antidemocratic).

Rousseau's mistake is thus not just to have put forward as an ideal a vision of democracy, at least in large enough states, where the sovereign is essentially mostly dormant, but one in which when the sovereign is awake, it only expresses itself through aggregative procedures, whose institutional translation is bound to look like a variety of plebiscitarian regimes. Additionally, if one further accepts some plausible interpretations of Rousseau's distinction between sovereignty and government as a distinction between constitutional and ordinary politics, Rousseau's mistake is perhaps even worse. Not only did Rousseau seemingly believe that sovereignty was simply about having the final say (a voting right about predefined options). He might have even thought that sovereignty was merely about having the final say *about the rules of the game*, rather than a final say in the game itself. Surely, contemporary democrats should aspire to a more ambitious ideal of democratic sovereignty than one where the people have a say only on constitutional matters, and even then, only at the end of the process and through purely aggregative procedures. Rousseau's ideal of direct democracy is not only very far from what contemporary advocates of direct or deliberative democracy have in mind, but it is also normatively unappealing.

Representation, Modernity, and the Problem of Size

In this section, I submit another argument against direct democracy, even when it is understood as comprising an agenda-setting and deliberative component, as opposed to being reduced to the act of voting: its unfeasibility at scale. However, I argue that this unfeasibility is not a problem for mass societies specifically but for any group of citizens beyond perhaps a few hundred people. In making this argument, I thus argue against a common misconception, one that is not specific to Rousseau (though he also held it) but pervades more largely democratic theory: the belief that representation was invented as the institutional solution to the emergence of mass societies. This belief, I suspect, is a classic case of confusing correlation with causation. I turn to this point first.

For most people, representation is what made democracy possible in the modern age of mass societies. Whereas the Ancient world lacked a concept of representation, the modern world, or so it is assumed, was built on it. Thus, a common view, famously expressed, for example, by the Founding Fathers in the United States, is that direct democracy is just not available to us moderns due to the size of our polities. Hannah Pitkin, for example, admits that exactly this assumption underlies her seminal *Concept of Representation*:

> Like most people even today, I more or less equated democracy with representation, or at least with representative government. It seemed axiomatic that under modern conditions only representation can make democracy possible. (2004, 336)

By "modern" conditions, authors like Pitkin generally refer to the age of empires and nation-states, polities too large to be ruled directly. Rousseau himself believed that the idea of representation was a modern invention inherited from feudal government. By contrast, he argued, "[i]n ancient republics and even in monarchies, the people never had representatives; the very word was unknown" (Rousseau 1997: 114). Is there any reason to believe, however, that representation was invented as a solution to the problem of governance in mass societies?

If we turn to the history of the concept, we find that the term "representation" itself comes from Roman law, where it simply meant a more intense version of presenting something. Respectable sources trace the first widening of the term's meaning to debates on the Christian Eucharist of the Middle Ages (e.g., Pitkin 1989: 133ff.). The then central theological question—whether and how Christ could be said to be "embodied," or represented in the Holy Communion—occasioned a conceptual breakthrough in making it possible to think of representation as a commonly agreed upon convention relating two objects without any kind of pictorial resemblance (Hoffman 1974: 80). Later conceptual evolutions brought in the notion of authorization (by the represented, of the representative) and, together with the birth of the concept of the corporation, the view that certain entities like Churches can exist and act above and beyond the sum of their individual members (Vieira and Runciman 2008). The specifically political meaning of representation emerged most recently, in the debates surrounding "the king's two bodies" (one mortal, one symbolic) in early international law (Kantorowitz 1998 [1957]) and in the English debates around the respective authority and powers of King and Parliament in the sixteenth and seventeenth centuries. The biggest breakthrough in this respect came with the publication of Thomas Hobbes's *Leviathan* (1996

[1651]). While on some level Hobbes merely synthesized available concepts (of representation, authorization, personification, etc.), he also radically altered representation from a derivative to a free-standing, specifically political concept, equating representation with political authority itself and grounding it on a secular conception of reason and equality (Vieira and Runciman 2008: 28–29). Representation would then go on to experience more tribulations in eighteenth-century debates around its connection or lack thereof with the comparatively simpler concept of democracy, with very different views held by Rousseau, Burke, Sieyès, and other prominent figures. These eighteenth-century debates paved the way for further debates and complications in the nineteenth and twentieth centuries (Vieira and Runciman 2008).

Nothing in the history of the concept, at least thus briefly reviewed, suggests that it was devised as a solution to the problem of mass societies. Representation appears instead to have emerged as a solution to the need to have something or someone systematically "stand for" something or someone else, whether the Holy Trinity as a representation of the Christ; the Church (as corporation) as a representative of its members; the natural and mortal body of the King as a representation of its political and durable one; or the great Hobbesian Leviathan as a representative of its subjects. Furthermore, it appears that the problems solved by representation initially existed at a variety of scales. The historian of democracy John Keane thus emphasizes that the origin of representative democracy was "in towns, rural districts [as well as] large-scale imperial settings" (Keane 2009: xix). It is only later that "representative democracy came to be housed mainly within territorial states" (xix–xx).

It thus seems to be sheer historical coincidence that the direct / representative democracy distinction has been made to map onto the temporal and conceptual break between the ancient era of small city-states (at most tens of thousands of citizens) and the modern world of nation-states (millions of citizens). It is certainly the case that the large-scale size of modern polities made representation seem all the more necessary. But the jump in size from city-states to nation-states and empires is not, or so it would appear, what *caused* the emergence of representation in the first place.

Advocates of direct democracy today—from Occupy Wall Street to the advocates of e-democracy or "liquid democracy"—seem to embrace this conclusion, seeing in representative democracies an essentially historically contingent and ultimately elitist version of democracy, while looking to revive ancient models of "direct" democracy. This vocal minority either discards the unfeasibility-due-to-scale argument or denies that there is something special about "modernity." Notwithstanding the impracticality of many of these direct democracy schemes and the so far largely unsubstantiated hopes of e-democrats, these movements are right to think that there is nothing special about modernity that makes the model of Ancient Greece or aspects of the

Roman or Swiss model irrelevant. But they are wrong to think that this means the possibility of returning to a golden age of direct democracy. It is simply not the case that democracy as a political regime can ever be truly direct, even at the small scale of a city or a canton, as opposed to being always mediated and based on some kind of delegation of political authority whereby some people stand in for others.

There are two overlapping arguments for why democracy cannot be direct. One relates to the unfeasibility of large-scale deliberation due to the time and cognitive constraints under which human beings operate. To the extent that we think democracy needs to have a deliberative dimension, *direct* deliberative democracy at scale is simply not an option (today at least and possibly ever). The second is a more general version of the unfeasibility argument, which doubles as a normative argument relative to the nature of politics and the desirability, in and of itself, of constituting interests through representative schemes.

Let me consider the first unfeasibility argument relative to the limits of deliberation at scale. If we accept that deliberation is a normatively desirable feature of democratic decision-making, because we owe each other reasons for the laws and policies that are going to affect us all, then democracy needs to include a deliberative phase. Deliberation involving every single member of the community at once and on equal terms is, however, impossible, at least if understood as the same thing as a deliberation among a handful of people but at the scale of thousands, or even millions, of people. Such a process would take too much time and be too cognitively taxing for individual participants. Democratic societies have thus long evolved the solution of representative assemblies, which allow for exchanges of arguments at a reasonable scale.

Much work by theorists of deliberative democracy similarly assumes the impossibility of deliberation among more than a handful of people and instead promotes, in lieu of deliberation among all citizens, the second best of minipublics that are minimally representative of the large one. These mini-publics are defined as "groups small enough to be genuinely deliberative, and representative enough to be genuinely democratic" (Goodin and Dryzek 2006: 220). There exists a diversity of mini-publics, including citizens' juries, consensus conferences, and AmericaSpeaks gatherings. James Fishkin's deliberative polls, which gather up to five hundred randomly sampled citizens for one- or two-day deliberations, offer what some have described as the "gold standard" in this respect (Mansbridge 2010), aiming to be as demographically representative as possible in order to replicate the preferences that the larger public would presumably hold were mass deliberation possible.

Most real, quality deliberations thus involve a handful of people. Even Fishkin's deliberative polls, which claim to have hundreds of people deliberating with each other, are in effect broken down into deliberative units of about fifteen people. In other words, deliberation within large groups is never all-inclusive in a direct way. Instead it is stacked, building on deliberative subunits that are then represented at the larger scale. Even among groups of a hundred people or so, deliberation occurs through mechanisms that closely resemble representative mechanisms.

Could new digital technologies solve the problem by economizing on costly cognitive processing of information and allowing for the distribution of deliberation over time? This is the hope entertained by cyberdemocrats, some political and communication theorists, and visionary engineers (see, e.g., Bohman 2004; Dahlgren 2005; Hindman 2010; Velikanov 2012). Online deliberation permits the recording and archiving of all people's thoughts, comments, and ideas while economizing on the necessity of being present all at once. As long as everyone can access the same virtual "room" (the platform they sign in for), individuals are able to read the same content when it is convenient for them and at their own pace. Assuming a sufficiently long window of time before the decision is made, deliberation among all can thus be distributed over time in a way that fosters great inclusivity. Online, text-based deliberation thus potentially takes care of some of the constraining time and space aspects of face-to-face direct deliberation.

At the moment, however, even the most promising existing platforms—for example, Mark Klein's Deliberatorium—only succeed in expanding the number of people who deliberate directly with each other in this way to several hundred people (Klein 2011). A few hundred people enabled to deliberate in a direct manner with each other is a clear improvement over the limits of face-to-face deliberation. This is nonetheless a far cry from the millions that would need to be included for direct democracy to be possible in existing polities. Current promises of true "mass online deliberation" (Velikanov 2012) are at best conceptual prototypes at this point.

Direct democracy, to the extent that it involves an inclusive deliberative phase, is thus only feasible for very small groups.[6] If this is true, then the possibility of direct democracy breaks down as soon as the group expands beyond a few hundred people.

The second argument against the meaningfulness and possibility of direct democracy pertains to the nature of politics, rather than human or physical limitations per se. The claim is that representation is necessary and desirable, in and of itself, as a way to constitute interests and preferences. It is sometimes expressed as the view that "representation is always constitutive of democracy

---

6. Though some have argued that one could make direct democracy *more* deliberative, for example by requiring votes to be justified in order to foster public debates and internal deliberation. See, e.g., Vandamme 2018.

and democratic practices" (Plotke 1997: 10; Urbinati and Warren 2008, among others). Or, as Plotke puts it even more explicitly:

> Representation is not an unfortunate compromise between an ideal of direct democracy and messy modern realities. Representation is crucial in constituting democratic practices. "Direct" democracy is not precluded by the scale of modern politics. It is unfeasible because of core features of politics and democracy as such. (Plotke 1997: 19)

What Plotke and other proponents of the so-called constructive turn in representation theory argue is that interests and preferences, unlike, say, a taste for vanilla or chocolate ice cream, are not given. Only on a very crude (or economistic) understanding of politics can one expect individuals to be able to state their interests and preferences (let alone judgments) off the top of their heads and without prior elaboration. This elaboration will usually require the creation of interest groups, associations, or parties, which can then enter in a meaningful and informed manner the deliberation, negotiations, and bargaining taking place at the collective level. Figuring out, clarifying, and articulating interests is, in other words, a prerequisite to deliberation altogether (see also Rummens 2012). If this is so, representation is fundamentally unavoidable and will remain so even if deliberation could be made to scale to millions of people. In other words, except perhaps for very small groups whose interests can be identified in the course of a direct deliberation, direct democracy is just not an option.

I now turn to Ancient Athens, the Ur-model of direct democracy, to question the idea that it lacked representation altogether.

The Myth of Classical Athens as a Direct Democracy

A common vision of Classical Athens depicts a city where thousands of citizens directly self-ruled through regular face-to-face meetings in a public place large enough to contain them all. During these meetings, important decisions were made and laws passed through public deliberation followed by voting (by show of hands). Democracy was direct in that there were no intermediaries between the public and the regime's laws and policy outcomes. It was proper self-government.

Most prominent accounts of the way Athens was actually run (such as Hansen 1999; Ober 2008) paint a picture of Athenian democracy as much less direct than such naïve preconceptions assume. Indeed, I will suggest below that the fundamental legislative institutions of Classical Athens had a democratic representative character in that a subset of the polity was acting on behalf of the larger demos with the de facto authorization of the latter. Given the definition of democratic representation I use here, it matters only partly that this may not have been exactly how Athenians themselves pictured their own system, or what psychological beliefs they held about their roles as citizens.

The main legislative institutions of Classical Athens were the Boule, or Council of 500; the Ekklesia, the People's Assembly; the Nomothetai; and (in the fourth century BC) even the Courts. The Council was a body of 500 citizens randomly selected among the willing and able. It was "a linchpin institution that was given control of the vital agenda-setting function" for the meetings of the People's Assembly and was also responsible for the day-to-day administration of state affairs, "including meeting foreign delegations and reviewing the performance of outgoing Athenian magistrates" (Ober 2008: 142). The People's Assembly, by contrast, was an open assembly where up to 8,000 citizens were able to gather in order to deliberate and vote about the Council's proposals. The Nomothetai were the boards of "legislators" appointed by lot to review and revise existing laws in a trial-like process once the People's Assembly had deemed it necessary. The Courts, finally, were also randomly selected but non-deliberative bodies of hundreds of citizens in charge of deciding on public and private judicial issues. In the fourth century BC they were entrusted with laws themselves (acquiring powers previously belonging to the People's Assembly).

Assuming for now that the People's Assembly can legitimately count as an institution of direct democracy, this assembly was thus largely dependent on agenda-setting by the Council of 500.[7] According to Josiah Ober, the institution of the randomly selected council was in fact the key institution in Greek democracy and may even have been more central to the Greeks' concept of democracy than the Assembly (Ober 1997 and 2008). From this perspective, the People's Assembly may even appear as a mere rubber-stamping institution rather than an all-powerful sovereign. The Courts may, in fact, have been more deserving of the title "most democratic" Greek institution. Far from being, as we anachronistically often imagine, countermajoritarian institutions meant to constrain the people's will, courts were, she claims, the best, least corruptible, and most genuinely popular vehicle for it, in contrast to the People's Assembly, which was easily manipulated by the gifted, connected, and often rich orators (Cammack 2018). One could finally remark that since non-democracies, such as Sparta, had assemblies in which the agenda was controlled by the aristocracy, the existence of a People's Assembly is, by itself, no guarantee of popular sovereignty (Bouricius 2013). All of this relativizes the power of the Athenian Assembly and suggests that Athens was not the paragon of direct democracy that popular imagination and some neo-populists like to depict.

---

7. Sometimes, to be fair, suggestions from the populace at large were allowed to be added to the agenda as well.

Finally, should the People's Assembly itself be considered directly democratic? Even ignoring the fact that women, metics, and slaves counted for nothing, at no time did more than a small fraction of the male citizenry of Athens gather to deliberate and vote in the People's Assembly. As Mogens Hansen describes it, "Decrees of the Assembly *were treated in principle as decisions of the entire Athenian people*, but in practice not more than a fraction of the citizen population were ever present" (Hansen 1991: 130, my emphasis). Hansen estimates that no more than between 6,000 and 8,000 people ever showed up to the Assembly (as its location first changed from the agora to the Pnyx and the Pnyx itself became more spacious over time) out of an estimated 30,000 eligible attendants. In other words, between one-fifth and one-fourth of the entire population made decisions for the whole. The number of participants was anyway limited in practice by the finite size of the Assembly place. In the fourth century, when attendance was financially incentivized, a number of citizens were actually *physically prevented* from entering the Assembly once it was judged to be at capacity (Hansen 1991: 132, who reports on ropes dipped in red paint encircling the last row of persons allowed inside the assembly). Thus, regardless of the desire of the demos to participate, only a fraction of it could ever really make decisions—at most roughly one-fifth of the actual number of eligible participants.

What is striking in this alleged direct-democracy institution is that, despite the fact that it was physically impossible for all to be present, the decisions of whoever showed up and managed to enter the Assembly place were taken to be those of the demos at large. In other words, the 6,000–8,000 who actually showed up de facto acted as representatives of the other 22,000–24,000 missing free Athenians, even as the legal and political concepts of "representation" were not available just yet.

In the People's Assembly, therefore, those present made decisions on behalf of the absent, just like elected representatives make decisions on behalf of their constituents in our modern democracies. The main differences are that the representatives in the Greek context were not elected but self-selected; the ratio of representatives to represented was much higher—and more reasonable (between 1 to 10 in the fifth century when participation wasn't financially rewarded to 1 to 5 in the fourth century when it was)—than what it is today in our modern democracies, where one representative rather absurdly stands for millions of people. But most importantly, the representation that it makes sense to envisage in this context is not in fact "one-to-one" but "many-to-many." It is the whole assembly of 6,000 that could collectively claim to represent the larger community of 30,000 and legitimately act on its behalf, even as each individual member could not be said to be, and did not necessarily see themselves as, representing any other individual.

This many-to-many dimension may help us address the objection that participants in the assembly couldn't possibly count as representative in the modern sense because when they spoke and voted, they were responsible in their own name for their speeches and actions and liable to prosecution as individuals, not as "representatives" in the modern sense. The objection is that individuals did not act as representatives, nor were they perceived by others or themselves as such. It is supported by the fact that one of the historical evolutions that the concept of representation went through was to entrench a clear division of responsibility between represented and representative (Vieira and Runciman 2008). A distinction between their private and representative persons—their two "bodies"—gives representatives leeway to act and speak without fear of consequences for themselves that the Athenians did not enjoy.

One can make two rebuttals to this objection. First, far from proving that ancient democracy was not representative in the sense of allowing some to stand for others in a way accepted by the relevant audience, it simply establishes that ancient democracy lacked a proper understanding of its own practices. Certainly, Athenian citizens did not enjoy all the advantages that come from a clear perception of the concept of representation and the division of labor and responsibility between the personal self and the representative one that such an understanding would have permitted. In this sense, Paine's famous remark that Athens would have surpassed itself had it been "representative" can be reinterpreted as saying that it is more advantageous to conceptualize properly one's own practices. This is true in the same way that some understanding of probability theory—which only developed in the seventeenth century—might have helped the Greeks make better sense of their intuitive, pre-theoretical (some say religious) use of lotteries.

But, second, perhaps we are blinded by our electoral understanding of representation, which is limited to one-to-one or one-to-many dimensions. Perhaps for Ancient Greeks, only the *group* of self-selected participants was acting as representative of the larger group, thus leaving *individuals* on the hook as private persons for whatever they said and did. In other words, the many-to-many dimension of this form of representation may have prevented individuals themselves from acting or perceiving themselves as representatives. It was enough that the group performed this function of representation, regardless of what individuals within did and thought. Thus, when the demos chose to invade Sicily in 415, the entire Athenian citizenry took responsibility for the disastrous decision, not just those who had showed up that day and made the decision. The fact that individuals remained liable on a personal level might seem unfair, but it does not make the system incoherent. It is even possible that Athenians had the notion of responsibility of group Y for the decisions of group X, even as they punished members of X.

There are several reasons why democracy in Athens could not be direct in the way often pictured. As stated above, none of the known Assembly places (the Agora, the various iterations of the Pnyx) could hold the entirety of the body politic at once, or even a majority of it. Second, even if it could have, it would have been impossible to have coherent deliberation among 30,000 people. If one assumes coherent deliberation to be a condition for meaningful democratic decisions, then direct democracy among such a large number of people is impossible. In fact, such a deliberation was equally impossible among the 6,000 who showed up. While 6,000 people is often presented as a small number, it is in fact larger than any of the assemblies that today we can, ironically, call "deliberative" (even one of the biggest Parliaments in the world, the Italian parliament, only counts up to 1,000 people, and everyone knows how functional that has proven to be).[8] As a result, "the vast majority of the audience of 6,000 were content to listen and vote and only a tiny minority came forward to make speeches or propose motions" (Hansen 1999: 143). And because speaking in public demanded rhetorical skills and courage that not everyone possessed, among this speaking minority "debate was dominated by a small group of half- or fully professional orators, some of whom had been trained by sophists or in the school of Isokrates or in Plato's Academy." Even though the Athenians liked to cultivate the ideal of the Assembly speaker as "the plain man who spoke his honest mind with modest infrequency and without circumlocution," the reality was that much of the talking was actually done by a small number of professional speakers (the rhetores) (Hansen 1999: 144).[9]

All the evidence, therefore, indicates that the practices of Ancient Athenians were doubly representative when it came to deliberation in the assembly. Only a subset of the citizenry ever participated in the assembly and, among those who were actually allowed to participate, only a tiny fraction of those 6,000 self-selected citizens (about 0.5 percent of them, or 0.1 percent of the entire citizenry!) actually spoke up. It is not clear whether the self-selection of speakers took place ahead of time or on the spot, or whether it was always the same people who spoke publicly, or whether a new, fresh set of voices were

8. See also Dahl 1970 for the point that direct deliberation among 6,000 people would be too time-consuming.

9. This reconstruction of the way the Assembly functioned is supported by textual evidence: far from deliberating with each other as contemporary models of deliberative democracy like to imagine, the 6,000 participants engaged at most in "internal deliberation" before voting and after being talked to by 20 to 40 self-selected orators (Cammack 2020). Additionally, it appears that the speakers cast themselves, by the very act of speaking, outside the deliberating unit and into the distinct role of "advisor" (Landauer 2019: 8–10). In other words, coming forward as a speaker distinguished you from the rest of the crowd to the point of seemingly excluding you from the pool of decision-makers or at least putting you in a distinct category where the exercise of your right to speak up almost supplanted your right to vote.

heard each time. In any case deliberation never involved the entire citizenry and only indirectly involved the sample that was actually present.

One could push back against all of these claims in the following way. One could first argue against the representative nature of the Council of 500 on historic or terminological grounds. For Rousseau and today's historians of ideas, lotteries are in fact the telltale mark of a direct democracy. According to Bernard Manin, for example, the practice of selecting magistrates by lottery is what separates representative democracies from so-called direct democracies. This is because, for Manin, it is not indirectness per se that is the mark of a representative as opposed to a direct democracy. It is four distinct principles: periodic elections; independence of the representatives from the wishes of their electorate; freedom of expression; and public decisions being put to the trial of debate (Manin 1997). The Athenian system as a whole of course does not fit the four principles listed by Manin as characteristic of representative governments (mostly the electoral criterion). The limit of Manin's account, however, is that it is descriptive and that there is no reason why history should dictate our normative principles. There is no reason why the fact that representative government has been historically identified with such principles should make representation bound to them only.

Regarding the representative nature of the People's Assembly—an even more difficult case to make—one could ask: Why does the fact that not all showed up, or even could show up, disqualify the assembly meetings as a form of direct democracy and turn those who were present into ipso facto representatives of the absent? After all, to use a contemporary example, if I fail to show up at the faculty meeting one day, that does not mean I feel "represented" by their decisions in my absence. Nor does it mean that my colleagues see themselves as acting as my "representatives." One could thus argue that while the larger Demos was bound by the decisions of the people who showed up physically at the assembly, it does not mean that this assembly acted as "representative" of the larger group in any meaningful sense. The absent just accepted that they were tied by the decisions made, not that they were represented by the decision-makers.

But first notice that it does not really matter how individual members of the assembly or those failing to show up "feel" if they are not the relevant audience for the claim to representation.[10] Who was the relevant audience whose accep-

---

10. To take up the University departmental meeting example, what matters is that those present, as a group, claim to speak on behalf of the whole department, even if I, as an individual, missed the meeting and even if individual participants in the meeting did not feel or claim to represent me. Equally important, the upper hierarchical echelons at the University will accept this group's claim to be representing the whole department. By the definition used in this book (see chapter 4)—representing is standing for someone in a way that is accepted by the relevant

tance mattered in the Greek case? Ultimately, it has to be the people at large: the capital D-Demos, as Ober calls it, by opposition with the small d-demos present in the assembly (Ober 1996). If it is indeed the case that the larger Athenian people did not see the Council or the People's Assembly as "standing for them" in some way, it would be very hard to claim the Council or the People's Assembly as representative institutions on my own terms. The problem is that it is very difficult today to figure out what the capital D-demos really thought. Available sources suggest that they identified the People's Assembly and "the people of Athens," though it is a matter of controversy among historians whether this identification should be understood in the modern terms of a representative relation.

Here it is worth bringing up a fascinating debate between two prominent historians of Ancient Greece, Mogens Herman Hansen and Josiah Ober. Though they ultimately seem to agree that Athenian institutions such as the People's Assembly and the Council of 500 (as well as the Nomothetai and the Dikasteria [the popular courts]) could not be said to have been "representative" of the People, their hesitations leave the door open to a different interpretation.

Hansen vacillates the most on this. He initially argued in various articles that the Dikasteria did in fact "represent" the demos in the sense of "acting on behalf" of it and, as mentioned earlier in this section, he similarly used language about the members of the assembly with respect to the larger group of citizens that suggests a representative relation. It is only when prodded by Ober's critique that Hansen feels obliged to retract a view he had persuasively argued for before.[11] Ober, for his part, believes that the relationship between the Demos and the Dikasteria, or the Council of 500, is better understood in terms of the rhetorical figure of speech "synecdoche," which is "a figure of speech in which a part *stands for* and refers to a whole, or vice versa" (Ober 1996: 330). When it comes to the relationship between what he calls capital D-demos—the entirety of the Athenian free people—and the demos effectively gathered in the People's Assembly, Ober calls the relationship not one of synecdoque but one of "symbolism," whereby "decisions made by those who attended [. . .] certainly *symbolized* the will of Demos; but the participants at a given Assembly were not identical to Demos (Ober 1996: 330, my

audience (here the University)—the members who attended the meeting represent me, whether individuals in the group see themselves as doing so and whether I accept it or not.

11. In a stunning appendix called "The Idea of Representation." It turns out that upon rereading, the Greek texts Hansen had used as evidence for a representative relationship between demos and dikasteria in particular may simply mean "for the good" or "in favor of" the demos, not "on its behalf" (Hansen 2010: 536).

emphasis).[12] It is striking that even though Ober rejects the term "representation," he nonetheless cannot help but emphasize the distinction between the part and the whole and define the part and the whole in terms of one "standing for" the other.[13] What Ober thus describes under the terms "synecdoche" and "symbolism" strikes me as exactly what most political theorists since at least Hannah Pitkin (1989 [1967]) would acknowledge as representation, i.e, the act of "standing for." If Ober's description of the psychological disposition of Athenians to accept the decisions of the parts as decisions of the whole is correct, then Ancient Athens was decidedly a representative, not a direct, democracy, including on the definition of representation defended herein.[14] And indeed, in another of his works, Ober comes close to admitting as much (Ober 2017: 19).[15]

All in all, and the vacillations of the historians of ancient democracy notwithstanding, it seems to me at least permissible to entertain the thought of Classical Athens as a proto-representative rather than direct democracy, including in its most iconic practice: the People's Assembly. Far from involving all citizens at once, the People's Assembly was based on a form of self-selected

---

12. Ober then concludes that "[s]ince Since H[ansen] argues that the authority of the law-courts was not delegated, and since the Athenian jurors *were not appointed or elected* to represent a larger constituency, 'representation' does not seem the best way to conceptualize the relationship between lawcourts and Demos" (Ober 1996: 30; my emphasis). But of course, this reasoning only works on a narrowly electoral understanding of representation. Hansen's argument that the authority of the courts was not "delegated" might be more convincing, though one has the suspicion that Hansen too may have used an overly restrictive definition of what counts as "delegation."

13. "Each of the various institutional "parts" of the citizen body [ekklesia, dikasteria, nomo-tetai, boule] could thus *stand for* and refer to the whole citizen body. Orators could speak of jurors as having made decisions in Assembly because both a jury and an Assembly were parts of the whole" (Ober 1996: 330–331).

14. Hansen unfortunately still happens to disagree, mostly because once he retracts his own previous argument for a representative relationship between demos and courts, he cannot accept the one offered by Ober for the symbolic or synecdoche-like relations. Hansen rejects in particular Ober's distinction between the capital D-Demos—the ideological construct that he compares with Benedict Anderson's "imagined community"—and the small d-demos who gathered in the People's Assembly (a distinction seemingly accepted by Manin above). I do not know if this dispute can be decidedly resolved one way or another, but I am personally tempted to side with Ober, minus the semantic disagreement about the proper term to be used.

15. Even as Ober insists that "Athens was a direct form of government by citizens," he also writes: "the common notion that representation is a uniquely modern concept, utterly foreign to ancient democratic thought [. . .] is misleading. The Athenian demos (as the whole of the citizen body) was imagined as present in the persons of those citizens who chose to attend a given assembly. So the demos was *conceptually represented, pars pro toto, by a fragment of the citizenry* (Ober 2017: 19, my emphasis).

representation by which the subset of the citizenry that showed up at the meeting was effectively, and perhaps consciously, making decisions on behalf of the rest.

Direct versus Open

Direct democracy is either normatively undesirable or unfeasible. Rousseau himself, perhaps the most important proponent of direct democracy, seemed to acknowledge as much since (1) he did not consider Ancient Athens to count as a democracy and (2) he thought that "a true democracy has never existed and never will" (*Social Contract* III.4).[16]

If, as this chapter has argued, direct democracy cannot really exist as an autonomous regime form, what should we make of things like referendums? Do they not count as direct democracy? In this last section I offer a distinction between regime forms and elements or moments of a regime form. A democracy can have elements of direct democracy, like referendums, without ceasing to be representative as a whole. Second, numbers and participation ratios matter. Based on them we should distinguish between elements of direct democracy, which depend on mass participation, and what I propose to call "open" representative democratic practices, which are based on self-selection, compatible with low turnout, and must be understood as involving forms of representation.

Direct democratic moments are distinct from open democratic moments, in my view, in that they typically require mass participation. Referendums, like most elections, are typically meant to involve all, or at least a majority, of eligible citizens and indeed are not seen as very legitimate if less than half of the population shows up on the voting day. *Landsgemeinde*—Swiss direct democratic assemblies—are also meant to gather a large number of people relative to the community at stake (the canton). To my mind the Greek People's Assembly could only have qualified as a direct democratic institution if everyone had been able to gather on the Pnyx (which they never could) and, additionally, if it had been a common expectation and practice, most of the time, for most of the relevant population to show up (a counterfactual we unfortunately do not have access to).

By contrast, open democratic moments always involve fewer people than a majority and should be interpreted as representative (albeit non-electoral) in nature. They are occasions for what Mark Warren calls "citizen representation" whereby "lay citizens represent other citizens" (Warren 2013), including

---

16. In fairness, Rousseau's reason to think a true democracy unfeasible was a bit distinct, i.e., the supposed counter-natural principle of having the majority govern and the minority be governed.

without the explicit delegation of authority that elections typically allow for. This form of democratic representation is very much undertheorized in part because it tends to be confused with "participatory democracy." As Warren convincingly argues, however, using the category "participatory democracy"

> fails to identify what is perhaps the most important feature of cases of citizen representation: each involves a form of representation that depends upon *the active participation of a relatively few citizens who function as representative of other citizens.* (2013: 51)

It is thus the small number of participants relative to the population at large that tends to distinguish moments of citizen representation from moments of direct democracy (such as referendums). The democratic credentials of citizen representation in open democracy moments come not from mass participation but the fact that the representatives tend to be ordinary citizens as opposed to professional politicians (i.e., elected representatives).

Among open democratic moments I would count crowdsourced policy processes, participatory budgeting, and initiatives, where access is open to all and people participate based on self-selection, usually in relatively low numbers compared to the overall population.[17] For the same reasons, initiatives seem to me to qualify as "open" democratic moments rather than direct democratic moments. The threshold of signatures that an initiative needs to cross is a few percent of the population—hardly mass participation. A difference between open and direct democracy moments is that participants in the former are rarely given final say on any decision and their role is seen more as complementary to other representative or direct democracy moments. In crowdsourced processes, the crowd involved is not meant to have final say over the decision, even as it is able to influence it. Additionally, whereas in referendums citizens are supposed to vote what their conscience dictates, initiatives and crowdsourced contributions gain legitimacy only to the extent that the participants say things that are at least minimally representative of what other people think and care about.

Initiatives serve in part a remedial function, to compensate for the inevitable blind spots of a legislature (even a randomly selected one would have such blind spots). But they are also useful methods for citizens to put on the agenda propositions that would intentionally not be considered otherwise. With respect to classically electoral representatives in particular, these devices can force them to change arrangements whose flaws they see very well but that they have no incentives to change (regarding their own compensation, gerrymandering rules that benefit them, or the possibility of cumulating

---

17. For example, crowdsourced policy processes can be considered successful even if less than 1 percent of the population shows up.

mandates) or may have even put in place for their own advantage. Initiatives are about allowing citizens to shift the balance of power between represented and representatives and preventing an entrenchment and ossification of this distinction, ultimately resulting in a closure of power. Such devices thus would prove particularly useful in removing political obstacles in the transition to open democracy and in prefiguring it, even as they would be meant to play less of a role (hopefully) in a fully realized one.[18]

What are the benefits of the (possibly radical) reconceptualization offered in this chapter? Am I not harming the cause I claim to want to serve—recovering the meaning of popular rule and empowering ordinary citizens—by dismissing the idea of direct democracy as either unfeasible or undesirable, except as ordinarily infrequent moments of mass participation in an overall representative scheme? My sense is, on the contrary, that I am paving the way for democrats to reconquer sites of real power by disabusing them of the notion that gathering in public spaces in large numbers, marching against authorities, or letting popular social media personalities end up as de facto leaders is enough, or even all that democratic in the end (though it may be at the beginning).

Accepting that democracy is always, in some sense, representative (including when it has direct and open democracy moments), and indeed needs to be, would save a lot of these social movements from the sort of conceptual and practical dead ends that the Zappatistas, Occupy, the Indignados, and other proponents of assembly democracy in the Arab Spring, in Turkey and elsewhere could not find a way out of (Tüfekçi 2017). It would allow for the civic energy mobilized by these movements to be channeled into constructive decision-making beyond demonstrating and occupying, and generally go from noise to signal. From this perspective the Spanish party Podemos, who turned the Indignados movement into an effective political machine, the Pirate Parties in Europe, the Five Stars movement in Italy, the Partido de Internet in Spain, and the Partido de la Red in Argentina have pragmatically recognized that achieving their goals demands employing representative means. Some of them went back to classic electoral models (Podemos); most, however, tried a slightly different route, embracing what they call "liquid" democracy, which hybridizes referenda-like moments, classic representative democracy, and voting by proxy. This model is sometimes advocated by its proponents as a type of direct democracy, but it opens the more interesting possibility of a different kind of representation. These movements, however, have yet to try and practice new forms of democratic representation, for example based, as in ancient Athens, on sortition and self-selection.

But more important perhaps than the risks of impotence carried by efforts to stick to direct democracy are the real dangers, under the guise of immediacy

---

18. I thank Lisa Disch for helping me recognize the usefulness of initiatives in that way.

and spontaneity, of actually self-selected groups illegitimately speaking in the name of the whole—the danger of a certain kind of populism (Werner-Müller 2016). Social movements like Occupy could somewhat plausibly claim to be the 99 percent in an age when most of the economic gains of the last thirty years had gone to just a few people. But even such groups failed to include the very poor. Movements claiming the mantel of direct democracy quickly turn exclusionary.

This is a danger I also see with McCormick's "Machiavellian democracy" and his defense of a modern Tribune of the Plebs from which socioeconomic elites would be excluded, which thrives on a problematic distinction between "the people" identified in Aristotelian fashion with the poor majority and "the rich," as if the members of each economic class were not equal citizens of the demos. Despite the noble goal of fighting back the plutocratic tendencies of modern democracies, there is something unsettling about such proposals, and not just because instruments of direct democracy are always at risk of being highjacked by individuals with time, money, and intense preferences, i.e., the very people McCormick aims to protect the people from (see Shapiro 2016: 176 for a critique).[19] While McCormick is probably right that populism as a "cry of pain" has a role to play in the reconquest of our democratic institutions, we should not confuse political tactics and normative ends. Criticizing the spoiled brats of the family, keeping them in check, and reminding them to pay their fair share should not lead to excluding them from the family entirely. My own view is thus that we should resist labeling McCormick's Tribune of the Plebs an institution of direct democracy, when it is in fact a representative institution. Only then can we begin questioning its democratic representativeness compared to that of other institutions and procedures. Only then can we ensure that a subset of the people is never able to claim to be speaking as "the people," with all the attending dangers that this entails. More generally, recasting certain forms of participation by ordinary citizens as new forms of democratic or "citizen representation" would be more likely to generate support and recognition from the rest of the public.

Direct democracy cannot be the solution to the crisis of representative democracy. Democracy must retain elements of representation, indeed take a representative form, both because not everyone can be involved together at all times in the consuming tasks of deliberating and setting up the agenda, and because interests and judgments need to be constructed and reflected upon. If I am right, we are now back to square one: democracy of a representative kind, even as we reject the historical paradigm of "representative democracy" per

---

19. As Shapiro writes, "Perhaps a Tribune of the Plebs would have gone after Silvio Berlusconi, but it might just as easily have gone after those who were trying to hold him accountable for his abuses of office" (Shapiro 2016: 176, fn11).

se with its problematic commitment to periodic elections as the central institutional feature and the resulting exclusion of ordinary citizens from politics.

If democracy as a political regime is always, and indeed should be, representative, then the interesting question is not: direct or representative democracy? But instead: What kind of representation should we favor? And what selection mechanisms would yield it? The real opposition is thus not between "direct" and "representative" democracy but between more or less democratic forms of representative rule, and more generally between more or less open forms of democratic rule. At the most democratic and open extreme, one finds a representative system in which ordinary people actually get to rule, though in turn and never all at once (as in Ancient Athens); at the other extreme the representative system is only accessible to an elite few. In other words, the contrast is not between direct and representative democracies but between those that are open to ordinary citizens and those that are closed to them. Our contemporary electoral "democracies" fall somewhere on this continuum and, arguably, rather close to the elitist, closed side.

What would more authentically democratic representation look like? We turn to this question next.

4

Legitimacy and Representation beyond Elections (Part One)

On January 10, 2020, a sixteen-year-old high school student and one of the 150 randomly selected members of the French Citizen Convention on Climate Change asked President Macron, their special guest for the night, the following question: "Do you think that the future of French democracy is to be found in a more deliberative democracy, in the image of this Convention?" President Macron offered a conciliatory answer: "At the same time that we invent deliberative democracy, we need to restore representative democracy."

By "representative" democracy the French president meant, like most people, electoral democracy, implicitly restricting to elected officials the status of representative of the people. Even as he considered a place in French democracy for deliberative citizens' assemblies, like the Citizen Convention on Climate Change, the French president wanted them to reinforce the power of elected officials, not be competition for it.

Another more radical answer would have been for him to concede that inventing deliberative democracy (or the version of it I call open democracy) entails the possibility of representation beyond elections. This implies that deliberative democracy is partly in competition with traditional, electoral democracy. In this chapter I seek to show the way toward a non-electoral form of democracy that is both representative and deliberative. I do so by expanding the concept of representation and specifically democratic representation to include non-electoral procedures and bodies.

More specifically, I argue that new forms of participation in the political process that are often nested under the label of "direct democracy" (also "participatory," "deliberative," or even "citizen" democracy) should be conceptualized instead as new forms of democratic representation. In contrast to the conventional view expressed above by President Macron, reducing democratic representation to electoral representation is both too elitist and simplistic. It is elitist because, as we saw in chapter 2, elections are a selection mechanism that is intrinsically discriminatory and has a built-in (i.e., not empirically contingent) oligarchic bias. It is too simplistic because it precludes the possibility of conceptualizing and implementing new and indeed possibly better forms of democratic representation.

In trying to complicate our understanding of democratic representation, I am following in the path of a growing number of scholars who have sought to pluralize our notion of what counts as a democratic representative. Following Michael Saward, I question the all-too-common assumption "that representative democracy is all about elections, and only elected officials can be classed as democratic representatives" (Saward 2008: 1002). Following Laura Montanaro, I also recognize that "for the most part we [political theorists] do not understand what it means for groups and individuals to function as democratic representatives outside electoral institutions" (Montanaro 2012: 1095; see also Kuyper 2016; Rehfeld 2006). Following Castiglione and Warren (2006: 14), I accept that "[a]s politics has become more complex, multilayered, and pervasive within society, so too has the question of *who* can legitimately claim to be a democratic representative." Finally, like Mark Warren, I seek to reframe the way we view certain types of "participation"—such as involvement in mini-publics—as new, non-electoral forms of "citizen representation" (Warren 2013).

Among the natural contenders for the title of democratic representatives are, besides elected representatives, the following: members of randomly selected mini-publics such as citizens' assemblies, deliberative polls, and citizens' juries, as well as self-selected participants in demonstrations, crowdsourcing or participatory budgeting experiments, social movements like Black Lives Matter in the United States or the Yellow Vests in France, and referendum and initiative committees made up of regular citizens (as opposed to, e.g., corporate lobbyists). These groups and the individuals in them do typically stand for other groups in the sense that they make claims for them and do things (deliberate, protest) on their behalf. They sometimes even explicitly conceive of what they do as a representative role. I propose to call the representation performed by mini-publics "lottocratic representation"[1] and the

---

1. After the adjective helpfully coined by Alex Guerrero (2014) to characterize what he defends as the "lottocratic alternative" to elections. I am generally in agreement with Guerrero's analyses, though I prefer a centralized, all-purpose legislative assembly over the myriad of single-issue mini-publics that he favors, essentially because of the necessity of dealing with bundled issues in order to reach a coherent set of laws and policies.

representation performed by self-appointed participants "self-selected" representation. I use these categories for analytical clarity, though actual practices will tend to be much less pure, with most mini-publics, for example, involving a mix of random and self-selection (on the basis of willingness to participate).

Various objections can be raised against treating mini-publics and self-selected crowds as new types of democratic representatives. First, one could argue that these groups fall under the category of "direct" as opposed to "representative" democracy. I already partly addressed this objection in chapter 3, where I suggested that both the Ancient Greek Council of 500 and even the self-selected participants in the People's Assembly could be characterized as forms of "citizen representatives" (as per Warren 2013). I revisit only some of the arguments here.

Others may challenge the claim that these alleged forms of representation are "democratic," since both lottocratic and self-selected representation, unlike electoral representation, are untethered from the explicit consent of other citizens (those that are not part of the mini-publics or those who did not choose to self-select into the process). In this respect, both lottocratic and self-selected forms of representation qualify as "virtual" representation—a notion with a notoriously undemocratic lineage. So, we have to ask: how can mini-publics or the self-selected members of participatory experiments—the usual suspects as alternatives to elected assemblies—claim the title of democratic representatives if they are not directly authorized by the rest of the citizenry? What, in other words, are the democratic credentials of these new forms of representation?

Consider that members of mini-publics may claim to be "representative" according to the definition used thus far, that is, in the sense that they stand for the larger public in a way that is recognized by a relevant audience, say, the government. But can they claim to be *democratically* representative? What is the difference between them and, say, an appointed body of experts? Why shouldn't we conceptualize mini-publics instead as a form of technocratic representation, especially as they are often formed via complex and opaque sampling methods performed by experts? Similarly, why should self-selected groups participating in open policymaking processes count as *democratic* representatives, if they count as representatives at all? What is the difference between the self-selected participants in an online crowdsourcing process and a random mob? And, ultimately, how do the democratic qualifications, if any, of mini-publics compare to that of self-selected crowds? How does the democratic nature of either compare to that of elected representatives?

My goal in this chapter and the next is to offer some analytical clarity as to how we could go about answering these questions. I do so by arguing that we can evaluate the democratic character of a representative assembly or position—its "democraticity" in my vocabulary—in terms of the degree to which access to that assembly or position is inclusive and equal (or fair). I will then point out the trade-offs between different types of democratic representation, particularly in terms of their relation to democracy-related but not as fundamental democratic values, such as accountability and responsiveness to the ruled. Finally, we will run into an unavoidable but separate question. Even if these new contenders to the title of "democratic representatives" are both representative and democratic, where does their legitimacy, and specifically their democratic legitimacy, come from? All these questions are so tightly connected that I had to address them under the same heading, "Legitimacy and Representation Beyond Elections." For readability I divide my analysis into two chapters, one more theoretical and one more empirical and speculative.

Clarifying these questions will first require disentangling various related notions, such as representation, "democraticity," and legitimacy. In other words, one needs to be able to distinguish between a mere representative, a democratic representative, a legitimate representative (whether democratic or not, though the former is of greater interest to us here), and even a democratically legitimate representative (again whether a democratic representative or not). Considering the major disagreements in the relevant literature about the meaning of at least two of those terms (legitimacy and representation), I am forced to stipulate some of these definitions, though I will try to provide a reasonable justification for each.

In the first section, I question the tight identification between democratic, legitimate, and *electoral* representation, briefly exploring the historical and conceptual reasons behind this intuitive identification. I argue that the eighteenth-century electoral theory of consent is, despite its intuitive appeal, confused and sufficiently unsatisfactory to justify trying to move past it conceptually.

Having cleared the ground for new intuitions, I then justify the non-normative definition of representation I use in this book and defend my use of a new concept of "democraticity" as distinct from legitimacy.

Equipped with these distinctions, I turn in the next section to a form of democratic representation that is in my view the most promising alternative to electoral representation, namely "lottocratic representation." The third section thus argues that the democratic credentials of lottocratic representation come from its egalitarian and temporally inclusive features. The combination of sortition and rotation indeed ensures that power is equally accessible to all over time.

The fourth section turns to another alternative—self-selected representation—whose democratic credentials come from its spatial openness to all, which renders it all-inclusive by default, and from the (formal) equality of opportunity to participate that characterizes it. Despite the obvious time burden of volunteering for public participation, access to self-selected representation is at least fully open in theory. The fourth section considers the objection from the lack of accountability of non-elected representatives as well as the lack of statistical representativeness of self-selected representatives.

The Problem with Consent Theory

Let us first try to comprehend why we have come to see electoral representation as the only form of democratic representation and sometimes even as the only (or at least the most) legitimate form of political representation, period. In other words, why is electoral representation exerting such a pull on our collective imagination that it is the first and often the only thing we can envisage when we think of "democratic representation"? Why is democracy symbolized, in the popular imagination, by lines in front of the voting booth? Why can we hardly conceive of democracy and democratic representation but through the prism of voting and elections?

One explanation is offered by Bernard Manin. He argues that the "triumph of elections" in the eighteenth century set much of the Western world on a path that led to our current identification of democracy with representative democracy and elections. This historical triumph is partly contingent and indeed surprising if we consider that, historically, sortition (random selection by lot) had previously been seen as the more democratic selection device. In fact, Manin argues, it is precisely because of its pure democratic history that sortition was deemed unsuitable for a modern, large republic of property owners like the United States. The more philosophical reason, however, has to do with the prevalence at the time of social contract theories that grounded popular sovereignty in a moment of unanimous consent. Against that background, elections were understood as transferring consent from the voters to the elected representatives.

The idea of actual or "voluntarist" consent (by contrast with hypothetical consent) as the main source of democratic legitimacy is among the simplest and most elegant theories that one could posit. Consent at the ballot box has the remarkable property of conferring double benefits. It confers democratic credentials to the extent that it expresses the equal principle of "one-person, one vote." At the same time, it confers political legitimacy as defined by "voluntarist" social contract theory. In other words, according to the social contract theory framework, consent at the ballot box confers both democratic credentials and democratic legitimacy.

Yet the consent theory of legitimacy is plagued with conceptual problems.

The main difficulty with the electoral theory of authorization is that it fails to explain why any number of elected representatives could legitimately claim to represent the whole body of citizens when at best a majority of citizens has voted for them. By what kind of alchemy does the consent of some turn into authorization of all? In other words, the view that legitimate representation requires authorization and that authorization requires voting ends up acknowledging the impossibility of any legitimate government, for unanimity is an impossible ideal to achieve, and anything short of unanimity would not transfer full consent. The American revolutionaries themselves encountered the dilemma in the following form: "it would appear that there are only two choices: to grant every citizen a veto over the election of representatives, and every representative a veto over the enactment of laws, or to accept the enslavement of large numbers of citizens" (Nelson 2014: 95).

If we reject the idea that people are enslaved when a majority imposes its decisions on all as opposed to just those who consented to the choice of representatives or even the choice of policies, then something other than individual consent must perform the legitimizing function here. What is this other thing?

A plausible candidate seemed to be prior agreement to the rules of the game, i.e., consent to the constitutional scheme whereby a majority can make decisions on behalf of the whole and elected representatives count as representatives of all, including those who have not voted for them. But if we go back to an earlier social contract as the foundation for the authorizing power of elections, we run into similar as well as other problems. First, the same conceptual problem afflicts this theory of an original grant of authority. Short of unanimous consent, how do we get an original grant of authority? How can the authorization of some, even a large majority, confer the authorization of *all*? Since there is no historical evidence for moments of unanimous consent to the rules of any political game—monarchical or otherwise—we are left, again, with anarchical conclusions. There cannot be any legitimate government in the world, because none of them can be said to have been consented to or authorized by all, in at least one original moment of unanimous consent to the rules of the game.

A second problem is that if we recognize an original grant of authority as being constitutive of democratic legitimacy, anything can now count as a valid mechanism for the selection of representatives as long as it has been agreed to as part of the "rules of the game." In other words, elections need not be the authorization mechanism, since almost anything that could be agreed to as part of the rules of the games will do. The reasoning could end up, as it did historically, legitimizing hereditary monarchy (Nelson 2014). One could in fact reach an even more pessimistic conclusion. The constitutional theory of authorization is as incoherent as the electoral one and for essentially the same reason.

Authorization via actual consent, though intuitive and appealing on the surface, turns out to be an inappropriate basis, *at least by itself alone,* for a theory of democratic legitimacy. This is why consent theory has fallen out of favor with political philosophers and theorists at least since Kant (except for anarchist thinkers like Robert Paul Wolff (1970) or John Simmons (2001), who remain glaring exceptions in the contemporary philosophical landscape because they are willing to bite the bullet of assuming the illegitimacy of all existing governments[2]). The "hypothetical" version of consent theory put forward as an alternative by contractualist theorists of political legitimacy from Kant to Rawls has also proven problematic, for an obvious reason: hypothetical consent is, simply put, no consent at all.[3]

I postpone to the next chapter the further exploration of the concept of legitimacy. It is enough for our purposes here to have dethroned individual consent to power, and thus elections of representatives, as the be-all and end-all of democracy. Liberated from eighteenth-century misconceptions, we can now approach, in the conceptual space thus cleared, the question of democratic representation and legitimacy anew. But first, we need to posit some definitions.

Definitions

There exist multiple definitions of (political) representation. As a result of this plurality of definitions, as well as the plurality of approaches to the concept of legitimacy, there is a vast array of positions about what can count as "legitimate democratic representation."

Most theorists understand representation as an inherently normative concept. Hannah Pitkin (1989 [1967]), in particular, who inspired what is sometimes described as the "standard account" (Rehfeld 2006), built in her definition of representation conditions of legitimacy, democracy, and even justice.

One problem with the standard account is that, as Andrew Rehfeld points out, "[b]y wedding representation with the conditions that render it legitimate, the standard account is doing double duty: not only does it tell us when a representative is legitimate or democratic, it also purportedly tells us when a person is a political representative at all" (Rehfeld 2006: 3). For example, an illegitimate representative is, on the standard account, not a representative at all.

Like Andrew Rehfeld, I believe the concept of representation should not have to perform multiple-duty in accounting not only for how an entity can act on behalf of another, but also for how it can do so well, how it can do so democratically, and how it can do so legitimately. I believe we are better off using

2. John Simmons maintains that an authority is legitimate only if it is successful at eliciting the unanimous consent of its subjects (Simmons 2001), which leads to utterly implausible anarchist conclusions.

3. See also Greene 2016 for a recent and devastating critique of both the voluntarist and contractualist consent-based theories of legitimacy.

the concept of representation in "a robust nonnormative descriptive sense" whereby representation refers to facts about the political world "without necessarily appealing to normative standards of legitimacy or justice" (Rehfeld 2006: 2) and, crucially I would add, without appealing either to a normative standard of democracy. In other words, I think we should not build into our concept of representation the normative requirements that the representation performed be "good," "democratic," or even "legitimate."

This is why I subscribe to Rehfeld's thin definition of representation as the act of standing for someone or some others in order to perform a certain function in a way that is de facto accepted by a relevant audience. Representation, on this view, "results from *an audience's judgment that some individual, rather than some other, stands in for a group in order to perform a specific function*" (Rehfeld 2006: 2, emphasis in the original). The "audience" condition in the definition is there to weed out absurd claims to representation that no one would or should take seriously (as if I, say, suddenly claimed to represent the people from Botswana at the United Nations with the assent of my mother) but it is not a normative condition of political legitimacy per se. The audience reintroduces a normative dimension only with respect to the nature of what counts as valid recognition by whom, not with respect to the legitimacy of the act of representation per se. This normativity when it comes to what counts as valid recognition is necessary to avoid over- and under-inclusion of cases.[4]

This definition allows me to specify *democratic* representation as a species of representation, specifically a kind of "standing for" that is an activity open to all on an egalitarian and inclusive basis. This is very different from the standard account. For Pitkin, for representatives to be "democratic" they must (1) be authorized to act; (2) act in a way that promotes the interests of the represented; and (3) be accountable to the represented. As should become clear later, from my perspective, the first condition is a legitimacy condition. The second one is a requirement of "good" representation but not democratic representation per se. And the third criterion is democracy-enabling rather than democratic per se.[5]

In other words, on the view presented here, a democratic representative is not someone who is doing a good job of representing the interests of the

---

4. When it comes to over-inclusion, consider a thief presenting my stolen ID to my bank's teller. He would not be an actual "representative" of my person because the proper audience, my bank, would only mistakenly recognize him as such, if it did, under conditions of deceit, invalidating the de facto recognition. Cases of under-inclusion would include racist politicians refusing to recognize, say, Malcom X as a representative of the Black community. Here we can invalidate non-recognition as in bad faith, though surely there will always be a grey area between claims to representation that simply fail and acts of actual representation that go wrongly unrecognized. Robustness of the representative claims over time may help adjudicate the cases.

5. See below for the distinction between primary and secondary democratic values.

people (an oligarchic representative could do that too), nor is it someone who is authorized by the people she represents to perform this representative function (an oligarchic representative also could be authorized that way). Instead, a democratic representative is simply someone who has accessed the position of representative through a selection process characterized by inclusiveness and equality. By contrast a legitimate representative will be someone who has been properly authorized to act as a representative. And a good representative will be one that serves well the interests of the represented.

In my view, representation can thus be democratic or undemocratic. Additionally, representation can be either legitimate or illegitimate, whether it is democratic or not, and good or bad, whether it is legitimate or democratic. These distinctions will allow me to say (here I give a preview of the next chapter's argument) that mini-publics or groups of self-selected participants may lack political legitimacy, and even democratic legitimacy, despite their democratic credentials qua representatives.

What do I mean by legitimacy here—another notoriously difficult and controversial concept?[6] At an abstract level I define (normative) legitimacy quite conventionally as the property by which an entity (person or organization) is morally entitled to rule (in the case of a state) or to issue binding commands (in the case of political bodies more generally). The real difficulty is in identifying the sources of legitimacy thus defined. What confers this property—legitimacy—on a person or entity? There is, to my knowledge, no consensual, stabilized theory of political legitimacy, at least when it comes to pinning down the sources of such legitimacy. I will return to this difficult question in the next chapter. Suffice to say for now that the kind of legitimacy we call democratic crucially relates to authorization by a majority of the represented (plus some substantive conditions).[7] But the important point here is that legitimacy is not the same as what I propose to call "democraticity"—or the possession of democratic credentials (which is, like legitimacy, a property that I see as on a continuum once certain minimal criteria are met). In my view, "democraticity" and legitimacy are thus two analytically distinct properties, such that a regime or representative may be democratically legitimate (popularly endorsed if you will) even as they are not democratic per se.

I will use here as the main criterion of "democraticity" applied to representation the degree to which a given form of representation satisfies or expresses the principle of inclusiveness and equality among citizens. I take it that such

6. For an exhaustive review of the history and multiple theories of legitimacy to date, see Peter 2017.

7. Note that this is crucially different from the consent theories of legitimacy criticized earlier, which assumed individual consent of all.

values are the most fundamental democratic values, over and above other values such as accountability or responsiveness to citizens' preferences.[8] Consider, also, that, in a small group, we regard the decision democratic to the extent that all are included on an egalitarian basis. Properties of accountability and responsiveness only matter when the group becomes too large to make decisions directly and we need to introduce some amount of delegation of power to a subset of the group. It is then and only then that accountability and responsiveness start to matter, and they matter as a measure of good governance rather than democraticity as such. For this reason, accountability and responsiveness seem to me to matter as remedies for certain inegalitarian and exclusionary features induced by representation. Accountability and responsiveness become important values in representative contexts, which may well be the only possible context for most democracies (as argued in chapter 3). But their importance should not let us forget the normative priority of inclusiveness and equality as democratic values.

I would thus argue that while responsiveness and accountability of representatives matter a great deal, they matter as extrinsic or secondary rather than instrinsic or primary democratic properties. They matter, as it were, as derivative and instrumental effects of democratic properties and as remedies for the risks caused by the very existence of a separate group of decision-makers. It is precisely because representation always entails a distance between represented and representatives that responsiveness and accountability are required as correctives to the inequality and exclusion possibly engendered by this distance. Consequently, responsiveness and accountability are not the first benchmarks that I want to use in order to assess the respective democratic credentials of electoral, lottocratic, and self-selected representation, although I will invoke them again later as democracy-enhancing qualities we do want in a good representative system.

To recapitulate, I define democraticity as the intrinsic property of being democratic, that is, expressive of the fundamental democratic values of inclusiveness and equality, above and beyond being approved by a majority (legitimacy) or otherwise serving democratic goals such as responsiveness or accountability. Note that if the democratic principles of inclusiveness and

8. Why do I consider accountability and responsiveness only extrinsically democratic values? Essentially, it is because they are goals that could be pursued, in theory, by any regime. An aristocracy may feature or want to include accountability mechanisms or norms (such as "noblesse oblige"). An autocracy may seek to respond to its people's needs and interests via frequent consultative methods, such as polling. Accountability and responsiveness are symptoms that the regime rules "for the people." But they do not guarantee at all that the regime is "of and by" the people. In my view, ruling "for the people" or being accountable or responsive to them is not sufficient to qualify as a democracy.

equality are perfectly realized, then we should see a representative body that is statistically identical with the demos.

If we understand democraticity to entail the values of inclusiveness and equality, the intrinsic democratic credentials of elected representatives become, as we already saw, questionable. The democratic credentials of electoral systems of representation essentially stem from the fact that elections include all adults of a given demos when the franchise is universal and from the fact that these elections publicly express the equality of citizens in the principle "one person, one vote" (Christiano 1996). As an expression of equality, however, elections are ambiguous (or "Janus-faced" as Manin puts it). Their egalitarian credentials are countered by the fact that elections are meant to identify individuals who differ from ordinary citizens by their "superior" or at least "extra-ordinary" qualities (where superiority is in the eyes of the beholder, namely the voter, but it tracks properties that are not widely and evenly distributed in the population). In the optimistic view of the founders, elections were supposed to identify a natural aristocracy of virtue and wisdom. According to a more realistic view, elections are good at identifying the charismatic, wealthy, and connected. But the real problem is that even under ideal circumstances (a perfectly egalitarian society in which money would play no role in politics), elections simply rely on human choice, which is inherently discriminatory and biased toward certain traits (charisma, eloquence, height, for example). In other words, even at the level of the ideal, elections operate as a "principle of distinction" (Manin 1997) between ordinary citizens and those fated to become a political elite of sorts. As a result, elections will systematically close off access to power to people who are too ordinary to stand out in the eyes of other citizens. No amount of periodic renewal of the pool of elected representatives changes this fundamental fact. Electoral representation is not "open" to all on an equal basis but is at best overly accessible to some (the ambitious, connected, wealthy, charismatic, etc.). The result of this selection mechanism is bound to be a demographically skewed representation of the people, under ideal conditions and even more so under non-ideal ones.

Lottocratic Representation

What about the relative democratic merits of lottocratic and self-selected representation? What grants lottocratic assemblies their intrinsic democratic credentials and what, in particular, differentiates them from technocratic, meritocratic, or appointed assemblies?

Lotteries—understood as a combination of random selection and periodic rotation—are historically *the* paradigmatic democratic selection mechanism (Plato, *Republic* Bk 8, 557a; Aristotle, *Politics* IV.9, 1294b8; Hansen 1999;

Manin 1997).[9] It is precisely for this reason that Aristotle defines democracy as "ruling and being ruled in turn," rather than, say, participating in the People's Assembly. This is probably why criminal juries in the United States and the jury d'Assises in France are seen as fundamental democratic institutions (despite their well-known flaws, especially in the US case), and celebrated as such by historians, political scientists, legal scholars, playwrights, and filmmakers alike.

The view that lotteries are the ultimate democratic selection mechanism rests on a sound conceptual basis. Lotteries express a strict principle of equality as well as a principle of impartiality between citizens. Random selection, unlike election, does not recognize distinctions between citizens, because everyone has exactly the same chance of being chosen once they have been entered into the lottery. Given enough rotation and a small enough population, actual access to power is strictly equalized over the long term.

Of course, one needs to assume here both the equivalent of a universal franchise in terms of the pool from which lottocratic representatives are chosen and compulsory participation once selection by lot has been performed. In practice these assumptions are rarely verified, so pure lottocratic representation—and the pure demographic mapping of the population—almost never happens. For example, the Classical Athenian system did not meet the assumption of a universal franchise, even once we allow for the restrictive notion of the demos they operated within, as the Athenians made participation in certain lottocratic functions voluntary and also placed age restrictions on eligibility for volunteering in the first place. In modern times only the modern criminal jury is based on the universal franchise and mandatory participation that can produce the purest form of lottocratic representation (though participation in modern juries is actually relatively easily avoided, and there are age restrictions here too). Most citizens' assemblies and other randomly selected mini-publics are based on voluntary participation, which introduces an element of self-selection into the process. Incentive schemes (such as paying an honorarium to participants) can reduce this element of self-selection. But ultimately mandatory participation, as in the case of jury duty, might be the only way to implement lottocratic representation in a satisfactory way.

Lottocratic assemblies, an objector might point out, are not really open to all, since those who are not randomly selected are de facto excluded. From a

9. Because this historical fact has recently been re-advertised, lotteries are now enjoying a bit of a conceptual revival among various so-called kleiroterians, sortitionists, or "lottocrats" (e.g., Burnheim 1985; Bouricius 2013; Carson and Martin 1999; Dowlen 2008; Guerrero 2014; Hennig 2017; Landemore 2012; Leib 2004; McCormick 2011; O'Leary 2006; Saunders 2008; Stone 2011; Sutherland 2008; Warren and Pearse 2008; Van Reybrouck 2016; Gastil and Wright 2019). Sortition is also at the heart of the empirical "deliberative wave" of randomly selected mini-publics recently documented by the OECD in some Western countries (OECD 2020 report).

synchronic perspective, lottocratic assemblies may seem less open and even less accessible than elected ones, since in elections at least people can affect the ex-ante probability distribution of being excluded, whereas in a lottery they cannot.[10]

Responding to this objection requires that we take the longer view: the combination of sortition and rotation that ensures equal access to all citizens over time. Lottocratic representation is thus a more open form of representation than electoral representation. Given the limited life expectancy of human beings, however, some thought needs to be given to the size of these assemblies, the number of citizens they are meant to represent, and the exact frequency with which they are renewed if we want citizens to have a meaningful chance (though not necessarily a certainty) of being chosen over the course of their lifetimes. Indeed, if the number of seats and the frequency of rotation are insufficient for everyone to plausibly expect to rule someday, then the comparative democratic advantage of lotteries over elections becomes quite thin.

Here a possible solution lies in the decentralization of power and the multiplication of smaller jury-like assemblies—fifty people or fewer—at all levels of the polity, hoping that the statistical representativeness one gets with large randomly selected assemblies is achieved at the system level. Decentralizing power such that important policies and laws get made as much as possible at the local level may increase the chances of being randomly selected for a lottocratic assembly. For example, at the scale of the Germanophone region of Belgium (76,000 inhabitants or so), a permanent council of twenty-nine citizens has recently been created to help the local Parliament make laws and policies (their recommendations are not binding, but the Parliament morally committed to follow them). The probability of being chosen over the course of a lifetime in this scenario is 67 percent.[11] Nevertheless, the solution of small mini-publics is problematic because it may result in samples that are too small relative to the size of the represented population. This means there might not be enough diversity in the resulting body relative to the question at hand, even if this diversity is artificially reinforced via statistical engineering. The

10. It is true that individuals can boost their personal probability of getting into the assembly, but given the principle of distinction that electoral distribution of power depends on, it is likely that for the vast majority of the population, their odds of being included are actually higher under sortition than under election. And if ex post people are excluded under both, and ex ante their odds are in fact *higher* under sortition, then it is a mistake to say that lottocratic assemblies are less open or accessible than elected ones. Lottocratic assemblies are less open and less accessible only to (broadly speaking) elites, who are in a position to *substantially* boost their personal probability of getting into an elected assembly, but not a lottocratic one. I thank Max Krahé for this point.

11. Min Reuchamp, Public Communication at the GIS conference, "Localiser l'épreuve démocratique. Assemblages, circulations, imaginaires," Paris, Maison des Sciences de l'Homme, November 4, 2019.

solution might be to have sufficiently large mini-publics at the local level as well (more than one hundred people), although it is unclear whether such a solution is practically viable, as questions of recruitment, cost, and logistics might easily get in the way.

Decentralizing to small or even large local mini-publics does not, in any case, solve the question of deciding on national issues in large countries. At that level, everyone has an equal but close to null chance of being chosen, even if we assume an extremely large assembly of a thousand randomly selected people, which seems a generous empirical upper bound for mini-publics. One might rightly wonder whether it is much better to have an infinitesimally small chance of participating in such a national mini-public than to have only the equal right to cast one vote among several million to choose a representative or a party that may or may not act on campaign promises. Perhaps not. But it is not obviously worse either. Additionally, if we did combine a lottocratic assembly at the national level with a multiplicity of local assemblies that set the agenda for the national one (for example by having a separate lottery-based assembly that performs the task of synthesizing the converging conclusions reached by local assemblies), then the individual chances of being influential via lottocratic representation become much more meaningful. At any rate, if inclusiveness and equality are our central democratic values, then lottocratic representation remains the ultimate form of democratic representation.

As is often the case, the genuine fairness of lotteries will depend on the manner in which the random selection is conducted empirically. In practice the ideal of "one person, one lottery ticket" can rarely be operationalized as such. The size of the sample (which is generally too small to produce descriptive representation without some additional tweaking) and practical difficulties in collecting the relevant data (people's addresses or phone numbers) make it necessary to resort to second-best methods. Most mini-publics thus select their participants using a limited pool of randomly selected individuals from a given population, on which they then conduct stratified random sampling (applying criteria such as age, gender, geographic origin, ethnicity in countries where this is legal, or education level). Most organizers now use mixed methods, from texting to calling to mailing people. Ned Crosby at the Jefferson Center, the inventor of the Citizen Jury (a random sample of twenty-five citizens sometimes used in consultation processes) used to proceed as follows: he and his team divided the community into forty census tracts and then randomly selected houses within each tract. They then randomly chose whether to ask for the man or woman in each house. Crosby argues that going door to door was very effective in convincing people to participate and minimizing the problem of people self-selecting out of the process. In Iceland, participants were selected from the official directory of inhabitants by means of quota sampling in order to ensure representativeness in age, gender, and geographic origin.

The selected participants were contacted by letter and subsequently by phone. Because the response rate was low, about 3,000 people had to be approached in order to yield the resulting 950 participants. Furthermore, for each of the 1,000 seats offered, there were four backup candidates in the same age / gender / geographic bracket to ensure that, should the first, second, or third candidate decline to participate, there was someone relatively similar to replace that individual. The selection process was thus technically near random sampling, subject to some self-selection combined with stratified sampling. In the case of the French Convention on Climate Change, the first random sample was created by generating 250,000 phone numbers via a random generator, then texting people to ask whether they would be interested in receiving a call, and then calling people, collecting their information, and eventually forming a stratified random sample of 150 citizens on the basis of that information (along criteria of sex, age, education level, socio-professional category, geographic origin, and territory).

The selection method may seem like a technical issue. But it is actually essential to the democraticity (and also legitimacy) of the process. Methods other than those mentioned above can surely be devised that would increase both the turnout rate and the transparency of the selection method.

Self-Selected Representation

The other model of "democratic representation" worth exploring is that in which the representatives are simply self-selected or "self-appointed" (as per Montanaro 2012).[12] As already pointed out, self-selection is an almost unavoidable element of all existing forms of political participation, except perhaps in places where voting is mandatory or in jury duty. Self-selection is also the mode of selection favored by proponents of what I have previously called "spatially open" democratic innovations, that is, democratic innovations that erect no barriers to entry and allow everyone who chooses to participate. Self-selection is the selection method used in town hall meetings, Swiss

12. Montanaro defends the democratic legitimacy of self-authorized representatives on the basis of authorization by, and accountability to, affected interests, as follows: "I consider self-appointed representation "nondemocratic" if the constituency empowered to authorize and demand accountability is different from the constituency whose interests the representative claims affect. . . . *By contrast I consider self-appointed representation 'democratic' if the affected constituency is empowered to authorize and demand accountability of the self-appointed representative.* Thus self-appointed representatives are *democratically legitimate* only to the degree that the affected are empowered to authorize and to hold accountable the self-appointed representative" (1096: my emphasis). I find this account problematic on two levels: one, because of the ambiguous lumping together of democratic credentials and legitimacy; and two, because of the strict focus on authorization and accountability.

Landsgemeinden, participatory budgeting, crowdsourced policymaking, and the popular assemblies of Ancient Greek cities, popular demonstrations and marches, and citizen committees that form to launch an initiative to bring an issue to Parliament or to initiate a referendum on an existing law (where such participation rights, respectively called Citizens Initiatives and Rights of Referral, are indeed available to citizens).[13] I distinguish open democratic innovations from moments of direct democracy, like referendums, in that the latter expect everyone or at least a majority of persons to participate. In open democratic innovations, by contrast, only a small fraction of the population is expected to participate.

First, let me say a word on the "representative" status of self-selected individuals and groups. It might seem odd to call participants in these open democracy practices "representatives," perhaps even more so than calling the members of randomly selected assemblies "representative." If these assemblies directly involve ordinary citizens without the mediation of election or random selection, then surely the participants are just individual members of the demos, speaking exclusively for themselves rather than standing for anyone else. Even if mini-publics are not a form of direct democracy, surely participatory budgeting and crowdsourced policymaking must be.

Yet we should keep in mind the case of the Athenian People's Assembly examined in chapter 3. There we saw that the decisions of a subset of the people who actually participated were actually recognized as the decisions of the whole "Demos" by the relevant audience, namely other existing institutions and, as far we can surmise, the whole demos itself (at least according to some defensible readings of the evidence, including the one offered by Josiah Ober). This is why it seems reasonable to see participation in open events in which a minority of the population participates as occasions for "citizen representation" rather than forms of direct democracy.

According to the same logic, participatory budgeting experiments and crowdsourced policymaking are not so much forms of direct democracy as forms of "spatially inclusive" representative democracy. Participation in these

---

13. There is a question as to whether classical interest groups who game direct democracy mechanisms like Citizens' Initiatives and Rights of Referral to place on a legislative agenda policy proposals that they could not get passed through the regular legislative process deserve the title of democratic self-selected representative. I tend to think they do not. I thus exclude from the category of democratic self-selected representatives business associations, industry lobbies, unions, parties, and even professionalized lobbyists of certain causes like Greenpeace. The boundary between what counts as a self-selected citizen representative and a professional lobbyist will probably be vague at times, but I think one criterion could be whether the person's sole source of income is working for the interest group in question (though it is probably a very imperfect criterion subject to many exceptions). For a more capacious concept of "self-selected representation" that includes such professional interest groups, see instead El-Wakil 2020: chapter 5.

experiments is a form of representation because the participants make budgetary decisions on behalf of others that are accepted as valid by the relevant
authorities. The self-selected aspect of this kind of representation comes from
the fact that there is no gate at the door and the status of representative is
open to anyone willing to participate, even though there is no expectation
that the entire population of persons with affected interests will show up.
For the most part, such democratic practices do rely on just a fraction of the
eligible population actually showing up or participating. In the case of participatory budgeting experiments, practitioners rarely use the vocabulary of
direct democracy. They usually prefer to speak of "co-governance"—where
the implied partners are the existing (electoral) representative institutions.[14]
In the case of crowdsourcing, the illusion of direct democracy is even more
unjustifiable in that, while participation is open to all, even fewer people tend
to participate and decision power remains in the hands of those in charge of
crowdsourcing, usually government officials. The role of citizen participants
in instances of "co-governance" is limited to the contribution of input for decisions to be made later by elected representatives.

Assuming that self-selected participation in open democratic assemblies
counts as a form of "citizen representation" (Warren 2013) rather than a form of
direct democracy, what can be said of the democratic credentials of such representation? The main advantage of self-selected representation is that, at least in
theory, everyone is able to participate. There is no qualification for inclusion,
whether social salience and ambition or luck. All it takes, if we temporarily set
practical constraints aside, is the will to participate. Self-selected representation can be usefully contrasted against elected assemblies, which are at best
accessible to the willing and ambitious, and against lottocratic bodies that are
only open to all over time (at least with sufficiently frequent rotation). The
Athenian Assembly again provides an example of self-selected representation.
In theory, every Athenian citizen had the same right to attend the Assembly
meetings and to say something and to be heard. These generalizations are of
course true only at a high level of idealization, which brackets the substantive
conditions for participation in general, such as time and economic resources.
Whether this idealization is tolerable depends in large part on the empirical
question of whether the substantive conditions for equality of opportunity to
participate can be plausibly achieved. If they cannot, then self-selection may
reinforce existing inequalities (see in particular Rose 2016 and Cohen 2018 on
the political value of citizens' time).

Even if self-selected representation can count as democratic representation,
shouldn't we be worried by its potential lack of statistical representativeness?
If our primary concern is inclusion on equal terms, then a lack of statistical

14. I thank Paolo Spada for this information.

representativeness may be a sign that something is rather undemocratic with the selection process. Unlike lottocratic representation, which comes close to offering a mirror image of the people it represents, self-selected representation typically leads to demographically skewed groups of representatives, just like elections. If we look at the composition of the Athenian Assembly, or rather what we can reconstruct of it, it appears that it skewed toward urban, navy-employed, and poor citizens (Hansen 1999: 125)—even as it was sometimes disproportionately responsive to rich, skilled orators.[15] If we consider other spatially open democratic innovations, such as participatory budgeting processes, we find a similar overrepresentation of certain categories of people.[16] In crowdsourced policy processes, which take place online, the results are biased in an arguably much more problematic direction, reflecting existing hegemonies rather than counteracting them. In the Icelandic constitutional process, most participants to the crowdsourced stage were male and highly educated (see chapter 6). Similarly, in the Finnish experiment (Aitamurto and Landemore 2016), the participants were mostly male (more than 80 percent of the survey respondents), educated, and politically active. The bias in these latter cases may have occurred because the experiment took place online, a space still predominantly male, and, in the Finnish case, the fact that the experiment was about the reform of a law regulating snowmobile traffic (a predominantly male activity). Regardless, self-selection hardly seems like a good way to obtain statistical representativeness. A recent survey article of experiments in "Crowdlaw," including those that have taken place in Morocco, Brazil, and Chile, remarks that "the track record for *inclusivity* is pretty dismal" (Langlamet 2018: 2314, my emphasis), both in terms of absolute numbers and in terms of the statistical representativeness of the participants.[17]

---

15. This is why, in fact, critics or opponents of democracy contemptuously identified the "demos" with "the poor" (Aristotle, *Politics*, 1303b10).

16. Participatory budgeting experiments in Brazil and in the United States typically, and not unlike the Athenian Assembly, overrepresent the poor and uneducated. Interestingly, this is not true in Europe, where participants in participatory budgeting experiments overrepresent the educated (Empatia 2018: 35).

17. For example, while about 200,000 people visited the website Reforme.ma in Morocco within two months of the launch of the platform, the number of active participants was much smaller. The Chilean constitution, the policy text that attracted the most user participation on the platform, "drew only fifty-five participants, and 243 comments for 129 articles." Plataforma Brasil, another online platform meant to facilitate citizens' participation in legislation, received approximately 35,000 votes but had a participation rate of only 250 people. The Neos Lab's website, the next iteration of Plataforma Brasil, could only boast a few hundred participants as well. Worse, the surveyed platforms "fail even more starkly at achieving a few of the practitioners' aspiration of

In response to this criticism about the lack of representativeness in self-selected bodies, one could first note that no method of democratic representation achieves perfectly descriptive representation because no method is entirely free of self-selection. Elections, obviously, will always screen out certain personality types (the unambitious, introverted, less articulate, etc.). Even randomly selected assemblies are not immune to biases. The randomly selected Council of 500 and popular juries selected from a pre-screened pool of vetted candidates and the participants were determined in part by self-selection. Deliberative polls, which are arguably the "gold standard" for such randomly selected assemblies today (Mansbridge 2010), end up underrepresenting some categories of people, such as busy, wealthy individuals for whom the financial compensation is not worth the trouble of participating. Because participation in mini-publics is not mandatory (though perhaps it could be made so, on a par with jury duty) and acceptance rates are generally weak, and because lot of self-deselection occurs, the population of participants is skewed toward the more politically active and educated. Finally, even if no one selected out, most of the randomly selected mini-publics experimented with today are arguably too small (usually in the range of 100–250 people) to be truly statistically representative of the larger population, except on very crude dimensions like gender, socioeconomic class, and perhaps race (for sufficiently large minorities). Arguably, such mini-publics would need to include at least 1,000 people in order to be truly statistically representative. From this perspective, the Athenian courts, which included between five hundred and a thousand people, were ahead of their times.

To recapitulate, the democratic credentials of self-selected representation come from the fact that everyone has a (formally) equal opportunity to participate. Nonetheless, all else equal, self-selected representation is as likely as electoral representation to suffer from important biases in the perspectives that it includes. This should probably count against its democratic credentials. Despite the fact that they share the problem of statistical underrepresentativeness, one important difference between self-selected and elected representation is that the former is open to all in a way that the latter is not, since in elections access to the status of a candidate is generally controlled by gatekeepers such as parties, whereas in self-selected representation, access simply depends on self-motivation (something that might not be evenly distributed in the population but is at least within each person's reach).

---

creating representative participation and expanding participation to excluded groups" (Langlamet 2018: 2314). For example, only 17 percent of the participants that contributed feedback on the Chilean constitution on legislation were women.

On the Accountability of Non-Elected
Democratic Representatives

For all the intrinsic democratic credentials of lottocratic and self-selected methods of representation, these also have their own vulnerabilities. One particular concern is that lottocratic and self-selected bodies may lack important extrinsic democratic properties, such as accountability. While accountability (like other values such as responsiveness) is not an intrinsic democratic value but rather an extrinsic one, it must nonetheless play an important role in a holistic assessment of any institutional design.

The problem is particularly acute for lottocratic assemblies, since they are more likely to be given important agenda-setting and even legislative powers (in contrast to self-selected assemblies to which only certain information-gathering tasks and limited decision-making should probably be crowdsourced). The members of mini-publics cannot be held electorally accountable to the larger public for two reasons: (1) the larger public has no control whatsoever over the selection of participants in mini-publics (so the members seemingly have no incentive to justify their policy proposals to the larger public), and (2) members of mini-publics do not expect to stay in power after their term is over. Retrospective voting and the fear that it inspires in elected representatives cannot be used to keep lottocratic representatives in check during their term of office.

Thus, even if large enough randomly selected assemblies are statistically "safe" (in the sense of having an infinitesimally low probability of containing a large proportion of crazy and evil people),[18] what about the occasional bout of terrible luck? This could mean the selection of an incompetent assembly or the selection of a group with an internal dynamic that leads it to make bad decisions. In any democracy worthy of this name, citizens should be able to call their rulers to account and to sanction them when doing so is necessary and justified.

First, we need to clarify the meaning and requirements of political accountability. At a minimum, political accountability is a relationship between rulers and ruled that ensures that the rulers are bound to give a proper account of their actions, including the policies and laws that they pursue, to the represented. According to one of the simplest existing definitions, public accountability means "the ways in which public officials (both elected and appointed) describe, explain, and justify the activities of governments to their wider audiences of legislatures and citizens" (Pollitt 2011: 81). Note that this definition does not build in either responsiveness to the preferences of the ruled or the capacity of the ruled to sanction the rulers. And indeed, it would make sense that accountability be present even in the absence of congruence between the preferences of the ruled and policies that rulers adopt (though congruence

18. See Landemore 2012 for some calculations.

can be a good sign that accountability is present) and even in the absence of an ability by the ruled to sanction their rulers. In keeping with this minimal definition, I refrain from building into the definition specific means or institutional mechanisms (i.e., elections) through which relations of accountability may obtain. Finally, I do not assume that accountability relationships necessarily take the form of a principal-agent relationship. As Philp (2009) points out, definitions of political accountability that are derived from the idea of a principal-agent relationship between citizens and the government are problematic because there may be institutions that function as intermediaries of accountability, so that a government may be accountable to citizens even if citizens cannot directly hold it responsible. Additionally, as Philp also points out, models based on principal-agent relationships convey an unnecessarily narrow theoretical understanding of political accountability, with the inevitable effect that it precludes conceptualizing accountability in richer, more creative ways.[19]

Nonetheless, it is important to recognize that when critics ask and worry about accountability, their concern is often with a range of additional desiderata beyond the ways political officials give accounts in the sense just outlined. Under accountability, most people lump together various goals that are technically distinct from accountability but are seen as equally desirable, including the capacity to sanction rulers; the capacity to prevent them from acting badly; and the capacity to nudge them into doing good—all of which, incidentally, elections are supposed to be good at. Despite my preference for a more minimal definition of accountability, I accept that the objection from accountability is really about this larger set of desiderata. Keeping these distinctions in mind, however, makes it possible to identify which political mechanism is best suited to delivering the better solution for a particular requirement. Elections seem a universal answer to all these issues only because they provide a blunt tool that does all kinds of things somewhat well. But disaggregating the tasks, one could perhaps use a variety of better, task-specific tools and mechanisms.

To summarize, what the objection from accountability really asks is that we show the ability of non-electoral forms of representation to deliver on the multiple fronts where elections are supposed to be useful, namely:

1. Political accountability *stricto sensu*: the capacity of the ruled to hold the rulers to account
2. "Sanctionability": the capacity of the ruled to sanction / punish or at least threaten to sanction / punish the rulers for misdeeds
3. Prevention of corruption and bad behavior
4. Promotion of good behavior (responsiveness, good governance)

---

19. For non-Western notions of accountability that do not seem to fit in the principal-agent format, see for example Jordan 2011, who describes two non-Western traditions of accountability, namely ritual accountability in the cultural tradition of Confucianism and the affective accountability of patron-client relations in some West- and Central African cultures.

I will argue that, in theory at least, a democratic system can achieve many, perhaps even all of these things—which I'll refer to as accountability in a broad sense—without electoral mechanisms. Electoral mechanisms, I contend, are not as essential to political accountability as is generally assumed. They are neither the only causes of political accountability nor necessarily the best mechanisms to generate it.

Let us first look back at the case of the first non-electoral democracy, Classical Athens. How were the many randomly selected and self-selected bodies of Classical Athens accountable in the absence of the electoral mechanism of "retrospective voting"? First, randomly selected bodies in charge of law-making were protected from the risk of corruption (bad behavior) by the very fact of their random selection. This made it impossible to predict who was going to be in charge and thus prevented the bribery of decision-makers ahead of time (under the guise of, e.g., campaign donations). Random selection also made it impossible for any person to facilitate through donations the accession to power of his or her underlings. Additionally, facing a randomly selected group, any would-be corrupter would have had to bribe each individual one by one, in retail fashion so to speak, rather than in bulk (as is made easier in elected assemblies in which buying off the party hierarchy gets you all the votes at once). An additional accountability mechanism was periodic and frequent rotation of those same randomly selected assemblies, which made it difficult to build over time the relationships facilitating the desired quid pro quo arrangements. Additional preemptive accountability mechanisms included vetting of citizen volunteers for lottery at the gate.

In terms of accountability *stricto sensu* (obtaining accounts from politicians), Classical Athens included a system of popular juries before which people accused of leading the city astray had to explain themselves and provide accounts of their proposals and actions and by which these accused people would ultimately be judged (this was, infamously, what happened to Socrates, who was accused of impiety and corrupting the youth). Accountability *stricto sensu* was also facilitated by the practice of *euthynai* (or "straightening"), the examination of accounts that every public official underwent on expiry of his office.[20]

In terms of a pure sanctioning mechanism (whose known existence also operated as a preventive mechanism), the Greeks resorted for a time to the practice of ostracism, which consisted in putting down the name of the citizen

---

20. According to the *Oxford Classical Dictionary*: "At Athens the examination fell into two parts: the *logos* ('account'), concerned with his handling of public money and dealt with by a board of ten *logistai* ("accountants"); and the *euthynai* proper, an opportunity to raise any other objection to his conduct in office, dealt with by a board of ten *euthynoi* ("straighteners") appointed by the council (*boule*). These officials could dismiss accusations or pass them onto the courts."

deemed most dangerous for the city for that year and whom, if enough people agreed on his name, would be banished for the next ten years. This is not a practice we would consider desirable today, but it illustrates the range of accountability mechanisms that can exist beyond elections. Later, some time after 417 BC, the Greeks replaced ostracism, perhaps because they themselves came to measure its brutality, with the *graphe paranomon*, which consisted in the legal action taken against citizens who proposed motions violating existing legislation. The *graphe paranomon* can be read as a built-in judicial review procedure that was performed by democratic institutions themselves, as opposed to a task assigned to an external body such as a Supreme Court. It ensured that people proposing new laws did their homework to confirm that their proposal was in keeping with the fundamental laws of Athens. The *graphe paranomon* thus served as a deterrent to proposals that could have upset the Athenian democratic system, ensuring its own internally generated self-regulation.

All of these practices and institutions served as "accountability" mechanisms in a broad sense and, as far as we can tell, worked reasonably well. They were in fact probably overly strict and punitive, in that Ancient Athenians were held accountable for their proposals, not just their actions, and could be punished for sheer bad luck, regardless of whether they had been demonstrably incompetent or dishonest (Elster 1999). At any rate their example suggests that lack of accountability need not be an issue even for a system where elections play no or less of a role.

What we can learn from the Athenians is thus that the random selection and rotation intrinsic to lottocratic representation are in and of themselves accountability mechanisms, just like elections and term limits are supposed to be for electoral representation. The ex ante vetting of any candidate to the status of representatives might also be an option worth exploring, although this would come at the cost of full inclusion and equality. With regard to self-selected assemblies, however, forced rotation is not an option, though vetting might be. Obviously, the practice of ostracism or the *graphe paranomon* would be a hard sell in our modern liberal democracies. Nevertheless, the idea that representatives should ultimately be legally accountable to popular juries in some form and for a limited range of actions or decisions is perhaps something that could also be revisited.

Another lesson from Classical Athens is that the most problematic assemblies, in terms of accountability broadly understood (specifically the capacity to prevent rulers from straying), were the self-selected ones. Open meetings in the People's Assembly proved vulnerable to demagogues and gifted orators seeking to subvert democracy, leading to the oligarchic coups of 411 and 404, both legitimated by a vote of the assembly. When rebuilding their democracy on the heels of these events, the Athenians decided to pass a series of reforms that transferred power from the People's Assembly to sortition-based courts.

While these reforms are often understood to have weakened Athenian democracy, the changes may on the contrary be interpreted as a way of strengthening it (Cammack 2018) along what I would argue are representative lines—though perhaps we should bracket the Greek restrictions on who could enter the lotteries for the courts in the first place (a problematic feature from a purely democratic point of view). The Athenians seemed to have empirically arrived at the conclusion that temporally open democratic institutions are ultimately more accountable than purely spatially open ones.

Let us now challenge the claim that electoral mechanisms, predominant in modern representative democracies, are the amazing mechanisms of accountability many observers imagine them to be. First of all, in terms of accountability *stricto sensu*, it is not clear that elections foster all that much in the way of justification of politicians' chosen actions and policies. When they seek power, electoral candidates make promises, which are not accounts. When they seek reelection, they can indeed be described as giving accounts—as they explain and justify their past choices and the reasons why they think their policies were validated or at least understandable in retrospect. This kind of temporary exposure to public scrutiny, however, is not nearly as grueling as the exposure of Greek politicians to popular juries. Political campaigns are as much a time for spin, manipulation, and strategic lies as genuine engagement with the reasons behind policy choices.

Let us turn to the "sanctioning" value of elections. Elections are supposed to produce accountability (as sanction) via the threat of defeat at the ballot box. This claim makes two assumptions: first, that voters cast votes retrospectively, punishing incumbents for past behavior, occasionally in ways that benefit new, untried newcomers; and second, that this threat effectively produces accountability of the politicians to voters. Empirically, however, both of these assumptions are dubious. According to James Fearon, elections are not about holding governments to account (i.e., sanctioning them) but instead about choosing good governments. They are about selection rather than sanction per se. Among other reasons, he points out that if elections were purely about sanctions, then the existence of term limits would in many cases render elections entirely ineffectual. Fearon thus suggests that elections are more plausibly seen as a future-oriented device to select for the right kind of political leaders and representatives (Fearon 1999).[21]

Even in theory, it is hard to see that elections are more than an extremely imperfect and blunt tool for sanctioning elected officials. As Ferejohn and Rosenbluth remark, "elections, the typical way of disciplining political agents,

21. See also Mansbridge 2009 for a descriptive and normative defense of the "selection model" of representation as at least as valid as the sanctions models.

are a crude and imperfect way to control officials; they happen infrequently and they can usually only punish or reward officials by withholding or awarding office" (2009: 273). Another reason why elections are too blunt a sanctioning instrument is the number of issues that are bundled into one vote on a candidate's legacy.[22] Elections are at most a way to weed out the worst candidates, namely leaders who failed on too many dimensions of importance. But as long as the candidates delivered on, say, economic performance, they are highly unlikely to be sanctioned for, e.g., corruption, nepotism, racism, antisemitism, sexism, etc. (or having been the object of an impeachment procedure for that matter)—and other specific issues on which they may never feel the pressure to give accounts for their violations simply because whether they do or not will make little difference at the ballot box, where all that matters is the overall bundle.

Being an imperfect sanctioning tool, elections may still be efficient accountability instruments for reasons that have nothing to do with their ability to punish or reward but instead for their ability to select for the right type of politicians (as on Fearon's or Mansbridge's view): namely, those who feel an internal pressure to justify their decisions to the public. This assumption that elections can select for the right kind of representatives (internally inclined to do the right thing and give accounts for it) is not entirely implausible, though it is frequently violated. At any rate it does not support the view of elections as offering a much more secure form of accountability than, say, random selection.

If these arguments are correct, then, elections are neither a great mechanism for sanctioning rulers (though they may be good at selecting for a certain type of person), nor are they, more generally, an ideal way to generate accountability. More importantly, however, elections are not the only mechanism that may induce governments in a democracy, representative or open, to give accounts for their actions and to act in responsible ways. This question of non-electoral accountability certainly deserves further research, both at a theoretical level and in the historical and empirical context of non-purely electoral democratic systems, whether past (e.g., Landauer 2019) or present (e.g., Mansbridge 2019). I return to it in chapter 7, where I consider the internal resources for accountability that an open democracy could have at the systems level (rather than just the level of democratic representatives considered here).

As a final point at this stage, let me explore a possibly controversial thought. It is that accountability, as a remedial virtue and what I have earlier called an

---

22. DeCanio 2014. This is not to say that voters cannot be seen as having ultimate "control"— see Ingham 2019—but rather that having control at this level of generality might be a lower bar than achieving actual accountability.

"extrinsic" feature of democracy, should not be fetishized or ranked above more fundamental democratic values. In contemporary democracies, we accept, after all, that criminal juries are unaccountable to anyone but themselves.[23] If democracy rests, at bottom, on a faith in the ordinary citizen, then this faith should be reflected in the ways in which we treat its most democratic bodies. By contrast, we may want to pause and ask: What is the accountability of unelected bodies such as independent agencies or supreme courts? It is not clear that the burden of proof should necessarily be higher on randomly selected or self-selected assemblies of citizen representatives. It is undeniable that an institutional designer considering the introduction of a lottocratic or self-selected assembly faces a trade-off between democraticity and accountability. This trade-off must be taken into account when assigning such assemblies a function in the political system as a whole.

Conclusion

I have tried in this chapter to distinguish the concepts of representation, legitimacy, and democraticity to show that other bodies than electoral ones, specifically randomly selected and self-selected ones, can also claim democratic credentials and need not suffer from a broadly understood accountability deficit. But what about the democratic legitimacy of non-elected representatives, a question we bracketed at the beginning of this chapter? I turn to it in the next chapter.

---

23. Unlike judges, who are at the very least accountable to their peers and the public.

5

Legitimacy and Representation beyond Elections (Part Two)

The previous chapter has established what I hope are plausible claims for the respective democratic credentials of lottocratic and self-selected representation. It has also argued for the possibility of keeping non-elected representatives accountable in various ways, even in the absence of an electoral carrot or stick. Granting now the conceptual possibility of various forms of equally democratic representation, where do the corresponding representatives and bodies of representatives acquire their democratic legitimacy if not from being elected? In this chapter, I attempt to determine whether non-elected bodies with intrinsic democratic credentials (according to my argument in the previous chapter), such as mini-publics and self-selected representative groups like social movements, also have the legitimacy to make binding decisions for the rest of the polity. I use the rest of the chapter to prolong reflections started in the previous chapter, using some amount of empirical evidence where possible, to speculate about the possibility of tacit legitimation, conflicts of legitimacy, and ways of democratizing electoral representation.[1]

The first section returns to the question of political legitimacy bracketed in the previous chapter and proposes that the democratic legitimacy of representatives comes not from individual consent, as eighteenth-century theory of legitimacy understood it, but a plurality of factors, including majoritarian authorization as a necessary but insufficient condition. I further argue that

---

1. This chapter is, as a result, closer to a series of offshoots of conversations started in the previous chapter than a fully integrated and coherent argument. I trust it will be of interest nonetheless.

majoritarian authorization need not be directly of individual representatives but, instead, of the selection mechanism through which they are selected (for example lotteries or the act of self-selection).

In the second section I turn to a problem raised by self-selected assemblies. I consider the circumstances under which self-selected representatives can acquire a minimal form of democratic legitimacy even in the absence of any explicit majoritarian authorization of the selection mechanism or of the individual persons thereby selected.

In the third section, I turn to the problems posed by potential conflicts of legitimacy between different democratic representatives and consider how these problems may be solved. I do so through the study of concrete empirical examples of legitimacy conflicts between different types of democratic representatives. I suggest that the legitimacy of various democratic representatives is in part something that must be built, conquered, and demonstrated over time.

Finally, in the last, more speculative section, I return to electoral representation and ask whether it could be sufficiently democratized through so-called liquid democracy schemes, which would create a system that I propose to label "liquid representation."

On Legitimacy Again

Political legitimacy is one of the most contested and difficult concepts in political philosophy (see Peter 2010).[2] Beyond the general definition of "the property of having a right to claim obedience to one's rules," there is simply no agreement regarding what factors enter into generating this property and this right and, in particular, whether or not democracy (or what I call democraticity) is part of it. There is some agreement that "monistic" theories of political legitimacy (Christiano 2004a), which seek to trace legitimacy to a single factor, are implausible. As I tried to show in the previous chapter, for example, individual consent is not a necessary, let alone a sufficient condition for it. But then what are other plausible sources of political legitimacy? The most convincing theories of legitimacy in my view combine multiple factors, some procedural and others substantive, or to use a common distinction, recognizing the necessity of both "input" and "output" legitimacy (Scharpf 2003). Input legitimacy concerns the question of who is involved in the decision process and output legitimacy pertains to what kinds of outcomes are generated. For example, one may consider that a decision process is more legitimate if it includes more voices. But one may consider that it is less legitimate if the generated outcomes systematically fail to deliver good governance. Some also

---

2. See also Knight and Schwartzberg 2019, a cutting-edge volume updating the literature on legitimacy, which I unfortunately did not have time to process for this book.

include a third dimension of legitimacy as "throughput legitimacy" (Schmidt 2013), which has to do with the nature of the process through which decisions get made. A process that is deliberative rather than purely aggregative, for example, would have more legitimacy in the eyes of deliberative democrats (including myself).

The factors that enter into a theory of legitimacy are not all like boxes to be checked or switches to be flipped. They are more like buckets to be filled to a minimum level or thermometers that need to reach a sufficient temperature in relation to each other.[3] Jane Mansbridge thus speaks of legitimacy as a "continuum from more to less" (Mansbridge 2012: 5).[4] The important point is that there could be cases in which some of the criteria are not met (the actual bucket not filled / the actual temperature not achieved). But the fact that an entity, person, or process claiming authority fills all the other buckets in the proper way (possibly by overfilling them to offset the unfilled buckets) more than compensates for it. For example, perhaps a political authority has very little input legitimacy and yet, because it is extremely good at meeting other criteria (such as output legitimacy), it should be considered, on balance, legitimate nonetheless.

Rather than try to sketch a general theory of political legitimacy, let me simply posit a definition applicable to representatives rooted in common usages and, I hope, common sense. Considering the legitimacy of political representatives per se, I will posit that it depends on who has authorized them as well as the quality of the governance they are expected to deliver and the processes they follow to make decisions. The first and third criteria are procedural while the second is substantive. Note that the way representatives are selected itself does not matter (defining instead in my view, as per the last chapter, their democraticity or lack thereof). Focusing now strictly on the procedural aspects of representatives' legitimacy, I propose to distinguish qualitatively between democratic versus non-democratic forms of legitimacy on the basis of who authorizes the political representative. For example, the representatives of non-democratic nations on the international scene are authorized by groups other than the people they represent (including heads of other states). Whatever procedural legitimacy they have, in virtue of this international authorization, this legitimacy is not rooted in the explicit support of their own population. By contrast, I will posit that democratically legitimate representatives are representatives who have at a minimum been authorized by at least a majority of the people they claim to represent. Democratically

3. I borrow the bucket metaphor from a conversation with Jane Mansbridge from a few years ago and the thermometer metaphor from what I vaguely remember as a talk by Amanda Greene given at Stanford Political Theory Workshop, circa 2013.

4. An idea she rehearses in Mansbridge 2014, p. 11, and Mansbridge 2020, endnote 5.

legitimate representatives are, in other words, authorized by their people. These distinctions allow me to identify cases of democratically illegitimate yet democratic representatives: for example, a randomly selected mini-public convened by academics for the purpose of creating a pilot experiment would be democratic qua representative body but democratically illegitimate, that is lacking the right to claim obedience to its decisions. By contrast, a democratically legitimate yet non-democratic representative could be a Supreme Court Justice, who has no democraticity qua representative (since he has been appointed on meritocratic grounds) but who could be plausibly described as having been democratically authorized, via a democratic constitution, to represent the people. To recap, a representative (whether democratic, meritocratic, or oligarchic) will have democratic legitimacy only if, at a minimum, she has been authorized by a majority of the people she claims to represent.

The point of this analytical hair-splitting is to clarify that, at least on my definitions, a representative can have democratic legitimacy even without having been elected (the case of my Supreme Court Justice above) as long as, at a minimum, the selection mechanism through which one is selected as a representative is authorized by a majority of the people one represents. Conversely, no matter how democratic a representative is, she can still lack democratic legitimacy if she or the selection mechanism through which she was chosen hasn't been properly authorized.

Nonetheless, if we primarily associate legitimacy with majoritarian authorization, then individual elected representatives, selected by simple majority rule or plurality, have an advantage over other democratic representatives. In elections, elected representatives get both selected and authorized in one move, so to speak, which partly explains a common confusion about the sources of democraticity and the sources of legitimacy. But there is no reason why one couldn't separate the selection and authorization moments. In fact, the individual members of lottocratic assemblies need not be directly individually authorized as long as the selection mechanism picking them (a lottery, an algorithm) is explicitly authorized. So, to answer the original question: the democratic legitimacy of mini-publics or self-selected assemblies (or any other political body really) should be traced to a majoritarian vote authorizing the procedure of random selection or self-selection, as a necessary but insufficient condition of their overall legitimacy. But we do not have to trace the democratic legitimacy of the randomly or self-selected representatives to a direct, individual authorization by voters or elected officials.

All in all, in a system that would legalize mini-publics and self-selecting assemblies, these new forms of democratic representation should be viewed as meeting the same minimal threshold of democratic legitimacy as assemblies of elected representatives. Beyond that threshold, perhaps one type of assembly has more legitimacy than another, depending on how we "rate" their performance on a number of other dimensions (for example, their expected epistemic performance or how deliberative they are).

Tacit versus Explicit Majoritarian Authorization

I have argued that majoritarian authorization is a necessary condition of democratic legitimacy, and I have assumed thus far that this authorization takes the form of an explicit vote (a referendum or an election). In this section I would like to consider an intriguing possibility for the case of self-selected groups, namely the idea of tacit majoritarian authorization. Self-selected groups do not always act with the direct and express authorization of the larger group; empirical observation suggests that an element of tacit majoritarian authorization might, in some specific circumstances, be involved on the part of the non-participants.

Consider, for example, one interesting finding that came out of the study of a Finnish experiment in crowdsourced policymaking. It revealed that one possible reason for passive rather than active involvement in crowdsourced policymaking processes is individuals feeling that other people have already voiced their concerns and that their participation would not add much to the conversation (Aitamurto and Landemore 2016).[5] Observed passivity should thus not necessarily always be interpreted as indifference, laziness, incompetence, disapproval, or disenfranchisement, but possibly as a form of tacit authorization of what other people are doing, at least when equality of access to the process is real. One hypothesis, to be verified with further research, is that even when only a few people typically participate actively in crowdsourcing platforms, their activities may be implicitly authorized and thus granted a certain legitimacy by a larger number, perhaps a majority, of the other, more passive participants on the platform (though, as I explain below, no such thing should be assumed from people not on the platform).

Among offline examples, social movements and demonstrations sometimes arguably count as examples of implicitly authorized self-selected representation. During the social movements of winter 2018–2019 in France, the Yellow Vests were taken by a large fraction of the population to stand for the voice

---

5. Indeed, when prompted to comment on the 10 percent active participation rate on the website of the Finnish experiment (about 700 registered users out of 7,000 visitors), an interviewee pointed out that, from his perspective, the opinions on the website represented "a rather good sample of the opinions that are in the air, even though there are only 700 active participants." He further speculated that if the other 6,300 "felt that their opinions had been greatly insulted, they probably would've become active too" (Aitamurto and Landemore 2016: 190). Another participant seemed to confirm this intuition: "I can't think of any set of issues that would have been left undiscussed. The discussion progressed rather well without me, from what I've seen" (ibid.).

and the interests of a significant fraction of the French people, in particular poorer people living in the periphery of cities and with difficult access to public services. In terms of their legitimacy, the Yellow Vests for a long time thus garnered the implicit support, as measured by opinion polls, of a vast majority of the population (up to 75 percent at one point, including 20 percent who counted themselves as Yellow Vests).[6] They began to lose this support only when the violence of some in their midst, as well as the racist and anti-Semitic positions of a few others, became too much to bear. In this case one could say that the tacit endorsement of a majority, measured by opinion polls in which respondents explicitly announce their support, despite the absence of a vote, legitimized the role of the Yellow Vests as self-selected representatives of the French people. This was especially true of their rejection of fiscal pressures perceived to be socially unjust (such as the carbon tax that ignited the movement) and more generally their diagnosis that political institutions were not sufficiently responsive to many people's needs and interests.[7] At the global level, Swedish high schooler Greta Thunberg, whose school strike against climate change ignited youth demonstrations around the Western world, is a classic case of self-selected representation. She has been legitimized as a global youth representative, or at least a Western youth representative, by the scope of the support she gathered from the youth population across countries (especially in the West, to be fair).

Of course, in many and perhaps in most contexts, one will not be able to assume, let alone measure, tacit authorization. It is likely in fact that the silence and absence of people who know about the process (or person) may express the exact opposite of authorization, namely, refusal to engage or even tacit disapproval of what is being said and done supposedly on their behalf. Additionally, there remains the problem of those people who are not even aware of the representative claims made in their name or taken to be made in their name. In the Finnish experiment, for example, the vast majority of people did not even log on to the platform once, most likely because they were not aware of the experiment and the opportunity to express an opinion about the issue. In many other cases, people do not join online participatory forums simply because they do not have access to a computer or because they do not feel digitally literate enough to participate. Finally, there are people who generally

6. See https://www.bfmtv.com/politique/75percent-des-francais-approuvent-les-gilets -jaunes-un-soutien-en-hausse-de-5-points-1576345.html. Last accessed January 15, 2020. Interestingly, 52 percent of people who voted for French president Macron also supported the Yellow Vests at one point.

7. Though of course it is hard to pinpoint exactly the message carried by the Yellow Vests because they themselves refused to be represented by anyone and proclaimed many different demands and messages.

refuse to engage in digital forms of participation as a form of political protest.[8] It would be difficult to say that this potentially large category of people is then legitimately represented in any meaningful way by whatever is being done in their name online.

The democratic legitimacy (or lack thereof) of self-selected representatives has also been a constant source of anxiety for the members of the French Convention on Climate Change, as evidenced in various episodes. One involved the status of the work done among the participants to intersession webinars on the Convention's online platform "Jenparle" compared to the work done in person during the official sessions taking place physically at the Iena Palace in Paris. Because only 30 percent of the participants had registered on the online platform as of the fourth session, the organizers decided that the work produced during those online meetings could not be seen as forming the legitimate basis for the discussions during the following session.[9] This point was also emphasized by the guarantors of the Convention, who expressed their concerns to the Governance Committee in terms of the "digital divide" between, among others, younger and older members of the Convention. Many citizens complained they did not know how to log in to the platform or join the webinars, even among those who had been handed a free tablet at the beginning of the Convention (if they lacked easy computer access). Among those tech-savvy enough to join, time was also cited as an issue.[10]

Tacit authorization can therefore only be assumed in extremely narrowly defined contexts and under very specific conditions: for example, during large-scale events with high media coverage that are also accompanied by regular and trustworthy polling of the larger population (such as Yellow Vest demonstrations or youth climate change protests); or, in the case of participatory budgeting experiments, at the local level; or, in some small communities where digital access is prevalent, people can be assumed to have the resources and time to participate, and knowledge of the events involved is almost universal. All of these conditions, it must be recognized, are perhaps more likely to be met on the small scale of tightly knit communities.

8. See Annany 2020 and Gangadharan 2020 for more on digital exclusions and, in particular, digital silence as active refusal and a form of civil disobedience.

9. As one of the organizers reassured the participants during a plenary session of session 5: "We start from zero at each session, as if no one had attended the webinars, so no one feels excluded. Online participation during intersessions is a bonus for those who participate, not a prerequisite."

10. For example, a young female professional complained that when she agreed to join the Convention, she had signed up for six weekends, but that this Convention was turning out to be a lot more work than planned. She jokingly questioned whether other people had jobs and families. She also reported guiltily "binge-watching" (her terms) the recorded webinars she had missed in the past month on the morning of the fourth session. Even so, she said, she felt she had barely caught up.

But even within the very small scale of a given democratic assembly, where self-selection may seem a tempting selection mechanism to use for the purpose of division of labor between the members (self-selecting on the basis of affinity for a given task), legitimacy issues may crop up. Here, another example from the French Convention on Climate Change gives us food for thought. It involves a clash about the status of a particular subgroup called "the squad" and the rest of the other citizens.

Recall that the 150 members of the French Convention were (quasi-)randomly selected from the French population on the basis of randomly generated phone numbers. They were further divided, still randomly, into five thematic working subgroups as well. But during the third meeting of the Convention a sixth group was allowed to form (by the Convention organizers, not the citizens themselves) in order to deal with trans-thematic topics that had emerged across the working subgroups, such as constitutional and budgetary and financial issues. This sixth group was formed on the basis of a mixed method: random selection from among volunteers from within each of the five subgroups. The intention was laudable. This "squad," as the sixth group became known,[11] was supposed to centralize the common reflections of the Convention that had emerged in a bottom-up way from the work of the other subgroups. The squad was supposed to synthesize the work of the other groups during the fourth session of the Convention, and finally to report back to the subgroups in plenaries during the fifth session. This squad had its own inter-session meetings on webinars made available to the rest of the groups on the convention platform, "Jenparle." Yet at the first plenary of the fourth session of the Convention (January 10, 2020), the one immediately following that during which the squad had been created, a subset of the 150 had a spokesperson publicly express their resentment that the squad had been allowed to take over central questions and that it wasn't fair to dispossess the other groups of fundamental, structuring issues like constitutional and financial questions. This spokesperson insisted that the attack wasn't personal or aimed at any of the members of the squad per se but simply at the concept of a group standing apart and above the rest, a group that they hadn't authorized in the first place. He insisted that the 150 needed to work on these questions all together and that "the social contract" had been "broken" between the squad and the rest of the 150.

The organizers tried to push back by using common-sense arguments and by appealing to the need for trust and a division of labor among groups: "We cannot all work on everything. We are looking for solutions. We are going to weaken the work of groups [if we do everything at once]. Trust us and trust

---

11. In fairness, it was not meant precisely as a "sixth" group on a par with the others but as something different and complementary to all.

yourselves."[12] They also reminded the group that the squad had no decision power, that its goal was simply to consolidate ideas, and that it was meant to report back to the 150 during the fifth session.[13] These answers did not appease the mini-rebellion. An emergency meeting was held the next day between the 150 and the Governance Committee of the Convention,[14] during which it was announced that the squad would be dissolved at the end of the weekend, after reporting back to the 150 during the last plenary.

One way to reconstruct the meaning of what happened is that self-selection can be a problem when it ends up creating visible inequalities within the group, especially compared with the way the group was formed initially. None of the 150 participants had objected to being assigned to a thematic working group because the assignment was purely random. But the creation of a group selected by a hybrid method (self-selection and random selection) produced what might have been seen as an elite within the Convention. Indeed, it became very clear that, for one thing, self-selection (even corrected by random selection) led to many of the natural leaders becoming part of the squad. The natural leaders are the twenty or so people who spoke most during plenaries and in small groups, who were more frequently interviewed by journalists, and who were more active on the online platform, on Whatsapp, and during intersessions. Everyone knew who they were. These leaders were generally appreciated by the other members and indeed seen as indispensable to the dynamics of the small and large groups. Nonetheless, these natural leaders, once concentrated in a new body, may have appeared to be a threat to the rest, or at least a new kind of body, above and apart from the group.[15]

This hypothesis, I hasten to say, remains a hypothesis at this point. A number of participants actually expressed support for the squad, usually on the basis of the arguments advanced by the organizers in the plenary session (the need for division of labor and trust among the subgroups) and did not really understand what the fuss was all about and why the squad ended up being canceled. Some of them complained about what they saw as a troublesome minority with intense preferences creating fake problems and wasting precious

12. Organizer: "On peut pas tout faire à tous. On cherche des solutions. On va fragiliser la production des groupes. Faites vous confiance et faites nous confiance."

13. Organizer: "On se retrouvera en session 5 pour consolider. Mais pour l'instant, pour cette session il faut rester dans les groupes et travailler. Je sais c'est pas satisfaisant, j'en suis confuse. C'est pas pour prendre des décisions mais pour consolider."

14. A meeting from which researchers were unfortunately banned so we had to reconstruct the exchanges indirectly afterward.

15. The squad, however, was not dominated by men (as the reader perhaps expects) because random selection was stratified on gender (men and women picked from a different urn) so that parity would be ensured in all the groups (including the squad as long as enough women volunteered, which seems to have been the case).

time on meetings about procedures. Since votes were never taken about the issue during the entire controversy, there is no way of knowing exactly whether there was an actual majority in favor of the squad. This strongly suggests that explicit authorization is much more reliable than implicit authorization and should be systematically sought after where possible.

Regardless of the specifics of the French case, what seems plausible is that the legitimacy of self-selected representatives will depend in part on existing norms for the selection of representatives. Where sortition is the norm, introducing self-selection or letting it carelessly happen without much justification, or without at least a vote to authorize it, might be a problem. In other words, the legitimacy of self-selected representatives will be highly sensitive to context and to previously accepted or formally explicit norms of authorization.

Assuming we could, however, conceive of scenarios in which tacit authorization makes sense—and this most likely requires instantiating a strong version of what I label "substantive equality" in the last chapter—it could allow for an interesting division of representative labor. I suggested at the beginning of the previous chapter that self-selected representation (like lottocratic representation) qualifies as "virtual" representation (or representation without consent). Contrary to eighteenth-century undemocratic virtual representation, however, this form of twenty-first-century virtual representation is meant to take place in the context of a genuinely inclusive process (unlike the eighteenth-century British Parliament, which neither the property-less, nor women, nor American colonists had any chance to enter). In the smaller communities of an open democracy, or perhaps a very advanced society where we could assume equal social capital, education, and self-confidence, many who decide not to participate could perhaps be shown to have done so voluntarily and, in some cases, because they felt that their views had already been expressed. But if tacit group authorization were real in such contexts, then self-selected representation should be seen less as a form of "virtual" yet democratic representation and more as an attenuated form of "actual" democratic representation—attenuated in the sense that implicit majoritarian support is much weaker than explicit support.

In other words, self-selected representatives may, under specific circumstances, be able to claim the legitimacy granted by the tacit authorization of a majority (of those who didn't show up for the role of self-selected citizen representatives). In fact, one could argue that self-selection is one of the more plausible ways to obtain citizens' majoritarian authorization, at least if the option to step forward is genuinely made available to all—through appropriate outreach and financial compensation for example.

In any case, as suggested earlier in the chapter, the question of legitimacy is most likely one of degree and multiple factors, beyond mere majoritarian authorization. It seems that from this perspective any democratic body,

BEYOND ELECTIONS, PART TWO   115

whether randomly selected, self-selected, or even elected, could have enough legitimacy to claim the title of most legitimate democratic representative. It ultimately depends on the theory of legitimacy one privileges. The reason to prefer a certain format over another might come down to pragmatic considerations of feasibility and empirical evidence about the practical trade-offs presented by each.

From this perspective, there is surely something to be learned from the Greek experience. Fifth century BC Athens never used elections to staff democratic offices. It is instead usually associated with the People's Assembly. Yet to counter the accountability problems that arise in open assemblies, the Athenians ultimately transferred a large degree of legislative power to popular courts of randomly selected and relatively rapidly rotating bodies of citizens. What this suggests is that mini-publics are probably the more reliable and accountable of democratically representative bodies.

This conclusion also runs against the forceful arguments made by some deliberative democrats that we should never entrust mini-publics with decision power. Cristina Lafont, for example, argues that democratic legitimacy requires society-wide deliberation and that the latter cannot be "shortcut" by the deliberations taking place in what she sees as small elite groups disconnected from the larger public (Lafont 2015; see also Lafont 2020).[16] There can be, as she pithily puts it, "no democratization without improved mass deliberation" (Lafont 2015: 45). Lafont would presumably reject the idea of a randomly selected body as the central legislative assembly in an open democracy.

While Lafont is right that deliberative democracy ideally requires mass participation as a condition of political legitimacy, the problem is that the only form of participation that works at such a scale is voting, not deliberation. As we saw in chapter 3, there is no such thing as direct mass deliberation (in my use of the term at least).[17] So it is hard to understand what "*improved* mass

16. I hope to do justice some other time to Lafont's intricate argument and, in particular, her sharp and interesting critique of the positions I defended in my previous book (Landemore 2013) as "epistocratic."

17. My disagreement with Lafont can be traced back, I think, to our different understandings of deliberation. I mean by deliberation *an exchange of arguments among free and equal individuals*. Lafont uses deliberation as what seems to me a much looser notion, covering both what I just described and also a metaphorical version of it, namely the exchanges taking place among aggregates of individuals (interest groups, parties, the media) and distributed over time, processes, and institutions, including elections and Supreme Courts (Lafont 2020: 20–32). On Lafont's extremely capacious definition, there is no meaningful difference between the micro-deliberations taking place among fifteen individuals on a citizen's jury and the society-wide exchanges of opinion occurring at the level of the public sphere itself. This conflation of micro-deliberation and macro-deliberation, however, ends up masking crucial differences between the two levels. Macro-deliberation of the kind covered by Lafont's definition is not a process involving free and equal *individuals* as such, in the sense that individuals in these macro-exchanges of arguments are on

deliberation" would look like (my emphasis) absent the very possibility of mass deliberation to begin with. As discussed in chapter 3, legitimacy-granting deliberation about public policies can only take place within smaller, representative bodies (even as it is crucial to make these representative bodies available to the larger public). If we can't have mass deliberation, why not at least have deliberation in a mini-public rather than not at all?

At any rate, I take Lafont's distinct and correct point: if we care about legitimacy, then the mini-publics engaged in the process of "mutual justification" need to be as "open" to the larger public as possible and ultimately connected to an authorization moment and sometimes, though not necessarily always, a referendum down the line. In other words, I agree with her that mini-publics should not be run as secretive lab experiments in complete disconnection to the larger public sphere and society-wide "deliberation." Nor should they be making the decisions on momentous issues. But surely, for regular policy- and law-making, it must be possible to authorize mini-publics to make decisions on behalf of the larger group, lest nothing could be done well, or indeed at all.

At the limit the most ambitious way to connect a legislative mini-public to the larger public would be to enroll the entirety of the population in as many sufficiently small randomly selected assemblies as needed. This would *not* be equivalent to mass deliberation, conceptually speaking (which I picture instead as the image of "all brains connected to all brains at once") but would nonetheless practically achieve something close to its expected effects. These groups would meet physically or online, in order to either generate the input and agenda for the nationwide open mini-public (if we are considering a bottom-up process) or to replicate the deliberations of the central mini-public (if we are considering a top-down way of diffusing the conclusions of the national level mini-public). For the first model, the multi-level, ascendant structure of the National Public Policy Conventions in Brazil, which build on local meetings all the way to a national meeting, is close to the ideal of what one would want to replicate, once combined with the principle of random rather than self-selection into the assemblies (Pogrebinschi 2013). Jim Fishkin and Bruce Ackerman have also proposed an idea similar to this one with their proposal of a nationwide "Deliberation Day" (Ackerman and Fishkin 2005). This kind of heavily structured, society-wide enrollment of the population in small-scale

---

equal terms and would be able to process all the arguments and make up their minds about them at their own individual level. Even with all the idealizations in the world, there is no society capable of equalizing conditions such that small-scale deliberation and large-scale deliberation would be qualitatively the same object. Deliberation of the kind I am interested in thus ontologically requires either a small enough scale or a division of labor allowing some to deliberate on behalf of others in a representative scheme of sorts.

deliberations would look much different than "deliberation in the wild" as theorized by Habermas and embraced by Lafont.

In practice, however, such large-scale deliberative experiments can happen only rarely, and no polity could be plausibly run in such a manner. The French Great National Debate put politics on pause for nearly two months. The Brazilian Conventions (more on this in chapter 8) take a whole year from the moment local meetings take place to the time the national convention in Brasília ends. Meanwhile, everyday politics goes on and these countries need to be run. Division of labor is unavoidable. This is why, though I share Lafont's concern for keeping the larger public as involved as possible, I do not believe that even a demanding participatory conception of democratic legitimacy can forbid ultimately granting properly legitimized mini-publics decision powers similar to those we grant elected assemblies.

Conflicts of Legitimacy

In the transition to an open democracy, conflicts of legitimacy are likely to arise between different types of democratic assemblies with different representative claims and different claims to legitimacy. How do we adjudicate between these claims? Here it helps to look at actual cases of such conflict to study the ways in which they were solved (or not).

Consider, first, the conflicts of legitimacy that arose in the Icelandic context, specifically between the Constitutional Council of 25 ordinary citizens and Parliament. The Constitutional Council of 25 directly elected ordinary citizens saw themselves, and were seen by their supporters, as in some way "more legitimate" than the elected assembly of professional politicians—the Parliament—that had authorized their existence in the first place. The Council members traced their legitimacy to various sources, including their moral purity compared to the alleged corruption of elites in power (to be fair, this claim seems to have been supported by the very fact that Parliament had banned politicians in power from running for elections to the Council); the fact that their work continued the recommendations of a demographic sample of the population (the randomly selected National Forum of 950 Icelanders); and their own closer proximity to ordinary citizens, compared to professional politicians. The truth, however, is that Parliament had legal precedence over the Council, if only because Parliament had authorized the Council into existence, not once but twice: once, as it passed the law organizing the elections to staff it, and a second time when, after the elections were struck down by the Supreme Court, Parliament had to reappoint each member of the Council individually. From the perspective of the Council and its supporters, however, its legal origin was irrelevant. In their view, whatever dependence on an existing order the Council had was rendered moot by the fact that they had been given a wide mandate to rewrite the constitution and a popular referendum had approved their proposal by a two-thirds margin. As they saw it, the fact that the referendum was defined as merely "advisory" was a legal technicality, which did not affect the moral weight Parliament and other institutions should have attached to the positive verdict. Meanwhile, the establishment parties and the opponents to the constitutional process saw the Council as less legitimate than a group of activists. They judged that whatever democratic legitimacy the Council may have initially garnered from being, like Parliament, directly elected by the population, was entirely annulled by the Supreme Court decision to strike down the elections as procedurally flawed, and not regained by the ensuing appointment process by Parliament. They consequently treated the Council as, at best, an advisory commission rather than as the legitimate democratic representatives of the people. They treated the popular referendum as a joke, further delegitimized by its relatively low participation level (47 percent) and proceeded to ignore its rather clear-cut outcome.

Similarly, in the French case, there was a competition for political legitimacy playing out between at least three institutional actors: (1) the official institutions of the French Republic, most notably Parliament; (2) the randomly selected Convention on Climate Change, whose existence was authorized by the president but whose functioning autonomy was real and whose proposals were potentially meant to be submitted, without any "filter" as per the President's promise, to a popular referendum, thus de facto bypassing Parliament; and, finally (3) the social movements protesting the politics of the government at the time (on pension reform). The participants in these movements, though only comprising a fraction of the population, were nonetheless widely supported by public opinion in various polls and put direct pressure on elected officials, even as their relation to the Convention on Climate Change and its work was very unclear. At least some members of the Convention agreed to postpone their fourth session from early December 2019 to mid-January, in part to maintain solidarity with the social movements that started then. Meanwhile, many protesters saw the Convention as a great idea in theory but, in practice, a manipulative tactic on the part of the government, which they saw as using both the carrot of deliberative democracy and the stick of police repression to get reforms passed. In other words, in the French case, we had an implicit confrontation between elected officials on the one hand and what this book has called lottocratic and self-selected representatives, with each of the latter groups standing in uneasy relation to one another.

Though the debates in France have so far been a lot less acrimonious than in Iceland (probably because, as of the time of writing, we are still far from reaching an actual decision), some voices, mostly from the camp of Parliamentarians, rose against the competition and the threat to their status and legislative prerogatives that they perceived as coming from the Convention on Climate

Change. Multiple calls were made for a clarification of the relationship between what these Parliamentarians saw themselves as incarnating, namely, "representative democracy," and what was variously described as an alternative to it—under the terms "participatory democracy," "direct democracy," "deliberative democracy," or even "citizen democracy."

Consider the fascinating question put by Senator Frédéric Marchand to Secretary of State Emmanuelle Wargon on January 15, 2020.[18] In his address, the senator suggested that representative and participatory democracy should not be in competition but rather should work together toward a common goal, including on climate issues. Yet he ended on a somewhat anguished note regarding the question of who should really be in charge of "taking strong options," as President Macron had encouraged the 150 Convention members to do during his visit with them earlier that month. The senator thus asked: "Taking strong options is also the prerogative of representative democracy. How does the Government see the articulation between this novel exercise of citizen democracy and the representatives of the nation that we are?" The phrasing of the question restricts the title of representative to elected officials alone. The question itself seemingly challenged the legitimacy of the 150 in making decisions in the stead of elected officials or citizens themselves.

Questions also arose among the 150 themselves, who pondered their own status with respect to the rest of the country and the place of an assembly like theirs in existing institutions. In their answer to the researchers' questionnaires during the first meeting of the Convention, only 43 (or 35%) of the 123 members who answered said that they spoke in their own name only. Twenty-two responded that they spoke in the name of the public as a whole; 25 in the name of themselves and people like themselves; 24 in the names of causes they cared about; and 3 in the name of other groups or interests (6 did not answer this specific question on the questionnaire). It is hard not to read these answers as an indication that most citizens (at least 60% of the respondents) took themselves to act as representatives of some sort.[19] When asked in interviews about how they saw their role in this assembly, some of them also evoked, unprompted, a role of "representative"—often qualified in a tentative vein when prodded about what they meant by the term ("I'm trying").[20] At the same time some of them understood the representative task as a collective rather than individual

18. My translation. See the minutes of the corresponding Senate session at https://www.senat.fr/seances/s202001/s20200115/s20200115_mono.html. The relevant passage is the last paragaph under the heading "Convention Citoyenne pour le Climat."

19. I thank Jean-François Laslier for sharing the results of the researchers' questionnaires and Angèle Delevoye for compiling the numbers.

20. Male, about 30 years old. Interview November 16, 2019, on file with author. Another one of the younger members (a seventeen-year-old male) said, "I represent my high-school" then "I represent the youth." When asked what he meant by that, he qualified this way: "It's a

endeavor ("When I say *I* represent the youth, I mean me, [another young member], the others [young members of the Convention]"). They conceived of the representative task itself as "saying what they [the French youth] think, being their loudspeaker, acting for them."[21]

Similarly, when asked about their legitimacy, some of them emphasized that they needed to "build it," including by reaching out to the larger public. They described random selection as "elections without consent."[22] Finally, some engaged in even higher-level speculations. For example, to return to the anecdote opening chapter 4, when the youngest member of the Convention directly asked the president: "Is deliberative democracy the future of democracy?,"[23] the president's answer suggested a mutually reinforcing relationship between the two, where citizen deliberation was meant to nurture and inform the deliberation of elected officials, buttressing them by improving them. But this interpretation is directly contradicted by the president's own promise to submit the citizens' proposal "without filter" to a referendum should the text meet the required accuracy and formal criteria, thus possibly bypassing Parliament altogether. A more ambitious reading could be that as we aim to redistribute representative tasks toward non-elected, deliberative bodies like the Citizen Convention, de facto taking away some of the powers of Parliament, we will in fact buttress the waning legitimacy of existing electoral institutions, as the new representatives can help them conduct more successful policies overall.

Ultimately, conflicts of legitimacy are likely to be settled by luck, power, money, and other less noble causes, and whether majorities decide to throw their weight behind a particular, contested claim. What worked for the United States' runaway constitutional convention did not work for the Icelandic Constitutional Council. The exact balance in terms of legitimacy and representativeness between the Convention on Climate Change, social movements, and established electoral institutions in France is still being determined. There is not much that normative political theorists can conclude from this, though political scientists may have a lot to say about the strategic mistakes made by the actors involved (e.g., the Constitutional Council in the Icelandic case, which refused, in a self-defeating way, to cooperate with parties and other political elites).

What normative political theorists can conclude, however, is that although democratic legitimacy requires periodically renewed moments of majoritarian

---

little arrogant to say that but I'm trying to represent them. Not everybody has the chance to be selected." Interview January 11, 2020, on file with author.

21. The same seventeen-year-old male. Interview January 11, 2020, on file with author.

22. Interview January 11, 2020, on file with author.

23. As it turns out this young member had read about deliberative democracy that very year in a political history and geopolitics class.

authorization, it is possible to envisage the democratic legitimacy of a system in which *there exist no stable elected representative assemblies whatsoever*. This is not to say that, even in theory, such a system is the most desirable, and much more experimentation would need to be done to ascertain the respective merits of various forms of democratic representation and the way to best combine and articulate them.

Liquid Representation

The previous chapter considered two forms of non-electoral democratic representation, lottocratic and self-selected, which we contrasted with the more closed-off form of democratic representation that we are most familiar with, namely electoral representation.[24] But have we not been too quick to dismiss electoral representation? Isn't there a way to democratize the latter by building on its egalitarian side—the principle of "one person, one vote," and minimizing the aristocratic side—the principle of distinction on which elections are based?

In this section I engage in some speculations about how far we can take this idea by looking more closely at schemes of so-called delegative or liquid democracy (already briefly encountered in chapter 3). While these schemes typically claim to want to get rid of representation altogether or strike a middle ground between direct and representative democracy, they can also be described as aiming to strike down the barriers to entry to the status of elected representative, thus rendering electoral representation more inclusive. This inclusiveness arguably constitutes such a radical break from electoral representation that I propose to conceptualize it as the distinct notion of "liquid" representation.

Liquid democracy is of recent vintage. The earliest documented use of the term is in a 2004 Wiki by "Sayke" (Sayke 2004).[25] The first theoretical sketch of liquid democracy, however, was arguably developed by Gordon Tullock in a 1967 book called *Toward a Mathematics of Politics* (Tullock 1967: 144–146). It was further defended in a paper by James Miller in 1969 explaining its merits compared to contemporary legislative and electoral systems. Both Bryan Ford, an engineer who called it "delegative democracy" in an influential though unpublished paper in 2002 (Ford 2002), and the anonymous Sayke (2004) seemingly reinvented it independently later. Political theorists Christian Blum

---

24. I thank Chiara Valsangia for helping me improve this section considerably by sharing her extensive knowledge of liquid democracy and the literature around it.

25. This pseudonym may be the covert identity of John Washington Donoso. See https://www.heise.de/tp/features/Direkte-Demokratie-Eurokrise-und-Probleme-der-Privatisierung-3399055.html.

and Christina Isabel Zuber finally put it on the map of political philosophy in an important 2016 *Journal of Political Philosophy* article (Blum and Zuber 2016).

Liquid or delegative democracy, sometimes also called proxy voting, is a system in which people can give their votes to anyone they like, either for a given term or just on certain issues, with the option of recall at any time and the possibility of retaining one's right to direct input throughout. Blum and Zuber formally emphasize four key components: (1) the possibility of direct voting on all issues; (2) the possibility of flexible vote delegation on one, several, or all issues; (3) the possibility of meta-delegation (my delegated vote can be further delegated by the person I delegated it to);[26] and (4) the possibility of instant recall of my delegated vote. The advantages of such a system are, among other things, that it gives maximal freedom of choice to individuals while making better use of widely distributed expertise, information, and knowledge than electoral systems by moving the decision point, via meta-delegation in particular, to the people deemed most competent on the issue by the entire group (Blum and Zuber 2016; Green-Armytage 2015; Valsangiacomo 2020).

All of this may sound wildly impractical, in addition to being dangerous. On the practical side, there already exist various proofs of concept, enabled in part by the digital technology and social media revolution that the core concept of liquid democracy—vote delegation—depends on. It would indeed be difficult to envision something like this on a mass scale using regular mail (though corporations have long used somewhat similar systems, called "proxy voting"). For example, the Demoex party in Sweden first used a liquid democracy system between 2002 and 2016 (Norbäck 2012). Around 2006, software platforms were created to facilitate not only comment functions and vote delegation but delegation-based online discussion and deliberation as well, under the names "LiquidFeedback" and "Adhocracy." LiquidFeedback, for example, was adopted and used for the past several years by the German Pirate Party (Swierczek 2011).[27]

---

26. There is disagreement as to how many rounds of delegation should be allowed. Bryan Ford, for example, who initially proposed transitive delegation as a way to address the scalability and individual-attention-deficit problems of pure direct democracy, has since backed off to the position that "delegation [potentially] *can be* transitive"—with the question of whether it *should* be transitive an interesting and important open question" (personal communication, August 29, 2018, email on file with author). While he still believes that only transitive delegation allows for the multi-level organic representative structures he and others envisioned to form, he has now been convinced to retreat to the weaker but safer version of liquid democracy that allows only one level of delegation, whereby the ultimate voter can effectively assemble a small ad hoc group of "advisors" that the voter is allowed to "follow" and vote with automatically, but those advisor-delegates can't (at least automatically) further delegate their vote. For a defense of meta-delegation on epistemic grounds, see Valsangiacomo 2020: 14–15).

27. The Pirate Party recently tried to get a foothold in the United States, to little effect so far: https://www.bostonglobe.com/ideas/2014/10/31/text-aye-matey-the-pirate-party-push-for -direct-democracy/X8dl2dKD73HiXGTXdlyuDP/story.html.

Theorists of liquid democracy see it as compatible with representation, here simply understood as vote delegation or the fact of voting on behalf of someone else, as authorized by this person (a minimal definition that is compatible, I believe, with the definition defended in chapter 4). Sayke, for example, considers that liquid democracy is "probably best thought of as a voting system that migrates along the line between direct and representative democracy" and "combines the advantages of both, while avoiding their flaws." For Bryan Ford, liquid democracy replaces "artificially imposed representation structures with an adaptive structure founded on real personal and group trust relationships" (Ford 2002: 1). In other words, whereas electoral representation is constrained and rigid, vote delegation or "liquid representation," as I propose to call it, is free and fluid, based on "the principle that each voter should have free, *individual* choice of their delegate—not just a choice among a restricted set of career politicians" (Ford 2014: 1). For Blum and Zuber, similarly, "[l]iquid democracy is a procedure for collective decision-making that combines direct democratic participation with a flexible account of representation" (Blum and Zuber 2016: 165). Liquid democracy thus lies between the immediacy and impracticality of direct democracy, where everyone should vote on every issue, and the solidity of representative democracy in its electoral version, where only a few career politicians make most of the decisions.

More specifically, how different is liquid representation from electoral representation? First, a new and unique feature of liquid representation is that each citizen can be represented by several proxies depending on the policy or policy area at stake. As a result, a liquid parliament is extremely volatile, as it potentially changes composition every time a new policy or policy area must be debated. As Chiara Valsangiacomo describes it:

> Today, a person can be a proxy [aka a liquid representative in my vocabulary] in matters of elementary education while delegating his vote on matters of tertiary education, but tomorrow, that same person could become a proxy for public health issues and give up delegation in matters of education. Or she could drop out from activism and delegate all her choices to somebody else. Moreover, that person could decide to vote, every once in a while, in single polls of particular importance to her. (Valsangiacomo 2020: fn 19)

Second, the number of representatives is neither limited nor fixed. Instead of a relatively small and stable Parliament-size group, assemblies of liquid representatives could number in the millions and their number vary from decision to decision. Third, whereas elected representatives typically hold one vote each, individual liquid representatives typically hold various degrees of voting power each (in proportion to the number of votes they represent). Fourth, the feature of instant recall ensures that citizens don't have to wait until the end of a mandate to punish or reward their representatives. Finally, a fifth difference is that individual citizens are allowed by default to participate in policymaking and decide for themselves about issues if they do not wish to delegate their votes.

How democratic is liquid representation? Recall that, in my framework, democratic representation is that which is open to all and based on a selection process expressing the values of inclusion and equality. From the above description, it should be clear that liquid representation considerably opens up the status of representatives to anyone trusted enough by their friends, families, and other acquaintances. Anyone has a chance to become a liquid representative. As a result, liquid democracy also diversifies the profile of people who are able to operate as representatives. Anyone, in theory, could occupy a spot on a liquid "open-seat" parliament. Unsurprisingly, advocates of liquid democracy tend to celebrate it as a democratic decision-making system, characterized by its egalitarian (as well as epistemic) features (Blum and Zuber 2016).

Note that there is an element of self-selection in liquid democracy. People can delegate their votes to me even if I didn't properly announce I'm interested in having votes delegated to me, but at some point I still have to accept the task of proxy voter. The level of self-selection is probably comparable to that of lottocratic representation performed on the basis of a universal pool of candidates (as opposed to a pool of volunteers), where selected individuals (those randomly called on the phone for example) still have to agree to accept the responsibility. Additionally, citizens do not have to compete with each other for the *status* of being a liquid representative. "[T]hey only compete for the votes of individuals and for recognition from other delegates" (Ford 2002: 5). On the face of it, becoming a liquid representative is genuinely open to all, not reserved to those with money, connections, self-confidence, or competitive or other salient traits.

Yet it is not clear that "liquid" representation can solve the inequality intrinsically introduced by the choice of a proxy for one's votes. Similar to election, voluntary vote delegation seems based on a principle of distinction between individuals, identifying those who stand out for their knowledge or competence on certain issues or questions. Votes would not be delegated evenly in the population. Worse, the main risk in such a liquid scheme is that most of the votes would be syphoned off by salient public figures, ultimately imposing a further restriction of access to representative status, rather than engendering more inclusion.[28] If we look at what happened in the Icelandic context, where

28. Given what we know of human psychological mechanisms, this seems rather likely. As Adam Smith argued in *The Theory of Moral Sentiments*, humans have a tendency to "sympathise" more intensely with the "rich and famous" than with the obscure. Additionally, the nature of what Schelling called "focal point" dynamics works in favor of socially salient candidates. It takes time to procure information about different candidates, even under liquid democracy. People with an

elections to the Constitutional Council were somewhat "liquid" in the sense that anyone could run for them and ultimately 525 people presented themselves, we observe that the usual dynamics associated with status, celebrity, and social media savvy were at play in selecting the final contenders. The persons who garnered the most votes were an economist who was already famous, a lawyer who had made a name for herself by being very active and vocal during the 2008–2009 protests in front of Parliament, and those who managed to create enough buzz, early enough, on social media. Liquid democracy might similarly prove as vulnerable to oligarchic capture as regular elections.

Advocates of liquid democracy often emphasize the need for strong norms to guard against this risk of superstar voting. Bryan Ford also sees promise in a technical solution: allowing voters to split their votes among several delegates that they trust equally or almost equally. He predicts that vote-splitting combined with multiple-stage vote delegation would free the model from the winner-take-all straitjacket into which it is currently forced by empowering a greater diversity of delegates rather than concentrating all votes on a small set of stars.[29]

Proposals for voting systems compatible with such delegated vote-splitting include Paolo Boldi et al.'s "Viscous Democracy" proposal (Boldi et al. 2011) and a model called "Structural Deep Democracy."[30] While these approaches make the algorithms for handling vote delegation more complex, they would arguably substantially mitigate the real danger represented by the superstar problem. More generally, given the range of topics covered by political decisions, liquid democracy with delegated and split votes would presumably distribute much more equally the status of "liquid representative." Most people would have a decent chance of acting as liquid representatives in their areas of specialty.

Additionally, the fact that people keep the possibility of voting directly on issues at any point considerably tempers this oligarchic danger. Even if inequalities develop among citizens in terms of their likelihood of becoming liquid representatives, the system remains inclusive of all. Even if I'm not someone noticeable, connected, or knowledgeable enough to have people transfer their votes to me, I at least retain throughout the right to vote myself and thus to be, so to speak, my own liquid representative.

If the solutions to the problem of star-voting proved effective in practice, the difference between liquid representation and classic electoral representation would be crucial. By rejecting the principle of a set of preselected career

---

already established level of fame will tend to collect all the votes in a winner-take-all dynamics, leaving the vast majority of citizens behind. I thank Max Krahé for this point.

29. While there might still be some celebrity to whom a large number of people delegate, that celebrity would likely be receiving only a fraction of most of the delegated votes they receive, as the celebrity will be competing with (and likely often getting their votes split with) other delegates closer to the ultimate voter.

30. See https://groups.yahoo.com/neo/groups/sd-2/info. Last accessed September 23, 2018.

politicians, groomed by parties and given particular salience in the public sphere in order to attract votes, liquid democracy could arguably overcome the oligarchic dimension of elections. More importantly, thanks to the possibility of permanent recall, accountability would be much stronger than in classic electoral representation.[31] Whether any of these putative benefits would outweigh some of the costs of this method of running things remains to be seen.

Star-voting is not, however, the only problem with liquid democracy. Even if liquid representatives are, as I now believe, viable candidates for the title of new democratic representatives, a number of other theoretical issues and normative concerns should give us pause if we are to find a proper role for such liquid representatives in an improved democracy (I will leave aside here security-related issues as part of a more technical debate about the safety of digital technologies, although they are of course essential).

First, the sheer size of a body of liquid representatives in large nation-states would presumably render difficult any meaningful deliberation among them, even if we assume they could be gathered in a general forum, whether off- or online. This problem of mass deliberation remains one that even current Parliaments do not address satisfactorily (since very little deliberation can actually happen among hundreds of individuals, at least not without structure that adds additional layers of representation, such as breaking up the large group into smaller groups who then report back to the larger group). One would therefore either have to delegate the task of deliberating in depth about issues to a different group (perhaps a mini-public chosen at random from the larger population) or add an additional layer of a sufficiently small number of representatives from among the liquid representatives to allow them to conduct meaningful deliberation.

Second, even if deliberation were an option among all the liquid representatives at once (because a small enough number of them were chosen, say), it is not clear how this deliberation could be organized to reflect the differing degrees of power of each individual liquid representative. For the case of bodies that are sufficiently small, Ford has nonetheless developed the idea of a "weighted open forum," whereby debates would be moderated either to give more opportunity to speak to the delegates that carry more votes or simply to entitle them to more votes after deliberation is over (Ford 2002: 7).

It is probably too soon to make any predictions about the likely success of liquid representation going forward. Let me instead playfully close with the speculations of Tim Reutemann, a science-fiction writer who allows us to imagine what a large-scale liquid democracy system would look like.

In *Liquid Reign*, the hero wakes up after several decades in a coma to face the brave new world of 2051. This world, as it turns out, is now entirely run

---

31. Thank you to Pierre-Etienne Vandamme for this point.

by digital liquid democracy schemes, applied at all political levels, from the local to the regional to the global, with some local variants (e.g., the Swiss people still vote in person in their *Landsgemeinden*). Here is how one of the characters, a doctor who supervises the hero's recovery and also works as a liquid representative, summarizes the system:

> I've got around two hundred million base voters to represent, but I also get a lot of support from high-level aggregators who forward delegate those votes to me. They do all the work of finding good compromise strategies among our base voters [patients, doctors, nurses and people related to them], while I focus on negotiating with high-level delegates from different bases. It's normally just a few days per month for politics. (Reutemann 2018: 117)
>
> The vast majority of [votes] come via other proxies. On average, a vote is delegated four times before I get it. (119)

This vision is inspiring in that the whole political system is both sophisticated and economical of people's time. It also allows for deliberation at various levels of the global polity among higher-level delegates, as well as both voting and controlling for the possibility of trolls and other problems. The system widely distributes power to individuals with the right credentials and motivations. Liquid democracy even facilitates global and even deterritoralized democratic representation.

Yet, even in the novelist's imagination, liquid democracy is not without issues. For one thing, this scheme presupposes a faith in the ability of a single person to represent millions of others. While this assumption solves the problem of the scalability of liquid democracy beyond small organizations like parties, it is at odds with many democrats' beliefs that there is a limit to the number of people a single person can represent. This problem, however, affects any kind of representatives, posing the more general question of the ideal size of democratic communities. Moreover, little is said about how the possible conflicts that emerge in the assemblies of high-level delegates are solved, especially given the different sizes of constituencies they represent. Finally, the problem of super-star voting is evoked as a real threat, even in this highly idealized and not particularly dystopian setting.
A lot more conceptualization and experimentation are needed with this form of representation before we know what to do with it, whether we should authorize it as a legitimate way of making collective decisions, and how to articulate it to other forms of democratic representation.[32]

---

32. See Valsangiacomo 2020 for a modelization of liquid democracy for the purpose of future investigations about its normative status. I engage in some speculations about the articulation between lottocratic, self-selected, and liquid representation in the opening vignette of Landemore 2021.

6

The Principles of Open Democracy

It is now time to expand from democratic representation to the more general principles of open democracy. When I refer to "institutional principles," I mean mid-level principles that are more concrete than abstract values such as equality or inclusiveness but less specific than, say, electoral rules or a choice of bicameralism versus unicameralism. These principles are supposed to inform institutional design without over-determining it.

I use the term "principle" in the same way that Bernard Manin and Nadia Urbinati use the term in their respective work *The Principles of Representative Government* (Manin 1997) and *Representative Democracy: Principles and Genealogy* (Urbinati 2006). Both Manin and Urbinati draw on history to derive in an inductive fashion the core features of the regime they identify respectively (the nuance matters) as representative *government* and representative *democracy*. While Manin's account aims to be purely descriptive and Urbinati's account is meant to be a normative reconstruction of historic realities, their list of principles is surprisingly convergent and amounts to an "ideal-type" in the Weberian sense (see chapter 2 for an analysis). My list of principles is more aspirational and normative than descriptive but it is similarly rooted in history. I thus borrow from the traditions that have disappeared—the classical Athenian model—as well as the traditions that lost the battle of ideas—the Anti-Federalist perspective on representation for example—to build a list of normatively desirable institutional principles.

To anticipate what the rest of the chapter will proceed to develop and argue for, the five institutional principles of open democracy are:

1. Participation rights
2. Deliberation

3. The majoritarian principle
4. Democratic representation
5. Transparency

I introduce them in what I take to be their chronological and logical order of importance. If we assume that the natural order for human communities to evolve is to start small and only progressively grow to the size of city-states, then nation-states, and then larger entities (despite the many counter-examples of historical empires collapsing and societies reverting to smaller-scale communities), then the primary building blocks of a democracy are individual participation rights that recognize all members of the group as equally entitled to participate in the decision-making process. What comes next must be decision-making procedures—deliberation and majority rule—allowing the group to establish a few key laws (about, say, constitutional fundamentals). As the group (or the franchise) expands and consequently the diversity and complexity of their problems and interests, we then quickly also need to institutionalize the principle of democratic representation already encountered in the previous chapters as that which allows for the preservation of democracy at scale. Finally, to make *democracy* and not just representation fully open, we also need to introduce a counter-balancing principle of accountability (transparency), which ensures that the represented can keep an eye on the representatives and mobilize their participation rights as needed.

The chronological order also maps onto the logical order. Participation rights represent the condition of possibility for the system as a whole. The second and third principles—democratic deliberation and majority rule—form the backbone of decision processes in a genuine democracy, at any scale. The fourth principle captures the open nature of democratic representation, when the latter is needed. The last one, transparency, is an accountability principle whose value is first and foremost instrumental to securing the proper functioning of the system and prevent the closure of open representative institutions between the moments when they are renewed. All together these five principles aim to institutionalize the ideal of popular rule as the equal right to participate in self-rule.

In the first section I contrast two analytical paradigms I build after the two historical versions of democracy with which we are familiar, respectively the model of assembly democracy implemented in fifth and fourth-century BC Athens and the model of representative democracy implemented in various forms from the eighteenth century onward in the West.[1] The second section builds on this contrast to derive the principles of open democracy by layering

---

1. This stylized comparison is of course simplifying historical realities in many respects, but it helps manage the complexity of the comparison by focusing on the relevant features that could

new practices and meanings onto some of these idealized democratic practices and institutional features and sometimes breaking from the latter altogether. Ultimately, I derive five core principles of open democracy, which are summarized in a comparative table. the third section addresses the status of political parties in a non-electoral system and what alternative bodies could play their role of information and interest-aggregation. The fourth section, finally, addresses the role of popular vote processes, referendums, and other "direct democracy" measures under this new paradigm. I postpone to the next chapter considerations of feasibility and incentive compatibility.

Assembly Democracy versus Electoral Democracy

In order to appreciate the novelty and radicalness of the five principles of open democracy, at least as a combined set, let me first go back in time and build an analytical contrast between the two distinct paradigms of democracy with which we are most familiar.

The first one, democracy 1.0 as we might call it, is the Classical Athenian model of "direct democracy." I prefer to label it "assembly democracy," though this is probably not the most accurate term either. I reconstruct the institutional principles of assembly democracy on the basis of what historians and democratic theorists tell us and with an eye to the relevant contrasts with modern democracies.

The second model is the historical paradigm that is currently failing us: "representative democracy," which I will identify by its salient feature as electoral democracy (although other features, like liberalism, are very much part of it) or democracy 2.0. I build here on the normative account developed in chapter 2 on the basis of Manin's and Urbinati's theories, assuming among other things that universal franchise is the normative aspiration of electoral democracy, even though its realization comes remarkably late in most existing representative democracies.

In both assembly democracy and electoral democracy, universal inclusiveness of the relevant demos can be seen as a characteristic feature, even as it applies in each case to very different conceptions of the relevant demos. The Greeks had a notoriously restrictive notion of who counted as a citizen, excluding all women, foreigners, and slaves. Electoral democracies, in turn, used to exclude women, the property-less, and various minorities. It took some of them close to two centuries to accept all of the latter as full members of the polity, but they eventually did. The next civic frontier is now whether to extend

---

still be relevant in the twenty-first century. Though I aim to construct analytical types, I try to respect the historical specificities as much as seems necessary and relevant.

voting rights to resident aliens and children, at least in some elections. I will briefly explore the ideal of inclusiveness in chapter 8.

The two models of democracy can also be contrasted in terms of how they understood political equality. In Classical Athens, this ideal translated into *isonomia* (equality before the law), *isegoria* (equal right of speech), and equal vote in the Assembly. The vote in the Assembly was either directly about issues put to the Assembly, about persons running for elections (for the very few positions thus staffed in ancient democracy), or about persons meant to be exiled (during the time when the practice of ostracism was in place). What is less often remarked upon is that democracy also meant an equal opportunity to participate in the agenda-setting Council of 500 for the willing and properly vetted (citizens had to volunteer for the job and were thoroughly screened by religious authorities). Under representative democracy, by contrast, political equality only means equality before the law and "one person, one vote" in the context of periodic elections. Voting equality itself is a relatively recent gain since, for a long time, Western democracies accommodated plural voting and some still do in indirect ways. Additionally, there is no strict equality of access to agenda-setting power under electoral democracy, where only the members of parties sent to power are in a position of setting the agenda, and the chance of being among those lucky few is very unequally distributed. Nonetheless, one could argue that ancient and modern democracies are, in the ideal, committed to political equality. Presumably neither paradigm would qualify as democratic if they lacked these two institutional features, i.e., inclusiveness and equality.

Individual rights available to citizens under assembly democracy were minimal. Indeed, the notion of individual rights, at least as understood in our modern liberal sense, was lacking. What the Greeks had, more accurately, were participation powers, some of which share some similarity with modern liberal rights. By contrast, citizens under representative democracy are able to claim a certain number of often constitutionally entrenched individual rights (voting rights, rights of association, religion, freedom of speech, etc.) that empower them as political actors, even as their actual access to the formal political sphere is in some ways much more restricted than under assembly democracy. Indeed, these liberal rights are for the most part designed to protect democratic citizens from abuses of state power, including by giving them a say on the choice of rulers rather than directly help them exercise any form of self-rule. They were meant primarily as trump cards against government rather than participation rights in government. As the right to run for elections gradually became universal, the participatory dimension of such rights increased, but with the unequal distribution of actual power entailed by the electoral principle, with only a minority of the population standing a chance of accessing power through elections.

Another contrast lies in the role of discursive exchange of arguments in each model. Public deliberation was an institutional feature of ancient democracy (celebrated most famously in Pericles' Oration). However, the fact that it was combined with exclusionary principles for the definition of the demos limited its democratic value. Additionally, deliberation in the Assembly seemed to have practically boiled down to a succession of speeches by gifted orators (Hansen 1991), arguably falling short of its own commitment to an equal right of speech or at least taking it only as a very formal and minimal constraint, with most of the actual deliberation taking place silently within each of the participants (Cammack 2020). By contrast though, representative democracy seems even less deliberative, in that if we follow Bernard Manin's historical account, a central institutional principle of representative government is mere "trial by discussion" (Manin 1997)—a much more minimal bar than what deliberative democrats call democratic deliberation.[2] Additionally, most of the actual discussion is restricted to the formal sphere of decision-making, within the walls of Parliament. It is only in Jürgen Habermas's (and other deliberative democrats') interpretation of the relationship between the first and second "deliberative tracks" that electoral democracy can be conceptualized as having meaningful, society-wide deliberation. Even then, society-wide deliberation remains a normative aspiration that representative democracy may not be able to deliver. Not only, as argued in chapter 2, can one be skeptical that this idealization of electoral democracy by late deliberative democrats captures anything close to the reality of what has been happening since the eighteenth century, but the very institutional principles of electoral democracy may be at odds with deliberative democrats' ideals. First, as long as agenda-setting is done by elected elites, there is only so much that the external pressure of public opinion as resulting from society-wide debates can do to shape the agenda from the bottom up (see also McCormick forthcoming for a similar reading).

Second, as Mark Warren puts it,

> [b]ecause representatives function within a context that combines public visibility and adversarial relations, they must weigh the strategic and symbolic impact of speech. Thus, representative institutions have limited capacities for deliberation, which requires a suspension of the strategic impact of communication in favor of persuasion and argument. (Warren 2013: 54)

---

2. In fact, public debates in Parliament are often no longer debates at all, but mere public speeches where MPs "perform" the positions that they actually staked, negotiated, and deliberated over in closed settings (closed meetings and informal settings). See, e.g., Willemsen 2014. However, see Bächtiger and Beste (2017: 108) for the deliberative nature of non-Westminsterian systems.

In other words, electoral systems do not necessarily incentivize representatives to deliberate so much as to posture, grandstand, and eventually bargain. Third, the civic qualities one would expect from citizens in a truly deliberative democracy—such as open-mindedness to other people's points of view and willingness to listen to the other side—are at odds with the main virtue that citizens need to cultivate under an ideal of democracy where parties and elections are seen as central, namely partisanship, which is a willingness to commit uncritically (at least up to a point) to a set of values and principles for the sake of political efficacy.

Let us now turn to each model's decision rule per se. In assembly democracy, the majoritarian principle was broadly used. It was initially approximated by estimating enthusiasm for a given proposal based on which raised the greatest number of hands (a rough approximation that did not involve counting them) and generated the loudest vocal support from the crowd. The decision mechanism was only later institutionalized as a counting mechanism (the counting of raised hands) (Schwartzberg 2014).

Under representative democracy, however, majority rule is held in suspicion for its alleged propensity to enable what Tocqueville famously labeled the "tyranny of the majority." Under representative democracy, the majoritarian principle is intentionally undermined by several counter-majoritarian procedures, such as the principle of separation of powers, checks and balances, veto points, supermajority thresholds, filibuster rules, and even federalism and bicameralism. These counter-majoritarian features were seen by the founders of this system (whether in France or the United States) as a superiority of representative democracy over ancient democracy and are still seen as such by many contemporary political theorists (especially Pettit 2016; but see also Urbinati 2016).

The main difference between assembly democracy and electoral democracy, however, is the role that representation plays or fails to play in each. According to the standard historical reading, political representation did not exist in assembly democracy where direct participation was an all-consuming activity demanded from all citizens and only rendered possible by the institution of slavery and the delegation of child-rearing and other "care" activities to women. By contrast, under electoral democracy representation becomes a substitute for political participation. As citizens grow to be consumed by their private lives and economic activities, it becomes necessary for them to delegate power to a separate class of full-time professional politicians. Unsurprisingly, therefore, the relationship of representation and participation is strictly reversed in assembly democracy and representative democracy, at least on the standard reading. My own reading, as presented in chapter 3, is that assembly democracy included representative or at least proto-representative features, if only in the role of the Council, which included 500 randomly selected citizens in charge of setting the agenda for the open assembly and, later, in the role of the nomothetai and courts (I also suggested that participation in the People's Assembly is best conceptualized as a form of citizen representation rather than a form of direct democracy per se).

All these important differences, I would argue, boil down to a simple one: a fundamental difference in the degree of openness of the sites of power to ordinary citizens. Under assembly democracy, access to power is open to all, either immediately or over time (through the strict equalization of chance offered by lottery and rotation), whereas under representative democracy it is gated at all times and largely closed to most people over their lifetimes.

The Principles of Open Democracy

Let me now propose a new model of democracy, open democracy or "democracy 3.0," as improving on and in some ways transcending these two existing models. This new model consists in layering new principles on top of the most normatively appealing ones in the previous models, expanding the scope of some of them (like inclusiveness), and occasionally replacing or reformulating some of these principles entirely. Building on the last two chapters and the stylized contrast above, I summarize the differences between all three models in the accompanying table, some elements of which I'll address further in the last chapter.

Let me proceed directly to the five main institutional principles I derive from table 1 (the items in bold in the table).

PARTICIPATION RIGHTS

The first principle of open democracy is the principle of "participation rights." This may seem like an obvious starting point and perhaps a principle we should assume is already widely implemented in existing democracies. Liberal societies arguably improved other ancient illiberal ones by turning certain powers of participation into actual political *rights* such as voting rights, freedom of speech, freedom of association, freedom of the press, etc. These political rights, however, were initially conceptualized as facilitating consent to power rather than exercise of power. Voting rights were meant primarily as rights to choose representatives, not to directly decide on issues or put questions on the political agenda. In that sense one could argue that voting rights do not count as genuine participatory rights, or if they do, they do so only in the relatively rare (outside of Switzerland) context of referendums. As to the right to run for office, we already saw that even when universally distributed, it questionably amounts, in an electoral system governed by the principle of distinction, to a robust participatory right for most of the population. Other political

TABLE 1. Models of Democracy

	Assembly democracy (5th/4th century Athens)	Electoral democracy (18th–20th Century)	Open democracy (21st Century?)
1. Inclusiveness	Universal relative to demos: All free, autochthonous men within the city-state	Universal relative to demos: All nationals (blood line or right of soil)	Dynamic: Universal relative to demos but also at least partially inclusive of other affected interests, including across national borders (see chapter 9)
2. Equality	Equality before the law. Equal opportunity of access to agenda-setting. Equality of right to speak. Equality of votes	Equality before the law. Plural voting to voting equality	Equality before the law. Equal opportunity of access to agenda-setting. Equality of votes. Substantive equality (see chapter 8)
3. Rights	Participatory powers (equal voice, equal vote, equal opportunities to be selected for the council and popular juries)	Political rights, e.g., voting rights. Freedoms of association, speech, religion, etc.	**Participation rights** (beyond political rights: citizen's initiative; right of referral, right to participate in political lotteries)
4. Discursive process	Public speeches, mostly by gifted orators	Trial by discussion	**Deliberation**
5. Decision rule	Shouting, murmuring, majority rule	Majority rule tempered by supermajority thresholds and checks and balances	**Majoritarian principle** (majority rule, majority judgment)
6. Representation	None (mainstream view)	Electoral representation	**Democratic representation:** lottocratic, self-selected, liquid
7. Participation	Intense and mandatory for some. Episodic but regular for others	Limited and episodic (mostly voting)	Regular (mini-publics, top-down referenda and at will (citizen's initiative, referrals)
8. Accountability mechanisms	Screening of candidates, rotation, ostracism, *graphe paranomon, euthynai*	Elections, courts	Courts, rotation, **transparency**, participation rights such as citizens' initiative and right of referral

rights—freedom of association, freedom of the press—were meant as trump cards against potential abuse of power by government rather than inroads for greater participation in and control of the government by the citizens.[3]

Open democracy, by contrast, means to preserve the ancient, positive ideal, or at least practice, of participatory powers and the modern, defensive ideal of liberal rights. But it reformulates and combines them as the principle of "participation rights." Participation rights are meant to ensure a proper functioning of authentically democratic institutions beyond ensuring the legitimation of power structures and protecting citizens from domination and possible abuse of power. The principle of participation rights thus may have a surface familiarity but is actually intended as new and radical. It should thus include more than voting rights and the right to run for office. On my proposal, participation rights thus include all imaginable rights that can clear a path from the periphery of power to its center. Participation rights, in particular, ensure access of ordinary citizens to agenda-setting power rather than just allow citizens to consent to power or protect citizens from power.

Among the new rights covered by this more encompassing category are: citizens' initiatives (whether direct or indirect), which allow citizens to have the first say on law- and policymaking by putting a proposal on the agenda of the legislature (in its indirect version) or to a constituency-wide referendum (in its direct version); rights of referral, which are the rights of individuals to trigger a referendum on any existing law (conditional on meeting a reasonable threshold of supporting signatures); a right to participate in any sortition-based political body (aka "mini-public"), and any other right that may facilitate access to the heart of power by ordinary citizens.

The best existing model for such rights is probably Switzerland, where participation rights in the form of citizens' initiatives are real and meaningfully practiced on a regular basis at the cantonal and communal levels and are now considered for the federal level as well (where so far only initiatives on constitutional matters are legal). Other good, though so far unapplied, examples can be found in the 2011 Icelandic crowdsourced proposal (more on this in chapter 7), which introduced a right of referral, by which 10 percent of voters may demand a referendum on any bill within three months of its passage, subject to some exceptions (such as the budget) and a citizens' initiative, which

---

3. Indeed, some representative democracies (like the United States) have historically deemphasized participation rights, with various hurdles created in the path of citizens' right to vote (like literacy tests, I.D. laws, and inconvenient scheduling of elections on workdays). The reasons for these anti-participatory tendencies of at least some representative democracies may have been historically contingent (and often racially motivated), but the fact is that the model of representative democracy is clearly conceptually unequipped to resist them. Some influential theories of representative democracy actually depend on voter apathy and low levels of participation (e.g., Schumpeter 1975 [1942]; Morris-Jones 1954; Lipset 1960; Brennan 2016).

allows 2 percent of the population to present an issue to Parliament, which Parliament is free to ignore, and 10 percent to present a bill to Parliament, which Parliament can either accept or to which it can make a counterproposal. In the latter case, if the bill of the voters has not been withdrawn as a response, Parliament must present both the popular bill and Parliament's counterproposal to a referendum.

Citizens' initiatives and rights of referral, it should be noted, have been conceptually available at least since the 1960s and are supposedly available to citizens in a majority of European countries, at various levels of application. Yet many of them are, in fact, toothless, apply to too small a domain, or are so unwieldy they are rarely made use of. France, for example, waited until 2008 to introduce, on a restricted category of issues, what has occasionally been described as a hybrid version of a citizens' initiative—similar to article 11 of the French Constitution—the so-called shared initiative referendum. In fact, the initiative not only must be shared with parliamentarians, it can only be triggered by parliamentarians (a good one-fifth of them). This shared initiative referendum is therefore, despite the hype, no *citizens'* initiative at all. Furthermore, its hybrid and hierachical nature makes it so hard for any proposal to get off the ground, as does the high threshold of signatures required (10 percent of the electorate in France means more than 4.5 million people!) that it has only been used once thus far, in 2019. Similarly, the European citizens' initiative right entrenched in the European Constitution allows one million citizens residing in at least one-quarter of the member states to call directly on the Commission to propose a legal act in an area where the member states have conferred powers onto the EU level. This right to request the Commission to initiate a legislative proposal arguably puts citizens on the same footing as the European Parliament and the European Council. Yet it has hardly been used, and to questionably successful outcomes, thus far.[4]

In order to be meaningful, participation rights need to be defined in ways that render them user-friendly (for example by not placing signature thresholds too high). They probably also must be accompanied and strengthened by measures to ensure that historically disenfranchised minorities can meaningfully exercise them. Participation rights could even take the form of sunset law types of affirmative action measures or oversampling of small, vulnerable minorities in the context of the random selection of mini-publics (as was done in British Columbia—see Warren and Pearse 2008—or in the Australian deliberative poll organized by Jim Fishkin where aboriginal populations were oversampled).[5] Par-

4. See https://en.wikipedia.org/wiki/European_Citizens%27_Initiative.

5. Because they would be targeting vulnerable minorities in a specific way, such rights would be less likely to be hijacked by powerful minorities, the way other classical counter-majoritarian measures can be.

ticipation rights are essentially a precondition for the other institutional principles of open democracy to work as intended. They also form, together with
deliberation (more on which next), the main purely democratic (as opposed
to liberal-republican) resource against the danger of tyrannical majorities. In
other words, whereas liberal rights were historically and are still often conceived of as fetters and constraints on majority rule, and were only later sal-
vaged as "co-original" with democratic procedures by theorists like Habermas
and others, participation rights are wholly and unambiguously conceptualized
as internal to democracy—the kinds of rights necessary for democratic procedures (deliberation and majority rule) to function as intended.

DELIBERATION

The second institutional principle is the discursive process that distinguishes
open democracy from both assembly democracy and representative democracy: deliberation. Deliberation is explicitly borrowed from the recommendations, over the last forty years, of deliberative democracy theorists, for whom
democratic decisions and policies can be legitimate if and only if they could
be (Rawls) or de facto are (Habermas) the product of a deliberative exchange
of reasons and arguments among free and equals. I here embrace an explicitly Habermasian version of the deliberative democracy ideal. In Habermas's
theoretical architecture, rational discourse or argumentation is a practice of
checking truth claims and claims to moral rightness or legal legitimacy.[6] At this
abstract level, deliberation thus carries with it a number of presuppositions,
for example inclusion, equal opportunity to raise questions and objections,
to make contributions of any relevant kind, as well as absence of power, coercion, lying, and fraud (see Habermas 2006: 138–183, especially the schemes
on pp. 160 and 166).

Political deliberation, as legally institutionalized discourse among citizens, MPs, etc., applies to various types of questions (depending on non-
generalizable interests, empirical and theoretical questions, moral and ethi-
cal questions, legal questions) and does make room, in a selective way, for
bargaining and discourses of various types. However, status differences among
participants are legally, if not practically, ruled out once political deliberation
is institutionalized within a democratic constitutional frame.

---

6. It stretches across a broader range of validity claims that do not go with the justified expectation of agreement in principle; that is where disagreement is expected even disregarding the
burdens of judgment. I thank Professor Habermas (personal communication July 18, 2018) for
helping me clarify this passage.

Unlike preceding paradigms, open democracy consciously embraces deliberation as a key institutional principle. By contrast, the historical paradigm of representative democracy, though compatible with deliberation, is not essentially committed to it, in that it can be realized in purely aggregative and Schumpeterian versions that emphasize elite competition and voting moments over deliberation.

One might argue, however, that deliberation is not fundamentally distinct from the institutionalized practice of public speeches in the Athenian People's Assembly, barring the fact that it applies in a context vastly more inclusive of affected interests. There is nonetheless greater theoretical and empirical attention given to what counts as authentic deliberation in open democracy than in Classical Athens. Democratic deliberation, whether direct among all or indirect among representatives, must involve all participants, not just gifted orators (Ober 1997). Efforts must be made to reach out to the shy, the less articulate, minorities, and the vulnerable. Lottocratic representation (see next principle) is one element of these efforts, though it too won't be enough on its own, because silence from the less articulate, minorities, and / or the vulnerable might simply be reproduced internally to these assemblies. Deliberation under open democracy, as per the now refined and empirically informed versions of deliberative democracy that have become mainstream, would thus be carefully curated and facilitated, rather than just allowed to happen in a public space. Open democracy, taking advantage of advances in the study of human psychology and the social conditions of proper equality, considerably improves (though it does not fundamentally innovate) on assembly democracy on the deliberative front.

Deliberation, as social scientists understand it better today, is in fact essential to democratic decision-making in part because it is a (partial) solution to the problem of cyclical majorities (the other one being formal rules and informal understandings that restrict strategizing, or what Kenneth Shepsle calls "structure induced equilibrium"). Deliberation has been shown to have the merits of smoothing cycles and, in the best-case scenario, rendering preferences single-peaked. Deliberation thus ensures that ensuing decisions, when taken by a vote, are meaningful (Miller 1992; Dryzek and List 2003; List et al. 2013; all cited in Curato et al. 2017: 29).

As summarized by a recent survey article, deliberation has been formally and empirically demonstrated to have the properties of inducing agreement restricting the ability of actors to introduce new options that destabilize the decision process and structuring the preferences of participants such that they become "single-peaked" along one dimension, thus reducing the prevalence of manipulable cycles across alternatives (Curato et al. 2017: 29; see also, e.g., Manin 1987; Knight and Johnson 1994; Farrar et al. 2010). The authors conclude that "[t]he more deliberative the communication, the better democracy works. Democracy must be deliberative" (Curato et al. 2017: 29).

Note that a commitment to deliberation as a central principle of open democracy is not a commitment to consensus democracy (contra critics like, e.g., Shapiro 2017). Consensus has been shown to be thought of more usefully as an anticipated by-product of deliberation than a goal of deliberators per se (Landemore and Page 2015). This is so because consensus as a goal creates the possibility of veto points, status quo bias, and finally, minority tyranny, which would be antithetical to another commitment of open democracy, namely the majoritarian principle. Deliberation is thus compatible with the careful cultivation of productive disagreement or "positive dissensus" (Landemore and Page 2015).

What deliberation points to, however, is the need to enrich existing aggregative practices, such as referendums, with deliberative components. A good example here are Citizen Initiative Reviews (CIR), which have been a legislatively authorized part of Oregon general elections since 2010. The CIR gathers a representative cross-section of two dozen voters for five days of deliberation on a single ballot measure. The process culminates in the citizen panelists writing a Citizens' Statement that the secretary of state inserts into the official *Voters' Pamphlet* sent to each registered voter (see, e.g., Gastil et al. 2018).

THE MAJORITARIAN PRINCIPLE

The third institutional principle, which follows deliberation, is the majoritarian principle as the main decision procedure. It is a principle rather than a specific rule (like majority rule) because it can be instantiated in various guises. Michel Balinski and Rida Lariki thus suggest substituting the traditional interpretation of majority rule as a collective ranking of the available alternatives with an interpretation of majority rule as a collective judgment or evaluation of these same alternatives (on this interpretation political candidates or alternatives would be "rated" as typically occurs in wine-tasting competitions) (Balinski and Laraki 2010). Open democracy is committed to the majoritarian principle in a way that undoes many, though not all, of the counter-majoritarian mechanisms of representative democracy and cuts through the paralyzing complexity of the latter. This will surely raise some concerns. Rather than tackle those directly here, though (I will address these worries in the next chapter), I suggest that the real question is always comparative. Counter-majoritarian rights, devices, and mechanisms raise their own set of worries. Though perhaps initially they were meant as protections of vulnerable minorities, history and empirical evidence show that they have been hijacked as often, if not more so, by already powerful minorities to entrench preexisting advantages and have thus proven misguided and counterproductive, even from a liberal point of view.[7] On a more cynical view, counter-majoritarian devices were put in place as protections for privileged minorities who feared that their privilege would not withstand democratic scrutiny, once democracy was properly instituted.

Open democracy thus returns to assemby democracy in that it embraces simple majoritarianism over supermajoritarianism. To the extent that voting is necessary to resolve disagreements where deliberation does not produce a consensus, some form of default decision rule must be in place. The most democratic one, barring any good countervailing arguments to posit voting thresholds and minority vetoes, is some version of majority rule (for which both strictly procedural and epistemic reasons can be adduced).[8]

DEMOCRATIC REPRESENTATION

We have already encountered the fourth principle, democratic representation, in chapters 4 and 5, so here I will just review its central features.

Democratic representation is where open democracy departs both most subtly and yet radically from the historic paradigm of representative democracy, in the sense that while open democracy is also representative, it is so in ways that are not centrally or even necessarily electoral. Thus, no mention is made, at the level of the five fundamental principles, of the principle of elections (not even periodic ones) because elections, far from being *a* single democratic principle, let alone *the* ultimate democratic principle, are merely one selection mechanism among others capable of translating the representative principle in a democratic fashion. Though it is possible to imagine elections falling closer to the democratic end of the spectrum than they currently do on the continuum between oligarchic and democratic devices (see liquid democracy models mentioned at the end of last chapter), the reality is that elections are a fundamentally Janus-faced selection mechanism (Manin 1997: 150). Because their democratic credentials are problematic, elections should not be raised to the level of a democratic principle. One could in fact imagine democracies that would dispense with elections entirely, if elections proved too difficult to reconcile with equality of opportunities to become an elected representative (implied by the equality principle).[9] Open democracies could

---

7. See Buchanan 1999 versus Rae 1969 on whether democracies should have universal consent or a 50%+1 vote decision rule. See also Shapiro 2016.

8. It is not clear what theoretical reasons exist behind super-majoritarian thresholds such as two-thirds or three-quarters of the vote, except the intuitive salience of these thresholds for eighteenth-century institutional designers. In practice such thresholds often happen to be extremely paralyzing, perhaps over and beyond the intended effects of their inventors.

9. A defense of election-less democracies was recently offered for example by Van Reybrouk 2016. My own view is that an election-less democracy model is mostly viable, at this point, for new

use other selection mechanisms with their own democratic merits, including lotteries and self-selection. Thus, whereas periodic elections are a defining institutional feature of electoral democracy, open democracy is not committed to elections per se. Instead it embraces a richer ecology of various forms of democratic representation.

Relatedly, I have not mentioned in my list of principles the nature of the relation between representatives and represented because in this new paradigm the trustee/delegate distinction appears simplistic and the question of the representative's independence vis-à-vis his or her constituents becomes moot. The representative relationship should be able to take many forms as long as it is broadly democratic.

A central form of democratic representation is lottocratic representation, which combines sortition and rotation. Rotation in particular ensures that the practice of politics as a profession and the view of politicians as a separate caste is not part of open democracy. This is not to say that there is no room for professionals and experts of politics under open democracy. There should still be plenty of roles for expert advisors and *administrators*. But the *law* should ultimately be initiated, supervised, contributed to, and vetted by ordinary citizens, not career politicians. To the extent that open democracy may still accommodate elected politicians, there should be ways to ensure a greater turnover of the personnel occupying these elected functions, not only through the periodicity of elections, but also, for example, through strict limits on the number of terms of office and the possibility of recall. Periodic rotation is then a corrective to any form of representation. To the extent that representatives become de facto elites of some kind in virtue of being given even temporary power, it becomes important to make this access to power short-lived. Periodic rotation is meant to ensure that ordinary citizens who are given access to power for the purpose of serving the whole body politic do not turn into a class of professionalized politicians or lose sight of the common interest.

TRANSPARENCY

The final principle, transparency, can be seen as a condition for the other principles to resist closure at any point in time, particularly between the periodic renewal of randomly selected assemblies or elected assemblies. Transparency, generally valuable in and of itself, is (like rotation in democratic representation) an accountability mechanism for the whole system of government, ensuring that political legislators and leaders remain aware of their responsibilities

---

countries or online communities (e.g., crypto-currency communities) looking for a governance blueprint. Established representative democracies will probably have to adapt a more hybrid model, grafting lottocratic features onto preexisting electoral ones.

and duties by keeping them under the vigilant gaze of their peers and fellow citizens. Without it, even open mini-publics of randomly selected citizens can become suspect. As one of their critics puts it, they risk creating "legitimacy without visibility" (Rummens 2016).

Transparency is thus very much instrumental to the openness of the larger system. It institutionalizes the notion that "light is the best disinfectant," even if inviting light into the political decision process may also have some paralyzing effects, including in terms of the quality of the deliberations that can be conducted in the system (Chambers 2004). Transparency, because it is instrumental, is a default principle that can be occasionally breached but only for good reasons and with a heavy burden of proof and justification on those who would want to minimize it.

Transparency, it is worth noting, does not require citizens' active participation and can, in fact, characterize a process that is actually closed to the public's input. But transparency still means that citizens are able to witness, observe, and thus make up their minds about the activities of the actors engaged in the political process. Conversely, it also means that policymakers are able to access the thoughts and input of the public, when judged necessary. Transparency is thus a window, if not quite a door, opened in the walls of politics. Additionally, transparency can apply to relatively closed activities, provided a record of what is said and done is made available to the public afterward (what one might call "lag transparency"). Transparency should mean *process* transparency much of the time, though not always transparency about substance. Whereas ancient Athens was de facto relatively transparent in virtue of the small size of its political body, which permitted social control of the rulers, open democracy is purposely so. Given the size and complexity of modern polities, transparency demands extra effort and an institutional push for it.

Transparency may sound like an empty catchword, and there is no doubt that it often is one. Depositing a lot of unmanageable and unreadable data online does not make a government truly "transparent," let alone "open" (Heller 2011).[10] Similarly, in what is perhaps one of the most visually ironic contradictions of the European Union, building a Parliament with transparent glass walls does not ensure the accessibility or navigability of the building

10. Writing about the Open Government Partnership launched under President Obama, which in part aimed to fight corruption through transparency and greater availability of public data about topics ranging from health indicators to public servant and representatives' salaries, Nathaniel Heller, the then-founder of a transparency and anti-corruption NGO, and later turned civil society steering committee member of the Open Government Partnership, wrote: "Open Data [may provide] an easy way out for some governments to avoid the much harder, and likely more transformative, open government reforms that should probably be higher up on their lists." The same concern about fake openness and transparency led others to conclude that open data and open government should be conceived of as entirely separate programs (Yu and Robinson 2012).

itself (notoriously maze-like[11]), or the institutions it represents. In other words, transparency does not always translate into readability, legibility, and general accessibility of what is made available for all to see. A lot more research is needed in order to understand the ways in which proper institutional transparency can be implemented and at what costs.

Open democracy is thus based on a combination of five principles, some of them partly novel compared to those undergirding either assembly democracy or representative democracy: participation rights, deliberation, the majoritarian principle, democratic representation, and transparency.

Despite the novelty I claim for it, this paradigm of open democracy shares with assembly democracy and electoral democracy a basic commitment to equality and inclusiveness, as indicated in the accompanying table. Inclusiveness and equality within a given demos are such fundamental presuppositions of any form of democracy that they can and should be assumed as lexically prior to all the other institutional principles. They should not crucially distinguish open democracy from electoral democracy, assembly democracy or, indeed, any form of democracy.

In the concluding chapter, however, I will argue that open democracy could qualify these core principles in novel ways. To give a preview of the argument to come, inclusiveness under open democracy could be qualified as "dynamic" inclusiveness, in order to reflect the changing dimensions and scope of communities of affected interests in a globalized and interconnected world. I will argue that in our globalized age, geographic boundaries taken for granted by both ancient and representative democracy increasingly appear as not only morally arbitrary to begin with but also as an obstacle to obtaining the relevant input on some issues of cross-national or global interest. Because this principle of dynamic inclusiveness requires a longer justification than I can provide in this book, I postpone a sketch of a defense to the conclusion.

As to equality, another fundamental democratic principle at the foundation of all three models of democracy contrasted in this chapter, it is instantiated under open democracy in ways that are not fundamentally surprising and that remain formal. Under open democracy, political equality is, as in representative democracy, both equality before the law and equality of votes. Open democracy modifies the Greek de facto power of "isegoria"—equal voice—by turning it into a modern right, whereby all citizens should be given an equal opportunity to be heard where deliberation is needed. Given the size of modern polities, the ways in which this right is likely to translate is not necessarily direct physical access to the Parliament. Instead it could simply mean the equal right to access an online forum. Or equal voice could mean that each

---

11. I speak from experience and on the basis of multiple complaints by the local staff during a short visit in November 2014 at the occasion of a talk at the World Forum on Democracy.

individual has the same chance of being a representative where representation is needed (as in lottery-based mini-publics). Another power carried over from ancient democracy and turned into a right in open democracy is indeed the equal chance of being selected to participate in the agenda-setting functions of the legislative assembly (the Council of 500 in Classical Athens). In the final chapter I will contemplate the ways in which formal political equality should probably be made "substantive" by offering some reflections on the economic background conditions of open democracy.

What about the Role of Parties in Open Democracy?

Open democracy is a paradigm that can be instantiated in electoral versions, retaining a role for elected officials and assemblies. To the extent that new forms of non-electoral democratic representations are introduced as supplement to elected assemblies and officials—the most plausible scenario in all fairness—there is no reason to think that parties would wane or their roles fundamentally change, though their internal functioning may evolve in light of new institutional possibilities.[12] Since it is hard, in particular, to imagine an alternative way of selecting the head of the executive power without some form of elections, parties would likely remain an element of the democratic landscape even in an open democracy.

Let me now consider the scenario of an open democracy where elected functions are minimized or even absent altogether (perhaps because the executive power is very much subordinated to the legislative power and itself more like a jury, randomly selected from, say, a pool of vetted candidates— something that might sound less strange if we think of it in a non-state context, like a digital community). What would happen to parties in such a system? And what other body, if any, could perform the useful function of offering justificatory platforms for policy programs? Here is where I have to admit the conceptual limits my paradigm run into, which may actually only reflect the limits of our (or at least my) political imagination.

But first let us clarify the term "party." A lot arguably depends on what we mean by it. If we take parties to mean historically organized groups of

---

12. For example they could make use of random selection to form their list of candidates to a position, as recently attempted by Cédric Villani in Paris, who promised that 48 of its 526 running mates in the municipal election in the capital would be drawn from (volunteer) Parisians invited to apply on a special online platform ("Decidim," a well-known open source tool created by the city hall of Barcelona). Nancy Rosenblum also suggested to me (personal communication) the possibility of having parties send their members to elected chambers at random (voters having been asked to vote for a party, but not for the specific representative of that party in the elected assembly), presumably forcing them in anticipation to considerably flatten their hierarchical structure and equalize relationships among party members.

the like-minded whose main purpose is the conquest of political power via electoral means, then parties would by definition have no place in a purely non-electoral open democracy where positions of power are distributed at random or, in some cases (like participatory budgeting), given to self-selected participants.

But if by parties we mean associations of the like-minded for the purpose of bundling various issues into a coherent political platform, then it becomes a real empirical question as to whether a democratic system can do without them. This is at least conceivable at the local level. Local governments (cities) often function without relying on parties. Similarly, probably due to its smaller size, Classical Athens functioned without parties, on the basis of popular assemblies and a number of randomly selected ones. Even the few elections the Greeks held (for the selection of generals or certain administrators) seem to have been run on the basis of ad hoc groups and campaigns, rather than bodies, with the permanence of what we now call "parties."

Political scientists and theorists alike, however, unanimously attest that a no-party is unthinkable and unworkable in general (and they typically have in mind large-scale polities). Robert Goodin, who explicitly engages in the thought experiment, predicts that a no-party democracy would be characterized by five undesirable features. It would be a world of (1) "personalistic politics," whereby voters would choose representatives on the basis of personal qualities (amiability, eloquence, competence, integrity—in the best case scenario) rather than ideological or programmatic reasons; (2) "clientelist politics" whereby "[i]n the legislative assembly [. . .] coalition-building is personal, ad hoc, and ad hominem (Goodin 2008: 210); (3) "patronage politics," where the main focus of politicians would be on constituency service rather than the pursuit of the common good; (4) "administration" rather than politics per se since absent parties there would be no basis for "any concerted action to institute any systematic, coherent set of policies" (ibid.); and (5) "identity-group politics" where people would vote for people "like themselves" rather than on the basis of arguments that are compelling no matter the shared interests. Summarizing this dystopian scenario, Goodin observes that the crucial thing missing in a no-party democracy would be "any systematic pursuit of 'principles' in politics" or the "politics of ideas'" (Goodin 2008: 211). He further concludes that a no-party democracy, unable to coordinate the intentions of the disparate legislators or voters (bundle issues in the jargon) and thus unable to properly self-legislate, would be "not democracy at all" (Goodin 2008: 214).

Political theorists Jonathan White and Lea Ypi also think that a no-party democracy is undesirable, emphasizing for their part the impossibility of justifying power properly (which is probably related to what Goodin calls the ability to self-legislate). On their view, in a no-party democracy the justification of power would fall to individuals or ad hoc groups without the historical stability and structure of parties and thus more prone to capture and manipulation.[13] The consequence would be a focus on "strategy" at the expense of "justification." They conclude that:

> In short, political justification in a no-party democracy is yet more difficult to sustain than in a democracy where citizens act together, aware of the potential pathologies of partisanship, yet still committed to the forms of reciprocal engagement it makes available. (White and Ypi 2016: 70–71)

Despite the acknowledged costs and pathologies of partisanship, White and Ypi therefore see the electoral principle and attendant party system as worth the trade-offs and indeed essential to the definition of democracy.

Finally, Frances Rosenbluth and Ian Shapiro (2018)'s more recent defense of a strong two-party system as the best possible answer to the crisis of democracy is also conducted in the name of what they describe as the "bundling" capacities of parties, which in their model is entirely conditional on the prospect of elections. For them, the only reason we can expect parties to turn a variety of issues into a coherent platform and long-term vision for the future, as opposed to pushing for issues in an ad hoc one-off manner, is the prospect of elections and the possibility of having to convince, and being held accountable by, citizens at the ballot box.

I confess not having knock-down arguments against what seem like consensual, compelling objections to a no-party democracy. Let me observe, however, that the no-party democracy envisioned here is a classically electoral democracy from which parties have been magically excised, holding "all other features of our actual world absolutely constant" as Goodin puts it (2008: 205). The same "all things otherwise equal" clause is implicitly present in the reasoning of White and Ypi and Rosenbluth and Shapiro. Yet the artificiality of such a thought experiment is problematic. Presumably, an open democracy would offer different incentives, some of which we have yet to imagine, and so there is no reason why we should deprive ourselves of the conceptual possibility of all things being otherwise very different, even as it makes predicting institutional effects in that world very difficult.

Some theorists have been less skeptical of the role transitory, fluid, and self-reconfiguring associations of citizens could play compared to that of parties and partisan practices, including in the justification of power. Russian political theorist Moisei Ostrogorski is one of them. Having discovered what he saw as an iron law of the party oligarchy, according to which the organized

---

13. In their own words, "in the absence of partisan practices one would need to rest one's hopes on morally committed individuals or ad-hoc groups—neither of whom can offer the epistemic, motivational, and feasibility potential needed to promote and sustain political commitment" (White and Ypi 2016: 70–71).

party machinery would necessarily dominate its social and parliamentary base, he thought democracies would be better off abolishing all permanent parties and replacing them with spontaneous ad hoc alliances (Erbentraut 2017). No doubt aware of the trade-offs, Ostrogorski nonetheless came down in favor of a no-party solution. In his own words: "Down with 'party'! Up with 'league!.'"[14] Empirically speaking, one could argue that various ad hoc political groups in advanced democracies—the Five Star Movement in Italy, "En Marche!" in France—have managed to offer actual justifications (whatever one thinks of them normatively) for their respective leaders' claim to power. In the 2017 French presidential election, the movement can even be said to have demonstrated "the epistemic, motivational, and feasibility potential needed to promote and sustain political commitment" in triumphing over all established parties.[15]

Ultimately it seems to me that it is hard to speculate out for good the possibility and desirability of a no-party open democracy. What is certain is that, as is already the case in electoral democracies, a plethora of associations and intermediary bodies not primarily motivated by electoral goals would still exist in an open democracy, and they could be expected to perform some of the functions of aggregating information, interests, and arguments so as to feed the deliberations occurring at various levels of the polity. Interest groups would likely form in order to influence the open mini-publics by submitting comments and suggestions on the online platforms, as we see that they do in the case of empirically conducted citizens' assemblies. Even if only a certain percentage of the suggestions submitted that way actually made it into law, the openness of the process would certainly seem to offer enough of an incentive for groups to form strategically and enter the conversation that way.

In fact, I surmise that the degree to which these associations would be capable of formulating coherent platforms and long-term vision for the future, as opposed to pushing for issues in an ad hoc one-off manner, would be directly correlated to the degree of generality of the task assigned to open mini-publics. In the context of an open democracy centered around a national citizens' assembly in charge of defining the future of the polity and its great political orientations, for example, why wouldn't groups interested in influencing their debates and nurturing them form, even absent the electoral incentive to provide exactly the kind of bundling platforms parties provide today? Why can't we imagine other incentives than electoral ones? And finally, couldn't it be that the lack of an electoral incentive would actually free such "think tanks" from

14. Ostrogorski 1903. I thank Hugo Drochon for the reference.

15. The movement founded by Emmanuel Macron has now de facto morphed into a party-like structure (*La République en Marche*). But this might be due to the larger party-based context in which it is forced to operate, rather than some internal necessity.

the temptation to lie, smear, and generally confuse rather than enlighten the public debate? Absent more experimentation with different forms of democratic representation, I think we shouldn't entirely close the door to the possibility of a no-party open democracy.

What about Referendums in Open Democracy?

The emphasis this book places on democratic representation and the need to recast direct democratic practices as representative in some fashion may wrongly suggest that referendums would not be part of an open democracy. And, indeed, in open democracy, referendums would not be the central decision mechanism. Unlike partisans of so-called direct democracy or strong democracy, who see referendums as hallmarks of genuine democracy and want to generalize them to all kinds of political decisions (see chapter 3), I see referendums as indispensable expressions of popular will that are meant to be rare relative to the frequency of decision-making that needs to happen in a sizeable polity (though less rare than they currently are outside of Switzerland). Referendums are not meant to be plebiscites in disguise (Lijphart 1984: 203; Qvortrup 2000), mostly used to allow the powers-that-be to obtain validation of laws or policies they intended to push through anyway. Neither are they a viable way to run a country.

However, referendums are only one class of a more general category usefully labeled "popular vote processes" by political scientists Francis Cheneval and Alice el-Wakil. These authors have recently emphasized the need for a better labeling of processes involving popular votes. Their term—"popular vote *processes*" (my emphasis)—has the merit of stressing the complexity and temporally distributed nature of what often involves other steps besides the voting moment, such as the prior phase of gathering a sufficient amount of signatures. Referendums, to paraphrase John Dewey's famous phrase about majority rule, are never just referendums (Dewey [1927] 1954: 207).[16] They are multi-step processes that culminate in a popular vote. I thus agree with Cheneval and el-Wakil's avoidance of the contested notion of "direct democracy" to refer to processes that involved what I would call "self-selected representatives" (the people garnering signatures for example).

Cheneval and el-Wakil (2018) also fruitfully propose a series of distinctions within the category of "popular vote processes," of which referendums are just one subset. Referendums in their terminology refer to "a citizen right to refuse (or accept) a decision or proposition of elected authorities"—as in a process that leads to a popular vote on a decision or proposition that has been written

---

16. The exact sentence reads: "Majority rule, just as majority rule, is as foolish as its critics charge it with being. But it never is *merely* majority rule."

by the elected authorities. It can then be top-down, mandatory, or bottom-up. Only in the latter case is there a signature collection step.

Referendums are thus distinct from another well-established category of popular vote process, so-called initiatives, which are agenda-setting or authorship devices of the citizens. Referendums, on Cheneval and el-Wakil's (2018) view, are more reactive than constructive, aiming to question an amendment to the status quo rather than create one.

What role, then, would popular vote processes, including initiatives and referendums, generally play in an open democracy? An important one, no doubt, though not necessarily a frequent one.

First, recall that initiatives are already included under the principle of "participation rights" as a right held by every citizen to initiate, under conditions of meeting a signature threshold, a law or policy proposal and bring it either to Parliament where the proposal has to be considered and at the very least debated; or, in some contexts where it could be empirically proven to work decently well, as a direct right to put a proposal on a constituency-wide ballot. Similarly, certain types of reactive popular vote processes, also known as bottom-up referendums, are also included under participation rights as a "right of referral" or the right to initiate a referendum (under conditions of a signature threshold) by the nation on existing laws deemed unsuitable or in need of reform.

Referendums, in open democracy, would be by construction "deliberative." Building deliberation into the design would ensure that voters do not simply reject some unpopular, yet needed, measure (such as pension reform or environmental taxes) or, if they do, it would give us some assurance that voters know what they are doing (by contrast with, say, the Brexit case, where there is cause for doubt). The same way that James Fishkin has rendered familiar the notion of "deliberative polls," we should cultivate the more recent idea of "deliberative voting" (Levy 2013) and, specifically, "deliberative referendums." We can and should do so even assuming tight constraints on resources since many of these constraints can now be circumscribed with the help of digital technologies.

Why wouldn't we want such popular vote processes to be extremely frequent? an objector might ask. For one thing, in open democracy much of the deliberation would take place upstream of the decision process. To the extent that the whole legislative process itself is open and participatory, from the agenda-setting stage to the final passing of the law, including, crucially, the drafting stage, the likelihood of a bottom-up referendum organized to challenge the resulting law would be low, both because the process would be unlikely to allow such a law to see the light of day and because only rarely, or at least much less often, would laws produced by such a process turn out to have unanticipated flaws.

This still leaves the question regarding "top-down" referendums, those generated by the central legislative assembly. The main argument against top-down referendums put forward by Cheneval and el-Wakil (2018) is that they are plebiscitary and manipulative, an objection that carries a lot of weight in many existing representative democracies (except Switzerland), where a gulf seems to have grown between the elected class and the rest of the population (a case in point, again, is the referendum on Brexit). But in open democracy we should be able to trust democratic representatives. Under such a reformed democratic paradigm, we should be able to give representative assemblies the leeway of initiating popular referendums, at least in two domains: where they themselves judge that they need society's explicit approval, especially on issues where civil society should, but is unlikely to, mobilize; or where they find themselves incompetent or illegitimate to make the decision (e.g., on electoral reforms or compensation policies for political personnel). Alternatively, top-down referendums (perhaps for big decisions) or abrogatory referendums could be conceived as accountability mechanisms, ensuring that there is no excessive distance between the sortition chamber and the wider public. Of course, then, the challenge is to avoid losing the deliberative benefits of representation by lot.[17]

There is thus a place for referendums in open democracy, and more generally for all kinds of popular vote processes that allow ordinary citizens to access the legislative process.

17. I thank Pierre-Etienne Vandamme for the latter point.

7

Let the People In! Lessons from a Modern Viking Saga

This chapter turns from normative theory to empirical reality by looking into real-life democratic practices that, in some crucial respects at least, mark a break from electoral democracy per se and form a step toward what I have called open democracy: the 2010–2013 Icelandic constitutional process. I choose to focus on this process because it is one that I am particularly familiar with and also because, although it ultimately did not result in the passing of a new constitution, it is to date the first and most ambitious effort at rethinking democratic practices in a systematic way and, indeed, at the foundational constitutional level of a nation. I see Iceland as the first domino of the classic electoral democracy model to fall toward a more open democracy model at the national level in an advanced democracy,[1] even as the process was not conclusive and was soon followed by much more successful experiments in countries like Ireland—the second main domino—and France—possibly the third one.[2] The Irish case, in particular, is at this point the jewel in the crown of deliberative democracy, having established that citizens'assemblies can be entrusted with complex, fraught, and profoundly divisive questions such as marriage equality and abortion rights and come out with recommendations for changes to the constitution that elected politicians could not and that the

---

1. The 2004 British Columbia Citizens' Assembly, though remarkable in many ways, took place at the regional level and did not result in actual change to the electoral law.

2. A first, older wave of participatory constitutional processes also deserves to be mentioned, including Nicaragua in 1986, Brazil in 1988, Uganda in 1995, South Africa in 1996, and Kenya in 2001. See also Landemore 2020b.

larger public can relate to and eventually endorse. At the same time the Irish case, for all its exemplary value, was more piecemeal in its reformist aspects than the Icelandic case, aiming to amend constitutional laws a few at a time and essentially experimenting with one type of democratic innovation (the citizens' assembly). As to the French experiments, the Great National Debate, though rich in the array of participatory methods employed, did not reflect a clear and coherent vision of how to articulate various democratic innovations and was ultimately extremely limited in the actual power delegated to ordinary citizens. And it is too soon to tell, at least for the purpose of this book, what will come out of the Convention on Climate Change, probably the most well-funded, sophisticated, and long-lasting citizens' assemblies to date, in terms of actual decision power. Ireland and France are worthy cases to study, as are myriad others around the world. But rather than string together superficial analyses of multiple examples that I'm only indirectly familiar with, I prefer to go into the details of a single one that I happen to have looked at very closely.[3] And so, let us begin.

In the fall of 2008, Iceland entered into a deep financial and economic crisis as all four of its national banks collapsed. This crisis in turn spurred political protests against a government perceived as incompetent and corrupt, and which was in effect largely in cahoots with the small number of Icelandic entrepreneurs that had brought financial disaster on the country. The "pots and pans revolution" was born, with people protesting loudly with various pieces of kitchenware in front of the Icelandic Parliament during the winter of 2008–2009. While their main demands had little to do with a constitutional overhaul per se, the topic of constitutional change had been discussed for many years in Iceland. The change in political personnel the following spring brought to power proponents of such a constitutional change and gave the topic political momentum. In the process of rewriting their fundamental social contract, however, Icelanders also helped rewrite democratic theory, or so I will argue, including by disproving some long-standing political science dogmas.

The three key innovations of the Icelandic process were: (1) a national forum of 950 quasi-randomly selected citizens that took place at the very beginning of the constitutional process; (2) an assembly of amateur politicians who were elected to write the constitutional draft; and (3) the assembly's use of crowdsourcing methods. All of these approaches testify to the possibility of "opening up" democratic representation in ways that the following chapter will more fully conceptualize. For now, the goal of this chapter is to pump intuitions in the following way. If a constitutional process can be reinvented in such innovative and inclusive ways, why couldn't processes for ordinary law- and

3. For more details on the Irish case see, e.g., Farrell, Suiter, and Harris 2018; Farrell and Suiter 2019; for the French case, see Buge and Morio 2019.

policymaking? It is thus with an eye to the general implications for ordinary politics that this chapter explores the institutional innovations of the Icelandic experiment. What the Icelanders did for constitution-making might serve as an institutional blueprint for the whole democratic system more generally.

The chapter is structured as follows. The first section sets the stage and briefly introduces Iceland and its history. The second section describes the events that led to the constitutional process as well as the constitutional process itself. The third section analyzes the three key institutional innovations just mentioned: The National Forum, the Constitutional Assembly of amateurs, and the crowdsourcing phase. In order to support the claim that more inclusion of ordinary citizens is actually a good idea, the fourth section examines the product of the constitutional process—the constitutional proposal—arguing that it proved marginally superior to competing drafts written by experts at the same time. The fifth section analyzes the causal mechanisms for this superiority, tracing it to the greater inclusiveness of the process.

Iceland as an Early Democratic Laboratory

Iceland, a long uninhabited piece of land, was settled by Vikings in the ninth century. The Vikings established a form of governance centered around a parliamentary assembly (the Althing) and characterized by participatory and democratic methods. A must-see destination in Iceland today is Thingvelir, a vast open field swept by icy winds, south of Reykjavik. It is right there on the continental rift, under the cloudy grey sky, that the first Icelandic Parliament was founded in 930. Because of it, Icelanders often claim to be the oldest parliamentary democracy in the world.

This Parliament should not conjure up the image of an actual building, not even an enclosed space. The original Icelandic Parliament was a purely immaterial and human affair, a temporary meeting of shepherds and farmers gathering together in a single space for a few months before dissolving at the end of summer. In this way it was much more like a less frequent version of the assembly meetings of Ancient Athenians.

Iceland had a fundamental written law as early as 1117, when it was first codified under the name of Greylag (*Grágás*), and which lasted for a brief period of independence known as the Old Commonwealth (930–1262) (Karlsson 2000: 21). After this period, Iceland fell under control of the Norwegian king and was later made a part of the Kalmar Union (1397–1523), which united all Nordic countries under one alliance. After the dissolution of the Kalmar Union, Iceland fell under Danish rule until the late nineteenth century. In 1844, however, an independence movement led to the restoration of the Althing, which had been suspended in 1799. Iceland finally gained sovereignty after World War I, on December 1, 1918. But it continued to share the Danish monarchy until

World War II, through a treaty with Denmark that finally expired in 1943. As Denmark was then under Nazi occupation, Iceland freed itself from foreign control and declared itself a republic. The Republic of Iceland was thus founded on June 17, 1944 as a fully independent nation. In the months before the independence proclamation, Althing had agreed on a new constitutional document, while also proclaiming a referendum, which was held between May 20 and 23, 1944. Voters were asked whether the Union with Denmark should be abolished and whether to adopt the new republican constitution. Both measures were approved with more than 98 percent in favor. Voter turnout was 98.4 percent.

The 1944 Icelandic constitution, however, is only a slightly altered version of the one granted by Danish rulers in 1874, the so-called Constitution on the Special Affairs of Iceland. The latter document was itself inspired by the Danish Constitution of 1849 and the Belgian Constitution of 1831 (Torfason 2009, cited in Bergsson and Blokker 2014). The "new" constitution is basically that older document with "King" replaced by "Elected President," and other limited changes. That is because the 1944 constitution was always intended as a temporary document (Jóhannesson 2011: 63–68; Arnason 2011: 345, cited in Bergsson and Blokker 2014) and as a result has been described as a "mended garment" with the flavor of an "imposed document" (Bergsson and Blokker 2014). Politicians promised to revisit it at some later point to give Iceland a truly custom-tailored document, but various governments came and went over the years without ever delivering on this promise (Gylfason 2013). Since 1944, the Icelandic constitution has nonetheless been amended seven times, mostly to accommodate changes in Icelandic constituencies and alter conditions of voting eligibility. Additionally, in 1991 the organization of the Althing was made into a unicameral legislature. Extensive modifications were also made in 1995 when the human rights sections of the constitution were reviewed.

The 2010–2013 Constitutional Process

On June 16, 2010, two years after a spectacular financial and economic meltdown, the Icelandic parliament passed a constitutional act initiating a constitutional revision process. On November 6, 2010, a Constitutional Committee appointed by the parliament organized a National Forum, which gathered 950 randomly selected individuals tasked with establishing "the principal viewpoints and points of emphasis of the public concerning the organization of the country's government and its constitution."[4]

The next step, the creation of a constitutional assembly, was a major source of controversy. Born as an assembly of twenty-five delegates elected by direct

4. Kok 2011.

personal election in November 2010, this first assembly was then annulled in January 2011 by the Supreme Court, in light of various procedural irregularities in the election process. The government and parliament decided to ignore the Supreme Court ruling and individually re-appointed the elected members by Parliament to a new body named the "Constitutional Council."[5] The plan was for the Council to produce a draft in three months (from April 6 to June 6) with the possibility of a one-month extension. In the end, the Constitutional Council used the one-month extension and the draft was presented to Parliament a few weeks later, on July 29, 2011.

The last phase of the process consisted, first, of a non-binding national referendum on the constitutional proposal. Held on October 20, 2012, the referendum garnered substantial participation—half of the 235,000-strong electorate of Iceland participated—and secured a two-thirds approval of the draft as the basis of a new constitution.[6] The Parliament, then asked to pronounce on the validity of the draft as a constitutional document, found a way to avoid voting on the draft bill, which has been languishing in legislative limbo ever since.

The reasons advanced for the failure of the draft to be passed into law vary. Some blame it on a fickle Icelandic public who, once the worst of the economic crisis had passed, failed to rally around the project of a constitutional reform no longer seen as urgent or even needed.[7] Others blame it on the opposition, almost from the get go, from parties, politicians, and even academics threatened by the prospect of change or frustrated not to have had any control over it, as well as the hostility of powerful economic interests toward specific provisions of the new draft. For example, the lobby of the fisheries industry is said to have opposed the draft, essentially because the article on natural resources would render unavailable a great source of enrichment for them in the early 1990s.[8] Other explanations can be found, including in the ambition of rewriting the constitution in its entirety, as opposed to merely amending some articles. In any case, had the draft bill been passed, Icelanders would have had to vote in a second non-binding referendum on whether or not to adopt the new crowdsourced constitution in the Spring 2013, at the same time as parliamentary elections were held. The newly elected Parliament would also still have had to approve the new constitution.

5. Except for one person who declined to join this new body and had to be replaced by the next person on the electoral list.

6. Among the other questions put to the people of Iceland was, for example, whether natural resources that were not already privatized should be declared national property. This clause was approved by 87 percent of the voters.

7. Ginsburg and Elkins 2014.

8. These explanations are advanced for example by a former member of the Constitutional Council (see Gylfason 2013).

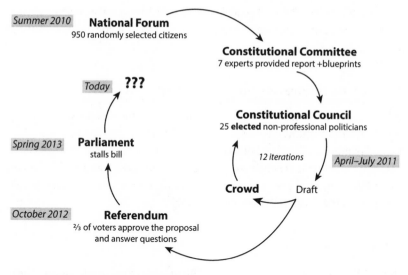

Summer 2010 **National Forum**
950 randomly selected citizens

Constitutional Committee
7 experts provided report +blueprints

Today **???**

Constitutional Council
25 **elected** non-professional politicians

Spring 2013 **Parliament**
stalls bill

12 iterations

April–July 2011

Crowd Draft

October 2012 **Referendum**
⅔ of voters approve the proposal
and answer questions

FIGURE 7.1. Icelandic experiment (2010–2013).

The following illustration encapsulates the steps and participants in the constitutional process (for more details on the process, see Skalski 2012; Valtysson 2014; Meuwese 2013; Fillmore-Patrick 2013; Oddsdóttir 2014; Landemore 2015; Suteu 2015; Bergsson and Blokker 2014).

What is unique and striking about the Icelandic process is that, contrary to what has historically been the case in all known constitution-writing processes, a concerted effort at including the population at large and in all its diversity was attempted at various stages. The Icelandic process strived to be as open as possible at every significant step, and particularly at the crucial stage of drafting the actual constitutional text.[9]

Constitutional processes are typically seen as processes best left to experts, at least when it comes to the crucial phases of agenda-setting and actual writing of the constitutional proposal. Ordinary citizens are usually involved only at the very end of the process, usually through voting on a referendum (that may not even be binding) on whether they approve the proposed document. In the last few decades, the practice and theory of "participatory constitution-making" have emphasized increased participation in the early phase of the process, through moments of "public consultation." Constitutional scholars are ambivalent about the role of popular participation in constitution-making and usually conclude that while upstream and downstream moments of consultation are welcome, the writing phase must be kept closed and in the hands of

9. Elster 2012.

professionals (Elster 2012). The Icelandic design, in that sense, is groundbreaking, violating a number of assumptions about the ideal shape of a constitutional process.

Democratic Innovations in the Icelandic Process

This section emphasizes the novel participatory features of the Icelandic process. Three innovations were key: the 2010 National Forum, the constitutional council of non-professional politicians as constitution-makers, and the crowdsourcing phase the latter chose to engage in. These three features went beyond the classic features of previous participatory processes and ensured a genuine openness of the process to ordinary citizens.

THE NATIONAL FORUM

The 2010 National Forum is, arguably, the most original aspect of this constitutional process. It was in fact the second iteration of a concept first developed by civil society in 2008. Shortly after the collapse of the Icelandic economy and the political revolution that ensued, a grassroots association self-labeled "the Anthill" had organized a large public event called a "National Forum" to discuss the future of Iceland. This earlier National Forum had gathered 1,500 individuals, most of them randomly selected from the National Population Register, in a one-day exercise that consisted of articulating the values and priorities that should guide the renewal of government and public administration. The results of the first National Forum were made public and discussed in the news media and the larger public sphere (Ólafsson 2011). The success of this first National Forum was such that Parliament decided to organize a second National Forum, together with the Anthill organization, as the first step of the new constitutional process.

National Forum 2010 took place on November 6, 2010. The Constitutional Act prescribed that the participants of the Forum had to be randomly sampled from the National Population Register "with due regard to a reasonable distribution of participants across the country and an equal division between genders, to the extent possible."[10] The Anthill group collaborated with Gallup Iceland, which then selected participants from the official directory of inhabitants by means of quota sampling. The idea was to ensure representativeness in age, gender, and geographical origin. The selected participants were contacted by letter and subsequently by phone. Because the response rate was low (20 percent), about 3,000 people had to be approached in order to yield

10. From the Act on a Constitutional Assembly, Interim Provision, Icelandic National Forum 2010.

the resulting 950 participants (Kok 2011). Furthermore, for each of the 1,000 seats offered, there were four backup candidates in the same age / gender / geographical location bracket so as to ensure that, should the first, or second, or third candidate decline to participate, there was someone relatively similar to replace them.[11] The selection process was thus technically near random sampling, subject to some self-selection, combined with stratified sampling.

The task of National Forum 2010 was to establish "the principal viewpoints and points of emphasis of the public concerning the organization of the country's government and its constitution" (Kok 2011). After a day of brainstorming, the answers were compiled under eight different themes.[12] These findings were meant to inspire a constitutional draft reflective of the preferences of the Icelandic people. The participants of the Forum sat in small groups of eight at round tables monitored by discussion leaders, all trained facilitators,[13] who did not contribute any personal views and were merely there to ensure that everyone had an equal opportunity to voice their opinions. While the setup lent itself to deliberation and the exchange of arguments, most of the discussions proceeded on the basis of brief speeches recorded by the facilitators. The tight schedule had been laid out by the members of a company named Agora that specializes in crowdsourcing. In the morning, the job of participants mostly consisted of brainstorming potential values and visions that were aggregated into eight main themes. The afternoon was spent on more concrete discussions between thematically specialized groups. This part of the event seemed to have been more deliberative, although its goal was simply to generate another ranking of the content proposals in terms of "importance" and "[positive] new ways of thinking." At the end, the participants split up across various tables for the theme discussions, then returned to their initial table to share the experience of the afternoon. This part entailed more casual exchange of the information than a proper deliberation about substantive issues. Based on these exchanges, each table drafted up to five recommendations, from which each table selected three by voting.

At the end of the event, the organizers extracted a series of key values that the participants wanted to see in a new Icelandic Constitution by applying the following procedure. They asked each table to select one-sentence thematic answers to the question: "What do you want to see in the new Icelandic

---

11. Thanks to Finnur Magnusson for this clarification. Personal communication, March 13, 2013, on file with author.

12. "*The main conclusions from the National Forum 2010,*" http://www.thjodfundur2010.is /frettir/lesa/item32858/, last visited August 21, 2017.

13. A special word was created in Icelandic to refer to these "facilitators"—*L'oðs* (the closest meaning in English would probably be "pilot")—to avoid implying that they were "leaders," the only word available until then. Thanks to Finnur Magnusson for this information. Email from Finnur Magnusson, March 12, 2013, on file with author.

Constitution?." Then they asked each table to jointly compose a sentence containing the most important input within the theme addressed by that given table. Then they asked each table to vote on three answers to the question: "What are our recommendations, advice, and requests to those who will continue and finish the work towards a new constitution?." Finally, they asked the participants as well as the facilitators to the Constitutional Assembly for their individual recommendations.

The output of the National Forum was synthesized in a 200-page report, along with expert recommendations and two blueprints for a constitutional proposal. These materials were transmitted to the twenty-five members of the Constitutional Council.

THE ASSEMBLY OF AMATEURS

The second democratic innovation of interest in the Icelandic constitutional process was the constitutional assembly in charge of writing the draft. In many ways this constitutional body can be described as an assembly of "amateurs" in the sense that it was open to ordinary citizens without prior experience with politics. In fact, not only was being a member of the Constitutional Council itself a job theoretically open to ordinary citizens, it was also a position from which incumbent professional politicians were excluded by law. The goal was to maximize the presence of ordinary citizens in the Council. Perhaps as a result of this openness, more than 500 people (522 in total) decided to run for election. Ultimately the twenty-five people who ended up winning a seat on the Council reflected an unusually diverse selection of profiles, *at least compared to more traditional constitutional assemblies.*[14] Instead of politicians appointed from among elected representatives or prominent political or administrative figures (e.g., the members of the constituent assembly created to produce a constitutional text for the European Union or the 2012 Egyptian Constituent Assembly[15]), the Council was made up of mostly amateur politicians. Only two out of its twenty-five members were former Parliamentarians (though several also held positions in various parties during their involvement in the Council). The Council consisted of ten women and fifteen men, meeting the required minimum of 40 percent women specified by Althing.[16] The twenty-five also included: five university professors (one in economics, one in applied mathematics, one in ethics who was also director of the University of Iceland Ethics

---

14. I emphasize this comparative point because it is true that in other ways the Constitutional Council was still elitist, as critics were quick to point out and as I'll mention where relevant.

15. The composition of the Egyptian assembly is described in Maboudi and Nadi 2016.

16. One woman had to be moved up in the ranking for this to happen. Had fewer women been elected, up to six women closest to being elected under the regular method would have been declared elected to fulfill the quota.

Institute, one in politics who also was a lecturer, and one in theology who was also a pastor), two media presenters (one also a student), three physicians (one of whom also self-identified as a filmmaker), a lawyer and radio presenter, one mathematician (working outside of academia), a farmer, a journalist, a manager, a pastor (distinct from the theology professor above), a reader of political science, the manager of the division of architecture at Reykjavik Art Museum, the chairman of an Icelandic video game developer and publisher, a theater director, a former museum director and teacher, a lawyer, a trade union chairman, a political scientist and university student, and a consumer spokesperson.[17]

While remarkably inclusive of Icelandic diversity, at least compared with historical precedents or comparable bodies in other countries,[18] the Constitutional Council clearly was not descriptively representative along a number of dimensions. For example, only three out of the twenty-five members were from outside of Reykjavik, compared to some one-third of the Icelandic population.[19] The academic community was overrepresented. There was only one farmer and he also happened to be chairman of the Farmers' Association, one of the most influential trade unions and lobbying groups in Iceland. There was only one member of the working class, the trade union chairman. Although he was a former electrician himself and proudly sees himself as a member and a representative of the working class,[20] he is also the father of the internationally renowned singer Björk. In an otherwise ethnically and religiously homogenous country, the socioeconomic dimension is one that should perhaps have mattered more than it did, and critics argued that there were too many highly educated, urban, wealthy individuals on the Council.

THE CROWDSOURCING PHASE

The most original and directly participatory part of the drafting stage was the "crowdsourcing" phase, which included a series of twelve crowdsourcing moments. The twenty-five members of the Council, far from isolating themselves from popular input, regularly posted online, for the world to see and for the Icelandic people to read, the version of the draft they were working on. All in all, they posted twelve drafts, all at various stages of completion. Anyone interested in the process could send feedback by posting comments on social

17. Wikipedia, "2010 Icelandic Constitutional Assembly Election," https://en.wikipedia.org /wiki/Icelandic_Constitutional_Assembly_election,_2010 (as of June 9, 2017, 21: 56).

18. Notable exceptions are the South African, Ugandan, and the Tunisian constitutional processes. See Moehler 2006.

19. As of January 1, 2015, about 211,000 out of 329,000 Icelanders lived in the greater metropolitan area around the capital city Reykjavík.

20. Email from Guðmundur Gunnarsson (August 15, 2016), on file with author.

media platforms like Facebook and Twitter, or by posting on the Council's own webpage or using email and regular mail. In fact, even foreigners were free to participate if they could find a way (e.g., GoogleTranslate) to overcome the language barrier. For example, an American citizen who owned property in Iceland wrote on the Facebook page that she hoped the new constitution would take into account the interests of people in her situation.

Roughly 3,600 comments were made online. Each of these started a conversation of varying length, with many response threads following initial comments. Ultimately, only about 360 suggestions emanated from a population of 320,000 or so. As in most other crowdsourced policy or law processes, online participation seems to have involved a demographically skewed sample of participants—mostly older, educated white males.[21] Ragnhildur Helgadóttir, a legal scholar at the University of Reykjavik, critically points out that "internet consultations during the drafting seem to have further empowered a politically strong group (native-born, middle-aged males) instead of the youngest voters or those who generally do not participate in politics." She emphasizes that, by contrast, "traditional" consultation in Parliament drew a somewhat different group of people to the table," including young people and women (Helgadóttir 2014). It is worth noting, however, that the traditional form of consultation by Parliament drew only ninety submissions (four times fewer than the online methods) from only fifty-three different individuals and legal entities. While online crowdsourcing does not tap the full diversity of a country's perspectives, it helps increase the quantity of possibly relevant input by engaging participants who might not have been reached through any other existing means. Rather than a rival mechanism for public participation, crowdsourcing should be considered a useful supplement to more classic consultation processes. Finally, unlike parliamentary consultations, whose impact on the final draft is not easily measurable, it has been shown that close to 10 percent of the online contributions to the various platforms consulted by the constitutional council make a causal difference to the final version of the text (Hudson 2018). If only for this reason, the Icelandic innovation of crowdsourcing constitutional proposals is worthy of our attention.

Was the Constitutional Proposal Any Good?

The participatory Icelandic constitutional process can only be inspirational if the constitutional proposal that resulted from it was at least minimally good and, specifically, if public participation can be shown to be at least partly responsible for its quality. In other words, the level of public participation

21. See, e.g., Aitamurto, Landemore, and Saldivar Galli 2017 for a comparable crowdsourced policy process in Finland.

in the Icelandic process and the various democratic innovations put in place to make it happen can only be rightly celebrated if it can be shown that this participatory design was sufficiently causally responsible for the quality of the outcome. Was the crowdsourced constitution substantially any good? And if it was good, was it because, or in spite of, the participation of ordinary citizens at all stages of the process?

Regarding the value of the proposal, the fact that it was approved by two-thirds of the voters in a 2012 referendum would seem to speak to its strengths. Conversely, the fact that the Icelandic Parliament ultimately shelved it would seem to speak to its weaknesses.[22]

The literature currently offers no unique and consensual benchmark of "goodness" for a constitutional text.[23] Legal scholars and constitutional theorists tend to focus on formal features such as "coherence," as they do not entail having to pass controversial judgments on the substance. It is mostly on such grounds, for example, that the Venice Commission members, a group of European legal experts consulted by the Icelandic Parliament, expressed some concerns over the quality of the proposal, pointing out inconsistencies between articles and institutional settings, and suggesting a potential risk of non-workability of the document as a whole. These concerns, emphasized in the Icelandic media, undeniably played some role in delegitimizing the proposal in the eyes of many.

But coherence is only one way in which a constitution should be assessed, a very academic and abstract one at that, and perhaps not the most essential or adequate for processes meant to involve a large number of people. Additionally, it is not clear at all that public participation (rather than lack of time, since the Constitutional Council was only given four months in total to draft the document) should be blamed for whatever lack of coherence was identified by the Venice Commission. It is also worth mentioning that the Venice Commission did not offer a comparable evaluation of the expert proposals, which leaves us unsure of the comparative performance of experts in this respect. Finally, according to Ginsburg, Elkins, and Blount (2009: 215), when it comes to examples of "poor drafting, internal contradictions, or errors," which abound in constitutions across the world, "no one has yet tied these directly to participation." Nor is there, to my knowledge, indisputable evidence of a causal relation between lack of textual coherence and unworkability of a constitution in practice (though to be fair the connection sounds plausible).

---

22. Unless Gylfason (2013 and 2016) is right and the failure of the constitution is simply a coup of the politicians, which is plausible from his account. But I want to bracket this possibility for now.

23. For an attempt to sketch an index-like standard, see Landemore 2016, and for a constructed standard of liberalism and smartness on the specific issue of religious rights, see Landemore 2017b.

In what follows I assess the crowdsourced constitutional proposal by two less formalistic and more substantive standards that have long been identified by the relevant literature as two relatively uncontroversial good outcomes. I call these respectively "rights-heaviness" and "democraticity."[24] "Rights-heaviness," as I use it, measures how well a constitution is likely to do one of the essential things a constitution is supposed to do, namely protect individual rights. Heaviness here means both to the number and quality of rights entrenched in the constitution. It seems intuitively plausible that the degree to which a constitution details and entrenches individual rights, while not a guarantee that the regime built on such a constitution will respect them in any way, should factor in our evaluation of its goodness. The second criterion is a common standard in the constitutional literature. Carey (2009) calls it "democracy" and characterizes it as "the most prominent among constitutional ideals" (156). By "democracy" Carey means both to the kind of ideal expected to be found in the text of constitutions themselves and the kind of inclusive and participatory principles that govern constitutional processes. This criterion has been recently relabeled, less elegantly but more accurately, "democraticity" (Landemore 2016), measuring specifically how far along on the continuum from less to more democratic a constitution is procedurally (in contrast to how rights-heavy it is).[25] That democraticity is a desirable substantive criterion by which to assess the ex ante goodness of a constitution is largely taken for granted by normative theorists and empirical political scientists alike and thus a plausible benchmark of goodness to use.

One interesting conjecture in the constitutional literature is that the more participatory a constitutional process is, the more rights and mechanisms for popular participation it should include. In other words, the more participatory a constitutional process is, the more rights-heavy and democratic the content of the constitutional proposal should be.

The quasi-natural experiment nature of the Icelandic experience allows us to compare the crowdsourced constitutional proposal to two constitutional proposals independently written by seven government experts at about the same time and thus test the hypothesis that participation of the public made the proposal better than it would have been if left in the hands of professional politicians and experts alone.[26] As in a controlled experiment, we have two

24. These two criteria are also used in Landemore (2016).

25. Contrary to Carey, I prefer not to include consideration for rights, including human rights, under the democracy criterion but file consideration for rights under a separate, previously mentioned category: rights-heaviness. It is, after all, possible for a liberal but undemocratic constitution to respect a number of rights, while violating political equality.

26. The quasi-natural experiment design offered by the Icelandic constitutional process is, of course, far from perfect. These imperfections are not sufficient enough, in light of various mitigating factors, to invalidate the lessons one can derive from the comparison (see also Landemore

comparable processes: one that involves only seven experts writing behind closed doors; and one that involves public participation, in the sense both of involving an (initially at least) elected constitutional assembly of non-professional politicians and of having opened up the drafting process to the larger public as well via crowdsourcing.[27] In other words, the treatment here is "public participation at the drafting stage," which lumps together the participation of non-professional politicians on the constitutional council and the participation of the online crowd at various stages of the writing process. The "control" is the writing of rival drafts by experts behind closed doors.

Let me now turn to the evaluation. In terms of rights-heaviness, the crowd-sourced proposal counts a total of thirty-one articles related to "human rights and nature," which makes it more rights-heavy than the original constitution or the expert drafts, yet only "moderately rights-heavy" compared to other constitutions worldwide according to external observers, where the measure is of the percentage of rights included in the constitution across seventy or so distinct rights that have been specified in constitutions since 1789 (Elkins, Ginsburg, and Melton 2012). The Venice Commission praises the proposal for "new provisions [. . .] aiming both to extend the scope of protection and to better reflect the international human rights obligation" (Venice Commission 2013, Remarks 27). The Venice Commission singles out in particular article 112 as being of "great importance" in that it stresses the obligations of Iceland under international agreements and requires that all holders of governmental powers respect rules on human rights (Venice Commission 2013, Remarks 26). The Venice Commission also notes that "the scope of protection has especially been widened by adding new socio-economic rights (articles 22–25), as well as more or less 'collective rights' (articles 32–36), called by the explanatory bill 'third-generation rights'" (Venice Commission 2013, Remarks 28).

The proposal also includes rights that are not listed in either the original constitution or the expert drafts, such as the right to access to the Internet (article 15) and various socioeconomic and collective rights that may even seem excessively generous and difficult to uphold, as pointed out by the Venice Commission (Remarks 32–33). The proposal mentions explicitly "sexual violence" as a type of violence the state should protect individuals from. Unlike

---

2017b for a defense of the setup). All in all, this quasi-controlled experiment offers a close enough approximation of more formal comparisons between the few and the many used in epistemic democrats' models (e.g., Landemore 2012 and 2013a).

27. Please note that I do not include the offline consultations organized by Parliament. Although the participants were arguably more diverse than the online participants (more female in particular), their number were small, the impact of their contributions impossible to trace at this point, and most importantly, their participation took place *after* the Council had submitted to Parliament the version of the constitutional proposal I am assessing in this chapter.

the original constitution or either of the expert drafts, the Council's proposal also devotes a separate and extensive article to the rights of children. The proposal mentions still more sources of discrimination than the first expert draft ("A"), including genetic character, ancestry, and political affiliation. Finally, the proposal offers a more "open and comprehensive approach to the right of freedom of religion" in that it extends the scope of this freedom to what the Council's proposal calls "view of life" and "personal conviction." According to the Venice Commission, this extension of the scope of religious freedom as well as the inclusion of the right to change religion or faith form "a substantial improvement compared to the current Constitution" (Venice Commission 2013, Remarks 55).

It is worth focusing on, for example, the religious rights provision.[28] Article 18 of the crowdsourced proposal reads as follows: "All shall be assured of the right to religion and a view of life, including the right to change their religion or personal convictions and the right to remain outside religious organizations. All shall be free to pursue their religion, individually or in association with others, publicly or privately. The freedom to pursue religion or personal convictions shall only be limited by law as necessary in a democratic society."

This is one of four passages in the text where the reference to democracy or a democratic society is expressly mentioned (democracy is only evoked once in the 1944 constitution and three times in both expert drafts A and B). The necessities of "a democratic society," a phrase possibly borrowed from article 9 of the European Court of Human Rights mentioned above, are the only constraints on the freedom to pursue religion or personal convictions. Gone, by contrast, are mentions of "public order" or "good morals" present in both the original constitution and the expert examples, which arguably considerably modernizes and liberalizes the text compared to all the others, including article 9 of the European Court of Human Rights (which was written in 1951 and is not particularly modern in many respects). The downside of eliminating any reference to public order and good morals is perhaps that it dis-aligns the proposal from the substance of an international convention with arguably quasi-constitutional status over Icelandic law. Legal experts critical of the draft made this point repeatedly. They argued that the Council went too far in rewriting the section on human rights, which they thought had been satisfactorily settled since 1995 (pride of authorship might have interfered with their objectivity, as the person expressing this criticism is also the person responsible for the earlier amendment). Second, the right to religion is put immediately in parallel with a right to a "view of life" and "personal convictions" that may or may not be of a religious nature. In this respect, the group of 25 accurately reflected

28. This analysis is based on Landemore 2017b.

the general stance of tolerance toward various worldviews characteristic of modern Iceland (and Nordic countries more generally). The Council refused to give religion a distinct and superior standing over philosophical views such as atheism. The Venice Commission praised this part of the constitutional proposal for offering a more "open and comprehensive approach to the right of freedom of religion" in that it extends the scope of this freedom to "view of life" (or "philosophy") and "personal conviction." According to the Venice Commission, this extension as well as the inclusion of the right to change religion or faith form "a substantial improvement compared to the current Constitution" (2013, remark 55). Given that both expert-written drafts merely reproduced the content of the original constitution, the Council's proposal is markedly better than all three.

While the superior rights-heaviness of the crowdsourced document over all competing proposals is undeniable, it is hardly perfect. Critics have rightly pointed out its excessive vagueness, resulting in a lack of clarity. The Venice Commission suggests that it is "regrettable" that "most of the provisions concerned are worded in general terms, not providing sufficient clarity on whether and which concrete rights and obligations can be derived from them" (Venice Commission 2013, Remarks 32). While the Venice Commission is mostly concerned here about the risks of disappointing the public, which is a valid concern, from our perspective the worry should be also that the constitution will not be "good" in the sense of having the kind of formal quality that ensures proper interpretability and thus usefulness.

Turning now to the second criterion of quality, "democraticity," one striking feature of the crowdsourced constitutional proposal is that it put *citizens'* rights at the forefront of the constitution, in contrast to the current constitution that still lists them last. This reorganization is in keeping with the recommendations that emanated from the National Forum 2010, which the expert drafts also adopted. Putting the Icelandic people and their rights at the beginning of the text, rather than at the end, seems, symbolically at least, like a democratic improvement over the past emphasis on state institutions (the President's powers, the Court' powers, etc.). Most important, the democratic superiority of the crowdsourced proposal over all competitors is the degree to which it creates institutional avenues for popular participation (Elkins et al. 2012: 2).[29] Important elements of direct democracy are introduced in the crowdsourced constitution, allowing the public a role in the determination of the status of the Evangelical Lutheran Church as the national church (any change to the status quo introduced by Parliament

29. Discussing the "[e]lements of direct democracy [that] appear throughout the proposed Constitution."

must be approved by referendum) and the approval of certain treaties (such as a treaty to enter the European Union). The text also includes a "right of referral," by which 10 percent of voters may demand a referendum on any bill within three months of its passage (article 65), subject to some exceptions, such as the budget (article 67). Additionally, and most innovatively, the draft introduces what is elsewhere sometimes called a Citizens' Initiative (article 66). This participatory mechanism allows 2 percent of the population to present an issue to the Althing, which the Althing is free to ignore. If 10 percent of the population present a bill to the Althing, the Althing must either accept or make a counter-proposal. In the latter case, if the bill of the voters has not been withdrawn as a response, the Althing must present both the popular bill and the Althing's counter-proposal to a referendum. The text also authorizes removal of the President by a three-fourths vote of the Althing, but only after a referendum (article 84). It further permits a referendum for constitutional amendments after a simple majority in the Althing (although it is possible to adopt a constitutional amendment without a referendum by a five-sixths majority in the Althing) (article 113). Finally, candidates for President must have the prior endorsement of 1% of voters (article 78).

These elements of participation are rather distinctive of the crowdsourced constitution and have been internationally celebrated, including by the Venice Commission. Article 128 of the Venice Commission's report thus states:

> The Venice Commission welcomes the clear intention that underlines the above-mentioned provisions, namely, to enhance citizens' opportunities to influence legislation and more generally the decision-making on issues of key interest of the public. It finds this aim entirely legitimate and understandable in the specific socio-economic and political context of Iceland, and recalls that, this is also a part of a certain tradition of direct participation that exists in Iceland. (Venice Commission 2013: Remarks 23)

By contrast, the 1944 constitution only contains one provision to allow the public to vote on bills that have been returned to Parliament by the president, thus proving inadequate both in terms of the specific socioeconomic context of Iceland and its participatory and democratic tradition, as noted by the Venice Commission. The expert drafts are notably more participatory than the 1944 constitution, but not to the same extent as the crowdsourced proposal. Expert proposal "A," for example, also has a Citizens' Initiative article (article 46), which allows 15 percent of the population to trigger a referendum on a bill (subject to some exceptions like the budget). Expert proposal "B" has an article in the chapter on national referendums that specifies that 15 percent of the population can force the President to refuse to confirm an act of law or resolution of the Althing and refer the matter to a national vote. Again, these participatory provisions are not nearly as expansive as those found in the crowdsourced document.

These elements of direct democracy arguably bleed into the criterion of what might be termed "deliberative capacity."[30] To the extent that they put "the public in conversation with their elected representatives" (Elkins et al. 2012: 2), these measures enhance the deliberative character and potential of democratic institutions. They render more porous and thus more effective the communication channels that are supposed to exist between the formal and the informal deliberative tracks of a properly functioning democracy (Habermas 1996). Beyond the deliberation between government and citizens, the draft also promotes intergovernmental deliberation, with for example article 108, which makes it a duty of the national government to consult local government for issues related to them. The crowdsourced proposal—to a greater extent than either of the expert drafts—thus meets the "democraticity" criterion along specifically deliberative lines.

Last but not least, another characteristic one may easily associate with "democraticity"—transparency—is a central theme in the Council's proposal, to an extent unmatched by the expert texts "A" and "B," let alone the original constitution. The word transparency is used three times in the Council's proposal. Article 15 on the right to information states:

> Public administration shall be transparent [. . .] Information and documents held by public authorities shall be available without exception and the access of the public to all documents collected or paid for by public authorities shall be assured by law. A list of all cases and documents held by public authorities, their origin and content shall be open to all.

Article 16 requires "transparency of ownership" in the media. Article 51 finally aims to make contributions to candidates and their associations fully public. The goal is "to keep costs moderate, ensure transparency, and limit advertising in an election campaign." At least two other articles explicitly aim for transparency, even if they do not contain the word. For example, Article 29 prohibits members of the Althing from participating in deliberation on parliamentary business that concerns their special interests, or those of persons with close ties to them. Article 50 on disclosure of conflicts of interest for Althing members and their duty to provide information on their financial interests similarly aim at transparency, without using the word. A similar article, article 88, exists for ministers, who have a "duty to disclose information on their financial interests."

---

30. See Landemore 2016 building on Dryzek 2009. For Dryzek, "deliberative capacity" is "the extent to which a political system possesses structures to host deliberation that is authentic, inclusive, and consequential."

I conclude that the Icelandic proposal was an improvement over the 1944 constitution and was also comparatively though only marginally better than the rival expert drafts in terms of both rights-heaviness and democraticity.

Causal Mechanisms

Can we more precisely pinpoint this advantage on the greater public participation at the drafting stage? Here I borrow a conjecture from the theoretical framework known as "epistemic democracy," which traces the superiority of more inclusive deliberation to the presence of greater cognitive diversity, that is, the diversity of perspectives and heuristics used in problem resolution. The assumption is that, including more people in a problem-solving process, in other words, making the process more participatory, is likely to introduce more cognitive diversity and thus ensure better outcomes (Landemore 2013a).

The available evidence suggests that greater public participation helped with the formulation of more expansive rights provision because it simply led to more individuals' interests and perspectives being taken into account. The twenty-five members of the Constitutional Council included, for example, a severely disabled human rights activist Freyja Heraldsdottir, who is generally credited for strongly influencing the human rights section of the crowdsourced proposal (and modifying it considerably from its last 1995 update). But even the greater diversity of the constitution writers did not fully track the range of interests in the larger public. According to internal reports, the Constitutional Council had originally set out to be as inclusive as possible on matters of human rights and specifically on matters of sexuality. Yet it took the influence of outsiders for members of the Council to write the text they ultimately wrote. Pastor Örn Jónsson reports that article 6, which bars "discrimination, such as due to gender, age, genetic character, place of residence, economic status, disability, sexual orientation, race, colour, opinions, political affiliation, religion, language, origin, ancestry and position in other respects" was directly influenced by emails, letters, and online posts from, among others, the transgender community, who made members of the Council realize that the first draft they uploaded on the Internet was not inclusive enough.[31]

Opening up the draft to the larger public thus led to the introduction of a concern for transgender people's and children's rights, as groups representing transgender interests and children's interests were able to voice their concerns about the initially less inclusive formulations by the twenty-five constitutional council members (none of whom identified as transgender or was a child, despite many of them being parents).

---

31. Personal email communication from Pastor Örn Jónsson, July 17, 2015.

Meanwhile, the group of seven experts did not include either a disabled or a transgender person or a child, or their representatives, though they did include the constitutional lawyer responsible for the 1995 amendment to the 1944 constitution that introduced human rights into the text (to align it with international treaties), which would be assumed to carry an important intellectual advantage. The expert-written drafts thus do not reflect as much of a concern for the rights of the disabled, transgender, children, and other vulnerable categories. This suggests that no matter how good and inclusive the intention of smaller, less diverse groups, it is likely that they cannot quite "see" and explore the entire landscape of possible and relevant rights provisions the way more inclusive and more diverse groups can. When it comes to rights and their formulation, it seems fairly obvious that involving more people will have the effect of increasing the number of perspectives taken into consideration and thus the number of rights offered in the resulting text. It may in fact lead to an inflation of rights, though this seems to have been kept within reasonable limits by the constitution-makers in this case.

How did the diversity introduced by greater participation impact the democraticity of the proposal? Here the evidence is less clear-cut, though it is very plausible that here too a greater diversity of perspectives helped the drafters come up with a more expansive interpretation of the National Forum's demand that the new constitution should include new avenues for citizens' participation. For one thing, the twenty-five members of the constitutional council chose a more expansive definition of those participatory rights and mechanisms than did the experts. More research would be needed to figure out how, exactly, the deliberations among the twenty-five constitutional council members and their interactions with the online crowd and members of the public more generally led them to such formulations.

A case can thus be made that public participation at the drafting stage in the Icelandic case made the resulting document better in a substantive sense, in that the proposal included more rights and democratic mechanisms than would have been the case without public participation.[32] A plausible mechanism accounting for this effect of public participation is the greater diversity of perspectives ensured by the greater number of participants in the process, via both the design of a twenty-five-member (initially) elected constitutional council and the use, by the latter, of crowdsourcing techniques to consult the larger public. This corroborates other information that finds the Icelandic constitution also more "liberal" and "smart" in the way it addressed difficult issues of religious rights (Landemore 2017b).

---

32. A hypothesis somewhat precluded by Elster himself, since he recommends making the drafting stage itself rather less than more participatory (for reasons that have to do with the various biases and pressures introduced by popular participation at this crucial stage).

Iceland as an Open Democracy?

Now that we have established that the Icelandic process did produce nor-matively attractive results, let us turn to the ways in which it can be read as instantiating a version of open democracy. I will now argue that the process instantiated four out of five of the principles of open democracy (albeit to a lesser or greater degree): participation rights, deliberation, democratic repre-sentation, and transparency. The only principle the process really failed to implement is the majoritarian principle, and this may help explain the reasons why the constitutional proposal failed to be passed into law in the end.

PARTICIPATION RIGHTS

The Icelandic process embodied the institutional principle of participation rights through two mechanisms: the mechanism of random selection that was used to select the participants in the National Forum and the crowdsourcing moment. The selection method used to staff the National Forum indeed gave all citizens as close to an equal opportunity as they had ever had to be part of an agenda-setting assembly on the fundamental matter of the value con-tent of a new constitution. Under "normal" constitutional processes, where the most ordinary people can hope for is to place an op-ed in some visible media outlet or to exert an unusually strong influence on some pivotal politi-cian, individuals' chances of influencing a constitutional assembly's agenda are, realistically, null. The revolutionary aspect of this Icelandic institutional design choice is thus worth emphasizing. Of course, the individual's chance of being selected for that particular assembly was not high. Even in a small country like Iceland, the chance of every individually registered voter being selected was only around 0.38%. But this chance was evenly distributed and, assuming we think of an equivalent form of participation for more ordinary decision-making at various levels of a genuinely open democracy (including for example the municipal level), the odds of being part of something meaningful could become more substantial over the course of a lifetime.

The other, more limited way that citizens were empowered is through the crowdsourcing moment, which allowed all willing and able to at least voice their concerns and share their ideas. The evidence indicates that about 10 percent of the online contributions proved causally influential in some man-ner (Hudson 2018).

Of course, the process could have more actively empowered citizens' participation. Not enough thought was devoted to how to conduct an elec-tion (to the constitutional assembly) where candidates would self-select from the population, and the time given for people to learn about the process and consider running for it was inadequate. People living in Reykjavik who were involved in the Pots and Pans revolution, first movers, and people with an already established notoriety benefited more than others from the openness of the process. The choice of a conventional electoral mechanism to select the assembly members only entrenched these inequalities. A lottery-based selection among the pool of 523 volunteers (which may have been much larger under such a rule) might have been more respectful of citizens' participation rights.

It is also worth mentioning that if the constitutional proposal had become law, both citizens' initiatives and a right of referral would now be available to Icelanders.

DELIBERATION

Deliberation was an important feature of the overall design both at the "system" level and in at least some of the groups in charge of setting the agenda and writing the document. At the system level, the public had a chance to deliberate about constitutional issues when debating the results of the National Forum, when following the campaign of the 525 candidates to the constitutional assembly, and in the period leading up to the referendum as well as the period between the referendum results and the final non-vote in Parliament. International coverage of the constitutional process spurred additional conversation among Icelanders about the meaning of the process in which they were engaged. All in all, it was a very deliberative process at the societal level. It is true that not everything was done to ensure perfect legibility, in part because of the resistance of the various political elites.[33] But, in comparison to most other constitutional processes, the process was characterized by remarkable efforts to educate the public and disseminate information.

Deliberation was also a central aspect of the twenty-five Council members' work. Per their report, they would separate into smaller committees charged with writing different parts of the constitution and reconvene in plenaries where they would intensely debate the proposals presented by each committee.

The National Forum, however, was not characterized by much, if any, deliberation. Values and preferences were elicited from the 950 individuals involved in the National Forum mostly through aggregation. As the name of the "Anthill" group (reminiscent of the idea of the "hive mind") suggests, and the crowdsourcing activities of the Agora group involved in the organization of the forum confirm, the whole event was governed by a faith in the virtues of mere judgment and preference aggregation, rather than an interest in the ways

---

33. For example, Parliament refused to pay for a translation into English of the constitutional proposal that would have allowed the conversation to go global, such that the Council had to raise funding for it on its own, without institutional support.

these judgments were formed and could be transformed through deliberation. Wherever this bias in favor of aggregation over deliberation originated (one suspects it may be related to the same blind trust in the market that made Iceland the most neoliberal Scandinavian country prior to the crisis), it would at least have been worth considering whether something closer to an actual deliberative poll might have been more appropriate to initiate the debate about constitutional reform and discuss the guidelines any resulting constitutional assembly would have had to follow.

However, since the point of the National Forum was to take a snapshot of the Icelandic people's shared values and norms in order to form the consensual background for the Constitutional Council's deliberations, judgment and preference aggregation were not entirely inappropriate. The purpose was to facilitate self-clarification rather than problem-solving debates, and to explicitly avoid controversial debates.[34] The question was, simply: "What values do we actually share?" (As opposed to: "What values *should* we share?") Besides, one could argue that the deliberative, more controversial part of the process had to an extent taken place in the two years prior to the 2010 National Forum, with the Pots and Pans revolution and months of ruminating on the collapse of the economic system.

There was an element of deliberation, albeit a limited one, between the crowd and the Council during the crowdsourcing phase. The crowdsourcing phase undeniably made the wall between the first and the second deliberative tracks more porous. But this opening of the process was not complete, where it was attempted at all. The Council's responses to individual suggestions, for example, were irregular, informal, and limited, probably because the process of giving feedback to the public wasn't properly institutionalized and funded. As a result, the Constitutional Council members did what they wanted with the proposals and comments they received, such that it is hard to know whether and how crowdsourcing made a difference to the result. Were novel ideas—in particular, those breaking from the preconceived notions of the Constitutional Council—taken seriously at all? It is worth emphasizing, though, that the latest study of the data suggests that about 10 percent of the suggestions had a substantial causal impact on the content of the draft (Hudson 2018).

All in all, the public had a chance to deliberate about constitutional issues when debating the results of the National Fora, when following the campaign of the 525 candidates to the constitutional assembly, and in the period leading up to the referendum as well as the period between the referendum results and

---

34. Thus, the National Forum "was not aimed at stimulating controversial discussions in the sense of exchanging pros and cons to a given proposal" (Kok 2011).

the final non-vote in Parliament. International coverage of the constitutional process spurred additional conversation among Icelanders about the meaning of the process they were engaged in.

MAJORITARIAN PRINCIPLE

The process arguably instantiated the majoritarian principle up to the point when the proposal was put for a vote in Parliament (where it died). Because the National Forum was almost a perfect mirror image of the country, the priorities it set for the constitutional council were largely representative of majority preferences. Down the road, when a referendum was held on the proposal, a two-thirds majority of the voters approved of the text, and the rate of approval for each independent question asked on the referendum was high. In terms of substance, the draft was on the face of it in harmony with majoritarian preferences in the country, at least as expressed during the National Forum—except perhaps about the status of the Evangelical Lutheran church (but see chapter 6 for the ambiguity of that point).

Yet if we take the process as a whole, including its parliamentary aspect, it can be seen as failing the majoritarian principle. Parliament, which had final say, was seemingly more responsive to the intense preferences of a few interest groups against the constitutional draft than it was to the will of a majority of the people who voted in the referendum in support of it. It is worth emphasizing that the Icelandic Parliament is, under the current constitution, not truly reflective of the majority of Icelanders' will, as it gives more weight to the conservative countryside. Finally, the threshold for approval of the constitution was supermajoritarian in ways that would have been difficult to meet even if the Parliament had decided to take a vote on the constitutional proposal. The conclusion of the Icelandic experiment was bound to resemble the fate of many other democratic experiments around the world, where the powers that be cannot relinquish control and insist on supermajoritarian hurdles that have proven insuperable.[35]

---

35. Similarly, in the 2004 British Columbia experiment of a Citizens' Assembly on electoral reform, the Assembly's recommendations of replacing the province's existing First Past the Post (FPTP) system with a Single Transferable Vote (STV) system was put to a referendum held concurrently with the 2005 provincial election. Although the recommendation garnered 57.7 percent of the votes and had majority support in 77 of the 79 districts, it failed to pass because the Parliament had set the bar at 60 percent of votes and simple majorities in 60 percent of the 79 districts (Warren and Pearse 2008). Had this process been more straightforwardly majoritarian, the recommendation would have become law.

DEMOCRATIC REPRESENTATION

The Icelandic case offers a good example of democratic representation since it intentionally multiplied the sites and forms of representation. The National Forum used what chapter 4 called "lottocratic representation"; the Constitutional Council used a slightly more open, and specifically more "liquid," version of electoral representation (though technically the members were eventually appointed, they were initially chosen by election from a pool of candidates that was open to the entire adult population); and the crowdsourcing moment corresponded to "self-selected" representation.

The respective legitimacy of these different forms of democratic representation was sometimes clearly spelled out. For example, the small number of people who self-selected into the crowdsourcing phase and contributed input were not given final say and their views were only integrated to the draft as judged necessary by the elected representatives on the Constitutional Council. As a result, the division of labor was clear and effective between the crowds, intervening in an advisory role, and the Council, which had final say over the formulation of the proposal, and there was no conflict over legitimacy. Sometimes, however, conflicts of legitimacy emerged. The tension between popular support for the proposal in the referendum and the elected representatives who decided not to implement it offers an illustration. The claim of those who said the referendum result should be ignored was that turnout was relatively low for an Icelandic election (47 percent). In a sense, they argued that the voters who participated were not representative enough of the larger population to ensure that what a majority of voters wanted was what the larger population truly wanted. Against this argument, however, supporters of the constitutional proposal saw the referendum result as the real expression of the general will and, despite the fact that its outcome was legally non-binding, judged that the Icelandic Parliament, which failed to act on it, had betrayed the people and lost all legitimacy as a result.[36]

TRANSPARENCY

The Icelandic process was, finally, characterized by a high degree of transparency in that the public was able to witness, observe, and thereafter make up their minds about the activities of the actors engaged in the constitution-writing

36. A fascinating debate on the legitimacy of the Constitutional Council versus that of the Icelandic Parliament was conducted at the occasion of "A Congress on Iceland's Democracy," California Constitution Center at Berkeley Law and the UC Berkeley Institute of Governmental Studies, June 3, 2017. From a purely legal standpoint, it appears that the legitimacy claims of the Council held rather well. For a summary of the debate, see the resulting book, aptly titled *The Icelandic Federalist Papers* and edited by David Carrillo (2018).

process. Conversely, the actual drafters of the constitution were able to access the crowd's thoughts and input, when deemed necessary. Transparency was a window, one might say, opened into the walls of the constitutional assembly and, more generally, into the whole constitution-writing process.

More generally, the drafting process took place under the almost constant and openly solicited gaze of the people. This was a fundamental departure from the earlier and most common model of constitution-writing, which entailed secret meetings among an elite few, as in the foundational examples of modern representative democracies like France and the United States. The first example of transparency could be found early in the process with the streaming on the Internet of the 2010 National Forum. While it is not clear how many people actually watched the activities and discussions of their 950 randomly selected fellow citizens, it is important to the inclusiveness of the whole process that this option was made available.

The crowdsourcing part of the process allowed citizens to access not only the work done by the members of the Constitutional Council, who posted their drafts online at regular intervals, but also each other's thoughts. Everything an individual wrote on the Constitutional Council's Facebook page, for example, could be viewed, commented on, and ranked (via Facebook "likes") by other citizens as well. Modern participatory technologies have arguably made it possible to transform what were usually closed and unidirectional processes into open and multi-directional ones.

In the case of the Icelandic process, though full transparency was never possible, the traditional walls separating what Habermas calls the first and second "deliberative tracks" (Parliament and the larger public sphere, respectively) were made more porous to each other. From the first to the second track came the draft of the constitution itself; at various stages of revision and response there were email responses to public inquiries; from the second to the first deliberative track came emails, Facebook posts, Skype chats, and tweets.

Transparency in the Icelandic case was made possible both by new technologies, including social media, and by a deliberate decision to make the process as democratic and accountable as possible. The Icelandic people had clearly expressed a desire to break with the shady deals and corrupt ways of the pre-crisis era (which is not to say that the new ways are so different). Despite the defensible benefits of closed and secret deliberations, Icelanders obviously judged that light was a necessary disinfectant. Of course, the light reached only so far: the deliberations among the twenty-five members were not actually visible. Only their general "open" meetings were filmed, recorded, and later released as PDF transcripts, in what is sometimes called "time-lag transparency." Their committee meetings, which involved the members of three subgroups of the Council that worked on different issues, were not open in the same manner. Only their minutes were recorded (i.e., in a general written report of the agenda and decisions). There were also "informal" meetings, the content of which went entirely unrecorded. Nonetheless, the larger public was given as much access as history has ever witnessed in a constitution-writing process. It would be hard to overstate the novelty of this transparency, especially in comparison with recent constitution-writing processes, such as the European or the Egyptian one.

One may also argue that, even where the process was transparent, it was not as transparent as it seemed to be or should have been. As already mentioned, the Constitutional Council held open general meetings, but closed discussion sessions or "committee meetings" and "informal meetings," where all the "real" deliberation arguably went on. Only transcripts of the "open" meetings were made available, and only weeks later—too late for an immediate feedback loop to take place between the Council and the willing members of the larger public (the crowd) willing to read the transcripts. The format in which these transcripts were delivered—non-interactive PDF files of more than 1,000 pages—was not the most conducive to easy analysis by outsiders.

Despite significant flaws, the Icelandic process was characterized by a great degree of openness. Openness to the participation of the public at large was essential to the extent that the movement for a revision of the constitution was born from popular mobilization—the Pots and Pans revolution. It was further prodded along by grassroots organizations like the Ministry of Ideas, a think tank that began with informal meetings among groups of entrepreneurs reflecting on the economic meltdown; and the previously mentioned collective known as "the Anthill," which organized the first National Forum or National Assembly in 2009. The movement was situated outside of the official political institutions—parliament, parties, and so on—and the public presumably would not have accepted being excluded from a process that they started and rightfully understood to belong to them. From that point of view, the fact that the second National Forum was organized by the Constitutional Committee did not so much signal a closing down of the process as it testified to the powerful momentum created by civil society in generating new demands and having them met by preexisting institutions.

The Icelandic process illustrates the potential of an open democracy. Although it is difficult to isolate one reason for the Icelandic experiment's ultimate failure, the process reveals several possible sources of weakness.

The modern Viking saga of Iceland's constitutional process is worth taking seriously, nonetheless, because it sets a precedent for the rest of the world. If even a constitutional process—the kind of law-making that even democratic theorists tend to think should be left to closed assemblies of elites—can be designed in open, inclusive ways, surely ordinary law- and policymaking can be made more open too. Jean Jacques Rousseau once wrote of the small and promising nation of his time (Corsica), "I have a feeling that someday this little island will astonish the world." I would argue that Icelanders have already changed it.

8

On the Viability of Open Democracy

The previous chapter sought to illustrate what open democracy could look like by delving into the details of an experiment that has already taken place in Iceland. Nonetheless, even the charitable reader may have a lot of remaining questions about the viability of an ideal of open democracy that has been only partly implemented in a small country and in ways that were ultimately not fully successful. This chapter therefore turns to a host of predictable objections, both to the Icelandic example per se and, more generally, to the open democracy paradigm. These objections include: (1) the fact that the Icelandic process ultimately didn't succeed in putting in place a democracy closer to the open democracy model this book advocates for; (2) the issue of whether the size and heterogeneity of a country would get in the way; (3) the issue of the competence of non-elected representatives; (4) the risk of capture of open institutions by powerful bureaucracies and interest groups; (5) the possible illiberalism of more majoritarian institutions; (6) the lack of accountability of a non- or less electoral democracy at the systems level (not just that of the representatives themselves, a question already partly addressed in chapter 4); and (7) the possibly time-consuming nature of decision-making under open democracy. The chapter ends on a more general reflection about the transition from classically representative to open democracy.

On the Alleged Failure of the Icelandic Experiment

The Icelandic process was, in some respects, a "beautiful failure."[1] But what does this failure tell us more generally about the viability—both the feasibility and the sustainability—of an open democracy model? One reading is that the failure *vindicates* the model, if Parliament stalled precisely because its members correctly surmised that existing representatives and parties would lose power, or at the very least face a considerable reconfiguration of it under the new constitutional scheme. If correct, this conclusion simply suggests that in order to get from existing systems to open democracies we need recourse to things like initiatives and citizen-initiated referendums in order to force reforms that chasten parties' and legislators' abilities to manipulate democratic processes to insulate them against citizen sanction.

On the other hand, the failure of the experiment may instead, or perhaps also, reflect some flaws in the version of open democracy envisioned in the Icelandic draft constitutional proposal. After all, it is not easy to draft constitutional provisions that are actually workable and enforceable. In the French Convention on Climate Change one of the main challenges citizens were confronted with was, similarly, the difficulty of attaining the degree of precision for their proposals to count as "legal texts" that could be directly implemented "without filter." While I personally do not think that the Icelandic Parliament's stalling had much to do with a problem of wording (though that was certainly used as an excuse by some critics), especially as legal experts were brought in to reformulate provisions at the end of the process, there is a genuine question as to what is the best way to tap citizens' collective intelligence and ensure that the laws, policies, and solutions they offer are actually workable. Here the answer is likely more democratic experimentation as we still have too little evidence, besides the obvious requirement of space, time, facilitation, and access to experts, about the kind of deliberative formats and work procedures that are most conducive to quality citizens' work. All in all, therefore, the Icelandic (relative) failure is not a definitive proof that open democracy is unachievable or unsustainable. Things could have gone differently.

Objections to the Generalizability of the Icelandic Case

Conversely, to the extent that the Icelandic case was, in some crucial respects, rather successful, its generalizability is far from obvious. Iceland is, in many respects, a best-case scenario, taking place in a rather stable and culturally homogenous democracy, one of the wealthiest, most educated countries in

---

1. I owe this central objection and suggestions as to how to answer it to points beautifully made by Lisa Disch in her wonderful and generous comments on the manuscript (personal communication, February 24, 2019).

the world, and one with the highest Internet penetration in the world. The fact that the process partly worked there does not guarantee that it would work anywhere else, in part or at all.

The empirical lesson of Iceland as this book describes it—that more truly democratic forms of representation (or more participation on some other people's readings) is a good idea—needs to be made with caution. If we consider that producing a good constitutional text is only the first step and that an equally important second step is to be able to implement the constitution in a feasible way, then the Icelandic experience may well suggest that when there is too much participation, or at least too much participation of a certain kind, then it is possible that the incumbent politicians will not implement the constitution. More research needs to be conducted to explore the ways in which the rift between actors of the constitutional process and incumbent political elites harmed the experience's potential. Some (Hudson 2018) suggest that one of the reasons why the proposal could be produced to begin with was because political parties were prevented from, or refrained from, entering the process. But many signs indicate that, on the other hand, losing the good will of the political class and the support of parties may have ultimately cost the Constitutional Council its credibility and a chance for its crowdsourced proposal to make it through Parliament.

But even if we assume that the Icelandic design could have accommodated incumbent elites better than it did, many authors have cautioned against public participation in constitution-making processes in a variety of contexts. William Partlett documents how the use of extraordinary "constituent" assemblies (distinct from ordinary legislatures) and popular referendums—characteristic of what he calls "popular constitution-making"—too often play into the hands of charismatic politicians with authoritarian tendencies and ultimately lead to constitutional dictatorships in many Central and Eastern European countries (Partlett 2012). Nathan Brown argues that in the Arab world the increasing publicity of constitutional processes from the second half of the twentieth century onward gave "a boost to the Islamic inflationary trend in constitutional texts" (Brown 2016: 385). "Publicity" is characterized by Brown as a type of formal popular participation and blames it for illiberal consequences in the Arab case. Abrak Saati (2015), finally, denounces the benefits of participation in constitutional processes as a "myth" in most of the case studies she reviews.

Such warnings should certainly be heeded when considering exporting the Icelandic model. That said, it is worth emphasizing that participation in these earlier case studies has a much looser sense and does not necessarily measure up to high standards of democracy (from the use of "referendums," which are easy to turn into plebiscites, to the practice of "publicity," which only very partially empowers citizens). In any case, it is indeed plausible that the Icelandic design is mostly likely to be replicable in already stable and advanced democracies, rather than newly born ones and transitioning regimes.

That said, there are two objections to the generalizability of the Icelandic case that are less well taken and that I would like to briefly touch on: the size and homogeneity objections. Do we have any reasons to think that the Icelandic democratic design would work for larger countries and less homogeneous populations? Let me take these two objections in turn.

THE OBJECTION FROM SIZE

Modern Iceland is a tiny nation of 329,000 people. The objection from size is consequently rather natural. Yet I think in some respects it is the least intelligible, unless one takes it to boil down to a second objection, the objection from homogeneity, which is addressed below. Indeed, on the face of it, the Icelandic combination of various democratic innovations (a National Forum, a Constitutional Council made up of regular citizens, the use of crowdsourcing platforms and social media, etc.) seems easily scalable. It is precisely the use of various forms of democratic representation, as opposed to an appeal to the masses at all times, that renders this model scalable to countries of all sizes.

There may indeed be issues of data manageability for the drafters seeking direct popular input in large countries where the crowdsourcing moment would be likely to generate hundreds of thousands or even millions of comments. But this is something that new technologies, such as data-sensing software, or trained armies of analysts who would sift through and organize the input, could arguably take care of so that the constitution-drafters would only have to process a manageable amount of structured information. Mark Tushnet remarks that the Icelandic exercise in constitution-making put an end to the idea that inclusiveness of the population can only be done vicariously, via the representativeness of the drafting body. Instead the Icelandic example showed, in his view, that it is possible to open the process to all interested in joining it, via the technique of crowdsourcing. As he puts it, "One can imagine similar crowdsourced drafting processes even for nations larger than Iceland" (Tushnet 2013: 1994).

As it turns out, France—with a population of 67 million people—succeeded in implementing, in record time (a few weeks) and on a relative budget (11 million euros) a country-wide two-month-long deliberative process, called the Great National Debate that involved a crowdsourcing moment that generated close to 2 million comments and suggestions, which were then synthesized to help public policymaking (it can be debated whether any of this was done well, but the point is that it seems feasible). Before I turn to this example, which I observed close-up and for which I can therefore provide some first-person perspective, I should mention two examples of inclusive democracy at scale that in and of themselves already validate the hypothesis that more inclusive forms of democracy at scale are perfectly conceivable.[2]

2. I thank Tiago Peixoto for bringing those important examples to my attention.

The first example are the *gram sabhas* of rural India, which regularly involve up to 800 million people (out of 1.3 billion), many of them illiterate and very poor. In a fascinating and richly descriptive book, sociologist Paromita Sanyal and economist Vijayendra Rao (2018) report on these village meetings taking place at least twice a year all over India in the silence between elections, ever since a constitutional amendment to the constitution in 1992 rendered them mandatory. In these open meetings, which the authors see as a form of "oral democracy," individuals of all education levels can air grievances about their leaders and bring them to accountability. *Gram sabhas* are also the place where individuals can more generally voice their needs and share personal stories of hardships as well as share practical information and provide elements of solution about local problems. Most important, *gram sabhas* allow people to contest government's measurement of poverty as well as definitions of exclusion and the allocation of public resources, therefore engaging in what it is hard not to see as genuine deliberation about the meaning of justice.[3]

The second example includes the National Public Policy Conferences in Brazil, which have been characterized as "the world's largest participatory and deliberative experiment known to date" (Pogrebinschi 2013: 220). They gather together millions of Brazilians at all three levels of the Brazilian federation with the main objective of providing societal inputs into the design and implementation of public policy on issues ranging from health to the economy to education to security to human rights and social assistance (and many other issues). Like the *gram sabhas,* they involve millions of people, though fewer in proportion to the larger population (to date around 5 million out of a population of 209 million have participated in the seventy-three national public policy conferences that took place since 2003).[4] But, unlike the Indian *gram sabhas,* the Brazilian conferences are designed to scale from the municipal to the state and, ultimately, national level. The National Conferences, first summoned to convene by the executive branch of the country, are indeed preceded by deliberative rounds at the municipal, state, and regional levels whose aggregate results are then the object of deliberation in the national conference, which is attended by the delegates from the previous rounds. The end product is a document containing the guidelines for the design of public policy.[5]

The Brazilian process is remarkable for its ability to translate bottom-up demands first formulated at the local level all the way up to the national level through various layers of representative deliberation between citizens and

---

3. The authors sometimes seem unsure whether the exchanges they observe measure to what they see as the demanding standards of deliberative democracy (in particular because of the inequality status between village members and government officials). My reading is that they often do, even as the conditions are not always ideal.

4. Source: https://participedia.net/method/5450.

5. Source: https://participedia.net/method/5450.

members of government. This process has been successfully conducted at the scale of the fifth largest and sixth most populous country in the world since at least the new Constitution of 1988 (and especially under Lula). Between 1988 and 2009, eighty such national conferences were held.

These two examples strongly suggest that meaningful participation of a discursive type at the large scale has long been possible in immense, populous, and diverse countries like India and Brazil. I now turn to the Great National Debate, which is in some ways an intermediary case between the *gram sabhas* and the Brazilian conferences. Like the *gram sabhas* the Great National Debate tried to cultivate local deliberation, though it failed to generate as much mass participation (proportional to the national population) and was not particularly successful at reaching the poorest or less involved in electoral politics. Meanwhile, like the Brazilian Conferences, the Great National Debate tried to scale up and connect the regional to the national levels but did so without resulting in a clear set of policy recommendations.[6]

I focus on the French case study rather than the other two essentially because of my first-hand knowledge of it (and my comparative lack of familiarity with the others). Taking place in a wealthy and advanced democracy with a highly literate and digitally well-connected population, the Great National Debate provides a sort of best-case scenario for inclusive democracy at scale but in a country that, unlike Iceland, is large and heterogenous. I now explore that case study in some greater detail.

In December 2018, President Macron decided to address the crisis of the Yellow Vests, which erupted over a gas tax increase, via a deliberative democratic strategy: the "Great National Debate." In addition to promising 10 billion euros in social aid (including a 100-euro raise of the minimum wage), Macron penned a letter to the nation published on January 13, 2019, in which he put thirty-five questions, grouped under four themes, directly to the public. The four themes included taxation, state services and organization, the ecological transition, and democracy and participation.

What did this experiment in large-scale deliberation look like? Part of the challenge the French government set for itself, besides the rushed two-month time line, was the sheer scale and scope of the event. It is one thing to organize mass referendums, in which all people have to do is cast a vote on a predetermined issue after a systems-wide "deliberation" taking place in the anarchic and self-organizing ways described by Habermas (1996). It is another thing to ask millions of citizens to deliberate with each other in an intentional and somewhat

---

6. Essentially for lack of a crowning National Conference in charge of doing that work of synthesis. Instead President Macron himself chose what he deemed worthy of implementing. This mistake was only partly corrected by the creation, a few months later, of a Citizen Convention on the topic of Climate Change.

structured way on the scale of a large nation, even on a restricted agenda of four but nevertheless large and important questions. Past democratic experiments of the kind were still few and far between at the time. The most promising ones had taken place in smaller and / or homogenous countries—Iceland (see chapter 7), Canada, Ireland—and often on single issues. The most recent precedent was barely a few months old, with about 1,000 town hall meetings across France on the topic of Europe, but those had been conducted largely under the radar of the media and public perception. Unsurprisingly, many observers could thus confidently predict that the Great Debate could not be successfully conducted within the announced time frame and was going to end in disaster.

Here is what ultimately happened. Around 10,000 town hall meetings involving anywhere between 10 and 300 people took place all over the territory; 18,847 grievance books were written in more than 16,000 municipalities; twenty-one randomly selected assemblies of (in expectation) a hundred citizens or so were organized, including thirteen in the thirteen regions of France, seven in the five French overseas territories, and one among the youth (35-year-old adults or younger) at the national level; and four thematic conferences (gathering intermediary bodies' representatives) were organized at the national level on each of the four themes delineated by President Macron. Meanwhile the online governmental platform gathered 1.9 million contributions; 16,874 emails and mails were received; and 5,400 contributions were gathered at "proximity stands" located in train stations and post offices across the country. In total, somewhere between 500,000 and 1.5 million people took part directly in some way in the Great National Debate and generated 700,000 pages of contributions.

At the end of the process, on April 25, 2019, Macron announced a series of measures in response to the first syntheses of the Great Debate, officially rolled out by the Prime Minister on April 8 in an hours-long state ceremony covered by French TV. These measures included further tax cuts, decentralization from the state to the regions and municipalities, a lowering of the threshold for the signature numbers that trigger the so-called "RIP" (referendum whose initiative is shared by parliaments and citizens), the implementation of the RIC at the local level, the abolition of l'ENA—the elite administrative school that trained Macron himself and which is frequently the target of anti-elitist sentiment in France—a reform of the CESE to include in its makeup a share of randomly selected citizens, and the creation of a randomly selected citizen assembly of 150 people to debate the green transition over the summer and fall 2019, with the goal of having their proposals submitted to Parliament and / or a referendum in the Spring 2020 (this assembly became the much delayed Convention on Climate Change).

The Great Debate—both process and outcome—has been criticized from every side, often rightly, and partly shunned by the very people because of

whom it was started (the Yellow Vests and corresponding demographic population). Yet the French Great National Debate also presents some very interesting
and successful aspects, if only in the execution and completion of what some
predicted initially was a logistical impossibility and a disaster-in-the-making.[7]
Let me focus here on the part that generated the most challenges.

One of the main logistical challenges was the organization of twenty-one
randomly selected citizens' assemblies of one hundred people. In practice
anywhere between 28 and 130 persons showed up, for a grand total of 1,400
citizens. The design was more ambitious than the Icelandic National Forum
since these assemblies met for a day and a half and were structured and rather
heavily facilitated in order to be deliberative and co-creative rather than mostly
aggregative. Unsurprisingly, the organization of these twenty-one regional
assemblies, which all had to be selected following the same procedures and
the same protocol, and had to take place at about the same time, was what
demanded the most work on the part of the governmental mission in charge of
organizing the Great National Debate. The recruitment protocol turned out to
be identical only in metropolitan France as for various reasons (including logistical) it turned out not to be possible or desirable (according to the authorities)
to apply random selection in the DOM-TOM (French ultramarine territories,
such as Guadeloupe or Martinique). Two established private service providers specialized in the organization of public and private consultations were
mobilized to run the meetings (Missions Publiques and Res Publica). In the
end, manpower was too scarce, so the assemblies had to be distributed over
two weekends rather than just one (March 15–16 and 23–24 respectively). But
remarkably, the process took place without major glitches for the most part.
Participants report high levels of satisfaction about the organizations of these
assemblies (except for places where the food or wine was judged bad or too
scarce—this is France after all).

The other major difficulty was the so-called restitution: the synthesis of
everything that was said during the Great Debate in a manner that needed to be
exhaustive, transparent, credible, and timely. The synthesis of the free contributions alone (made online, in grievance books, or reported through proximity
stations) required the collaboration of the French National Public Library,
which had to digitize thousands of grievance books (that alone took a month)

---

7. Full disclosure: I was among the initial skeptics and was stunned by the government's
decision to try and pull off something of this scale in less than two months. For anyone who
knows France and its bureaucratic, sometimes downright Kafkaesque organizational hurdles to
anything, this will not appear an unreasonable reaction. In fact, all the people involved in the
organization of the Great Debate I have interviewed since then shared this initial feeling and
describe the scheduling pace as "vertiginous," the workload as "demential," and various logistical aspects as "a nightmare." Many complained about not sleeping or not seeing their spouse and
family for two months.

and private service providers specializing in large data analyses. New technologies and concepts were mobilized in order to render readable what amounted to 100,000 pages of PDF input. The use of "knowledge trees," in particular—a concept invented by philosopher Michel Serres in the 1970s—made it possible to capture in a synthetic manner the participants' thoughts on various questions without losing the fine-grained distinctions between contributions (see also Landemore in progress for more details).

In my view, the French case, which is a rich trove of data still in the process of being analyzed by a consortium of researchers, proves that size need not be an issue, though it also suggests that it helps to have a strong state, an efficient bureaucracy, a competitive ecosystem of private service providers capable of working closely with government and innovating on the fly, as well a lot of political will and investment.

THE OBJECTION FROM HOMOGENEITY

The question of whether homogeneity of the population is a prerequisite for this kind of experiment to work is, in my view, the real crux of the matter. By homogeneity, here, I mean roughly value or cultural homogeneity. Very imperfect proxies for it include ethnic and religious diversity. Here again the case of the French Great National Debate—taking place in a globalized multicultural and in many ways polarized country—should go some way toward answering that question.[8]

First, however, let me explore an interesting thought. We tend to assume a little too quickly that the causal relationship between homogeneity and democratization goes only one way, namely that a certain degree of preexisting cultural homogeneity is what renders greater democratization of institutions possible. But it is entirely possible, at least logically, that the causal arrow goes the other way as well, from democracy to greater cultural homogeneity. Consider Iceland's own history of the conversion to Christianity at a time when growing religious pluralism threatened to destroy the community.

The medieval chronicler Ari Thorgilsson in his *Íslendingabók* (book of Icelanders) written in the twelfth century recounts how Icelanders peacefully switched from paganism to Christianity in the summer of 999 (or 1000).[9] At the time, the population was becoming increasingly divided between traditional pagans and the growing number of Christian converts. The king of Norway, who had vested interests in seeing Iceland turn to Christianism, got increasingly

8. The case of the Indian village meetings probably also offers some illuminating answers, but I do not know enough about the case to use it on that particular question.

9. A translation is available here: https://en.wikisource.org/wiki/Translation:%C3%8Dsle ndingab%C3%B3k. The key passage is in chapter 8.

frustrated at the pagans' resistance and was ready to use violence to enforce swift and full conversion of the island. Two local chieftains, however, convinced him to let them try a more peaceful method. They spoke at the annual Althing that year and, according to Thorgilsson: "it is said that it was amazing how well they spoke." Seemingly impressed by their arguments, Icelanders then entrusted the decision about what to do to their heathen priest and chieftain, Thorgeir Thorkelsson of Ljósavatn. After one night of meditation (perhaps more), Thorgeir called the assembly and rendered his conclusion that Icelanders should embrace Christianity for the sake of unity and social peace. Thorgeir's argument was that Icelanders should

> not let those prevail who are most anxious to be at each other's throats, but reach such a compromise in these matters that each shall win part of his case and let all have one law and one faith. It will prove true, if we break the law in pieces, that we break the peace in pieces too. (Karlsson 2000: 33)

Thorgeir then concluded that all men should become Christians and be baptized. He also decreed that pagan sacrifice, the exposure of infants, and the eating of horse flesh (all pagan practices) would be tolerated for the time being if practiced in private (Karlsson 2000: 33; see also Winroth 2012: 135). The people agreed and many were subsequently baptized.

This peaceful transition to Christianity is astonishing. From Thorgilsson's account, it appears that the Icelanders chose to convert to Christianism on the basis of something like "the forceless force of the better argument," as expressed in the public speeches of the two Christian chieftains and the heathen priest and chieftain. The proposal to switch was thus argued for and justified to the whole community, before the law was passed. While Thorgilsson's account leaves out the reactions of the participants in the assembly and the way the decision was ultimately made (it is not clear whether a vote took place or whether the heathen priest simply decreed the new law), it appears as if the community raised no objections to the decision, and something like a general consensus to endorse it prevailed. Iceland might thus be one of the very few countries in the world, if not the only one, that was Christianized by something like public consent. As a result of what appears to be as close to a consensual decision as was probably possible in the tenth century, today's Iceland is 90 percent Christian. Perhaps as an additional result of this early commitment to equality and consensus, Iceland is also one of the most tolerant and open societies in the world.

Consider also the much better documented history of Switzerland, a country characterized both by a long tradition of direct democracy, including frequent popular votes, and by the coexistence of a great number of linguistic, cultural, and religious minorities. One of the American Anti-Federalists gives us a possibly prescient hypothesis as to how these two features are related in his reply to the Federalists' constitutional proposal. Judging their proposal of a representative government inimical to his own preferred model of direct democracy, A [Maryland] Farmer, a nom de plume behind which plausibly hid John Francis Mercer, a non-signing member of the Constitutional Convention, evokes Switzerland as a much better model of a system, "where the people personally exercise the powers of government" (Storing 1981: 267).

Mercer first dismisses various claims invoked by his opponents to invalidate Switzerland as an example for North Americans:

> But we are told that Swisserland, *should be no example for us . . . they are few in number it is said*—this is not true—*they are more numerous than we are—They cover a small spot of territory*—this is also not true . . . But it is also said *they are a poor, frugal* people—as to their poverty that is likewise untrue. (Storing 1981: 48, italics in the original)

Though Switzerland was smaller and less populous than the United States already at the time, the difference in scale was not as large as it is today. In 1790, Switzerland counted fewer than 1.7 million people[10] versus 3.9 million for the United States.[11] Switzerland had roughly the same territory as today, but the United States only comprised thirteen colonies on the East Coast. So, in the late eighteenth century the comparison actually made sense.

Mercer then focuses on the main advantage of Swiss practices: the fact that they allow for the peaceful management of a great deal of disagreement and religious divides:

> they [the Swiss] soon banished the daemon of discord, *and Protestant and Papist sat down under the peaceful shade of the same tree,* whilst in every surrounding State and kingdom, the son was dragging the father, and brothers, their brothers, to the scaffold, under the sanction of those distinctions. Thus these happy Helvetians have in peace and security beheld all the rest of Europe become a common slaughterhouse. (Storing 1981: 267)

Mercer thus traces the peaceful coexistence of plural communities in Switzerland, at a time where civil wars were tearing apart the rest of monarchical Europe, to the practice of deliberative self-rule.

One may also want to contrast contemporary Switzerland and Belgium. Where modern Switzerland is "a paradigmatic case of political integration" (Deutsch 1976, cited in and translated by Moeckli 2018: 338), Belgium is profoundly divided between its two linguistic communities, to such a point that partition is a plausible future. Why the difference? It can arguably be traced

---

10. Source: https://en.wikipedia.org/wiki/Demographics_of_Switzerland.

11. Source: https://en.wikipedia.org/wiki/Demographic_history_of_the_United _States#Population_in_1790.

to another crucial difference, namely the fact that whereas Switzerland is to this day "the most elaborate system of direct mechanisms in the world, with numerous popular votes held every few months," Belgium by contrast is "one of the very few European states that provide for no popular vote processes at all" (Moeckli 2018: 338). In other words, the lack of mechanisms for popular voice and vote may well explain the greater incapacity of Belgium at dealing with pluralism.

These two brief histories are suggestive. Iceland's history points to an interesting possibility, namely that *political* practices and processes of egalitarianism, deliberation, and consensus created Iceland's cultural, social, and even religious homogeneity—rather than the other way around. What Switzerland's history suggests is that, to the extent that diversity subsists, it is rendered more manageable by the use of democratic practices, perhaps especially of a more participatory nature.

In other words, a certain degree of cultural, social, and religious homogeneity could well be the result of a widespread commitment to broad democratic principles, rather than a limiting precondition for it. If true, this conjecture would have important implications for answering the objection that Iceland is too homogenous to prove anything about the feasibility of open democratic practices in more divided countries. Indeed, it could imply that democratizing the political process could ultimately bring people closer together, culturally and socially, perhaps even religiously, rather than worsen existing divides.

Regardless of whether this conjecture is plausible or not, there is evidence that quality deliberation on sensitive political issues can occur even in deeply divided societies. Deliberative processes have been successfully implemented in divided societies such as South Africa, Turkey, Bosnia, Belgium, and Northern Ireland. In a recent survey article, Curato et al. generally document "growing empirical evidence that deliberative practices can flourish in deeply divided societies to good effect, be it in association with, or at some distance from, power-sharing arrangements" (Curato et al. 2017: 33). Under the right conditions, deliberation in divided societies can help to bridge the deep conflicts across religious, national, racial, and ethnic lines (e.g., O'Flynn 2007; Luskin et al. 2014; Kanra 2009; Vasilev 2015).

In the case of Iceland itself it is also worth remarking that distant observers may be prone to overestimate the value homogeneity and consensual nature of Icelandic politics. Iceland certainly is not Lebanon, Israel, or even the United States in terms of cultural diversity. Yet, as in many other countries, the surface homogeneity reveals, upon closer inspection, much more underlying, fractal-like disagreement. These disagreements were also reflected on the Constitutional Council, where intense discussions about the National Church or even more trivially whether the constitutional text should include a preamble, led to bitter rivalries, intrigues, disputes, accusations, and often tears. Again, it is in the use of certain procedures—including non-obviously "political" ones, like singing together at the beginning and end of meetings as well as going out for drinks after particularly unpleasant interactions, that the Constitutional Council members found a way to remain united even in the face of deep disagreement and to produce a text that they could all stand behind.[12] In that respect, the fact that the expert group couldn't agree among themselves and settled instead on producing two distinct documents suggests that finding consensus is a matter of procedures and commitment, not just of preexisting value or cultural homogeneity.

While Iceland's nearly ideal democratic circumstances, small size, and population homogeneity can be used as objections to the generalizability of the lessons that can be derived from it, they at least allow for a proof of concept. It is not thus impossible to imagine that radically inclusive forms of politics would be feasible even in more heterogeneous countries. In fact, it is precisely in that kind of context that inclusiveness would be most needed, as a key condition of the legitimacy of both the constitutional process and its outcome. As I have argued, the French case gives us some idea of what the efforts to make that happen could look like in a large diverse country.

The French Great National Debate of 2019 also illustrates the possibility of respectful, productive debates among people of all walks of life both from self-selected groups (demographically skewed toward the older, more educated crowd, but still) all the way to randomly selected groups, in which very different political views inevitably came in close contact. One could argue that the French case only proves so much given that immigration—the hot-button issue of French politics—was not officially on the discussion table (it was deemed too sensitive by the government). The reality is that it was discussed anyway in practically all venues (from the online platform, grievance book, and proximity stations to the twenty-one randomly selected assemblies), with a marked difference in tone and content depending on how anonymous and deliberative the context was.

The Objection from Incompetence

Let me now turn to more general objections to both the feasibility and normative desirability of an open democracy model. The first predictable objection to open democracy is that, given the increasing complexity of the world, it is irrational to want to increase the level of openness to ordinary citizens of our central political institutions. In the face of increasing complexity, what we

12. All these details were reported to me in private conversations with various members of the Constitutional Council.

need is increased specialization and division of labor, not putting the amateurs in charge.

This argument assumes that increasing complexity can only be faced with greater division of labor. My answer is that, first, at the general level at which polities must face increasing complexity, they need to address it as a bundle of its effects, which are largely unpredictable. At that level, what polities are really dealing with is thus better characterized as great uncertainty: uncertainty about the kinds of problems generated by increasing complexity, uncertainty about the kinds of solutions that could address them, and uncertainty about what is acceptable among those solutions for the populations at stake. In the face of uncertainty, I have argued in previous work that it is best to distribute power equally and inclusively (Landemore 2014c). Only then does one ensure that at any point in time one maximizes the probability of tapping the right perspectives, information, and ideas, in other words, the collective and distributed intelligence of the group.

Second, it is important to emphasize that increasing citizens' participation in policy- and law-making need not mean rejecting experts and specialists. It simply means giving them an advisory role rather than a decisional one. The idea is to have "experts on tap, not on top." Most democratic innovations involve the possibility for the ordinary citizens involved in them to consult extensively with a wide pool of experts, sometimes of their own choosing. For example, in the French Convention on Climate Change, more than 140 experts were auditioned by the citizens and a support group of a dozen experts (including economists, lawyers, and climate change specialists) was made available to the citizens when they had questions, or when they needed information or help to formulate their proposals as legal texts.

Second, it is not the case that opening up democracy to a class of political "amateurs" would necessarily entail amateurism of the resulting law- and policymaking. This conclusion is simply false and premised on a simplistic model of the mechanics of collective decision-making, assuming a linear relation between individual input and collective output. In fact, there are good reasons to believe that democratic decision-making is synergetic and the gains in collective intelligence it permits, under the right conditions, exponential (see, e.g., Landemore 2013a; Goodin and Spiekermann 2018). Let me rehearse the main point of my own research here. Our understanding of what makes for competence in problem-solving bodies like legislatures has long been premised on the wrong understanding of collective intelligence. If it is the case that the diversity of the deliberative and problem-solving body matters more than the average competence of its individual members (Page 2007), then political processes and bodies that involve ordinary citizens should actually outperform processes and bodies that include only experts (Landemore 2012, 2013a). Even as the individual participant's level of "amateurism" may increase at the outset, the level of collective expertise may rise during deliberation.

This theoretical point is borne out by a vast empirical literature at both the macro- and micro-levels.[13] At the macro-level, a growing body of research highlights the positive association between citizen engagement in rulemaking and economic prosperity (Johns and Saltane 2016; OECD 2009; Gurin 2014). A World Bank study surveying 185 countries shows that citizen engagement in rulemaking is associated with higher-quality regulation, stronger democratic regimes, and less corrupt institutions (Johns and Saltane 2016).[14] Of course, regulations are just one type of policy area, but the study nonetheless sheds important light on the quality of citizen engagement in policymaking and the economic and democratic consequences.

At the mezzo-level of supranational communities, studies also show a clear correlation between citizen engagement in policymaking and good governance outcomes. In an econometric analysis of 5,180 randomly chosen households from a subset of Indian villages, Besley, Pande, and Rao (2005, cited in Sanyal and Rao 2018: 6) find that when *gram sabhas* (local deliberative meetings) are held, governance sharply improves, as measured by the better targeting of BPL (Below Poverty Line) cards, which provide an array of public benefits in India, to landless and illiterate individuals who need them. Holding a *gram sabha* raised the probability of receiving a BPL card by 25 percent. The reason for this outcome is that the lists of beneficiaries identified by the national government are publicly verified and corrected by the members of the local communities during the meetings, including sometimes by reevaluating locally the criteria of who counts as poor.

Additionally, to the extent that success is measured by people's satisfaction with the results, studies have shown that there are also higher levels of public satisfaction with policies that have been developed in a participatory way (Fischer 2016). Voice and participation are also correlated with perceived trustworthiness of decision-makers and subsequent acceptance of their decisions (Terwel et al. 2010). Finally, participatory governance has been shown to increase willingness to pay taxes (Touchton, Wampler, and Peixoto 2019; Sjoberg et al. 2019).

At the micro-level, myriad experiments involving "democratic innovations" of all kinds show that involving ordinary citizens, when done well, usually improves the decision-making process and is time- and cost-efficient, including in comparison with the use of expert commissions (Dryzek et al. 2019; Fishkin

---

13. I borrow here from the exhaustive report by Claudia Chwalisz in *The People's Verdict* (2018).

14. The authors develop a composite score based on six factors: publication of proposed regulations; consultation on proposed regulations; reporting back on results of consultations; conducting regulatory impact assessments; presence of a specialized body to review impact assessments; and publication of regulatory impact assessments.

2018[15]). One goal of the chapter on Iceland in this book is to establish the ways in which including ordinary citizens in a constitutional process can improve the quality of the resulting constitutional proposal, over and above expert proposals.

Let me finally make a narrower point about the supposed need for greater professionalism in the face of increasing complexity. Assuming it is the case that complexity is increasing (as opposed to our perception and understanding of it), there are two possible attitudes one can have in response. One can choose to divide the problem into subparts that are easier to manage and let professionals handle those parts independently. Or one can face the complexity by *first* processing it as a package of variables and only then, after this first generalist processing, turning over certain portions of it to subcommittees and experts. The first solution has been tried in the economic realm, where legislatures have surrendered complete control over some key variables (interest rates as a way to control inflation and ensure price stability) to independent agencies (i.e., central banks). It is not obvious at all that this has been the right solution. Even some former central bankers now make the case that we may have gone too far in granting economic powers to independent agencies (Tucker 2018). Complexity need not entail a greater fragmentation of the first line of response at the level of the polity. On the contrary, societies need a unified way to look at complex problems so they can process and break them down differently, along differently salient lines, at different times. In the 1970s, the solution to economic instability was, probably, inflation control via an independent group of economic experts adjusting interest rates as needed. Today, however, the solution might look different, as inflation in stable democracies has moved off the agenda and experts' obsession with interest rates may have actually hampered growth and recovery in countries hit by the 2008 financial crisis. In order to retain their power of adaptation in the face of uncertainty, democracies need to keep a centralized and unified clearinghouse where they process the world's complexity as a whole and keep accountable the experts and independent agencies to whom certain powers are temporarily granted.

The Risk of Capture by the Permanent Bureaucracy and Interest Groups

Another worry, in keeping with the fear of incompetence and amateurism, is that even if ordinary citizens could measure up to the task, they would be too easily captured by the staff of enduring administrative superstructures

---

15. Jim Fishkin, "Can Randomly Selected Groups of People Decide Complex Issues, Bring Back Trust in Democracy?" *Wall Street Journal*, August 7, 2018, http://www.constitutionnet.org /news/op-ed-can-randomly-selected-groups-people-decide-complex-issues-bring-back-trust -democracy. Last accessed August 7, 2018.

and the experts, or by outside experts, interest groups, and lobbyists brought in to advise them. This kind of capture is possible and a risk to almost any institutional design. But wouldn't the institutions of an open democracy be even more vulnerable? If so, we would end up with a "simulative" rather than open democracy, where politicians consult the people on a growing range of issues but really most decisions would be taken "off the frame" and made by experts (because ordinary citizens can't deal with the complexity anyway). Popular participation in politics would be superficial window-dressing for the purpose of legitimacy-buying, with the obvious effect of reinforcing citizens' disenchantment and cynicism toward the system. The long-term effects would likely be a turn to either populism, authoritarianism, or a combination of both.

Similarly, elements of direct participation introduced under the principle of "participation rights" are often dismissed as overly populist or too easily captured by powerful interests. Frances Rosenbluth and Ian Shapiro (2018), for example, build on the California case to argue that citizens' initiatives are an unmitigated disaster which, under the guise of introducing direct democracy and empowering ordinary citizens and vulnerable minorities, ultimately empowers those who know how to game the system (corporations, powerful interest groups, and lobbies).

But note that the citizens' initiative, in my model of open democracy, as in the Swiss model that partly inspires it, is indirect rather than direct, allowing for deliberation and bargaining between the parties involved (democratic representatives and citizens) *before* the popular vote is taken. This is a very different model than the admittedly dysfunctional California one, which is too crude, probably too direct, and too purely aggregative. In the California system, the ballot initiative process gives citizens a way to propose laws and constitutional amendments without the need for an intermediary, let alone deliberative steps involving either the governor or the legislature. In other words, the citizens' initiative goes straight to the ballot. This direct system, as we know, is extremely vulnerable to capture by corporations and lobbies (Papadopoulos 1998).

By contrast, the built-in nature of deliberative intermediary steps, in open democracy, should make it much less attractive to lobbies to buy signatures and votes, since they might lose control of the law or constitutional amendment's exact formulation or even the referendum as a whole at the deliberative stage of the process. This is not to say that such a system is foolproof, especially when obscene amounts of money are involved. In Switzerland the Swiss healthcare industry has managed to game the system despite the deliberative elements just pointed out, swaying public opinions through well-financed public campaigns.[16] But at this point any system would need to rely on additional account-

---

16. See Immergut 1992.

ability mechanisms, including laws regulating the role of money in politics, and so it is not an indictment per se of an open democracy that it too might be vulnerable to some degree of capture absent such mechanisms.

Finally, let me consider the arguments developed by Arash Abizadeh in his own defense of a bicameral system for Canada, in which the current upper chamber, the Senate, would be abolished in favor of a permanent, randomly appointed and regularly renewed Citizen Assembly. Considering the danger of manipulation of the neophytes brought to power, Abizadeh argues that the available empirical evidence, from the effect of the imposition of term limits on elected legislators in the United States, which led to less experienced legislators, is not conclusive for randomly selected legislators. The clearest effects of introducing such term limits were "the decreased power of legislative-party leaders and increased executive power" (Abizadeh 2020: 12, citing Carey, Niemi, and Powell 1998; Kousser 2005; Carey et al. 2006; Powell 2007; Miller et al. 2011). But as Abizadeh argues, this is not to be feared for randomly selected legislators since "a citizen assembly is less partisan by design, and informational asymmetries with respect to the Cabinet are offset by the chamber's independence" (Abizadeh 2020: 12). In other words, the randomly selected Assembly's non-partisan nature and institutional independence from the executive power should protect it from takeover by the latter.

As to the evidence concerning the influence of outside special interest groups and lobbyists on neophyte elected legislators, Abizadeh reports, it is rather mixed, as the outsiders' comparative informational advantage over neophyte legislators can be offset by the break in the long-term networks and relationships of trust between legislators and lobbyists, leaving the net effect rather unclear (Carey et al. 2006; Mooney 2007; Miller et al. 2011; cf. Kousser 2005: 65–66; cited in Abizadeh 2020: 12). In any case, as Abizadeh further points out, the sortition mechanism inherently protects randomly selected legislators from the influence of lobbyists, which for the most part takes place during election processes, a natural protection that Abizadeh proposes to reinforce "with a legally enforced firewall" protecting lottocratic representatives (and related staff) from lobbyists and other representatives and limiting contact to "official and publicly transparent channels" as well as "an annual accountability audit of assembly members" meant "to ensure strict adherence to anti-corruption codes" (Abizadeh 2020: 12).

Lastly, Abizadeh touches on the risk of bureaucratic capture, suggesting that it could be partly addressed "by separating the assembly's support staff from the executive bureaucracy and protecting the impartiality of their selection process" (Abizadeh 2020: 12).

I naturally side with all these remarks and suggestions. It is also worth emphasizing that if we look at empirical evidence from mini-publics and citizen assemblies around the world, there is, to my knowledge, not a single case of demonstrated capture by elected representatives, experts, bureaucrats, or lobbyists—just the opposite, if anything. In Texas, the land of oil and gas lobbyists, a series of eight deliberative polls organized by James Fishkin as part of an energy planning process ordered by the Texas legislature led to a "renewable energy epiphany" (Galbraith and Price 2013). The fact that as a result of these deliberative polls Texas is now leading the way in renewable energies is not something that could have happened if lobbyists had had their ways.

The Icelandic case, in turn, suggests that genuinely empowered and sufficiently large groups of ordinary citizens[17] are both eager and able to resist a fair amount of external pressures, especially intellectual intimidation by bureaucrats and experts. Though they were handed perfectly viable texts on a silver platter with the intimation that they should simply tweak them at the margin, the twenty-five amateur constitution-makers in the Icelandic experiment rejected the expert drafts and ultimately wrote their own.[18]

The more recent case of the French Convention on Climate Change, as per my direct observations, similarly suggests that ordinary citizens, once empowered, are very protective of their prerogatives and will actively and vocally resist perceived attempts at manipulating them, whether subtly or not so subtly. The advantage of a large enough random sample is that even if a majority in it is (at least outwardly) deferential, there will statistically almost always be strong-headed rebellious personalities to push back on behalf of the group. Several of the 150 members of the Convention, nicely distributed (by chance) over the five working groups, thus heckled experts when they thought they were out of line, either in the form or substance of their recommendations. For example, in one of the plenary sessions of the second session of the Convention, an expert was explaining the benefits of a carbon tax, when he was loudly interrupted by a well-liked troublemaker (a surgeon and provincial notable with a strong, disruptive personality): "Stop treating us like children." It is not clear whether a majority of 150 members were actually entirely skeptical of a carbon tax as a possible solution to cutting carbon emissions.[19] But what is clear is that none of them wanted to be instrumentalized by experts to sell to the larger public a policy that the government failed to pass on its own (after

17. Although in the case of Iceland, the twenty-five Constitutional Council members were not randomly selected, they counted as political "neophytes" on many levels.

18. It is only to the extent that the design did not give them ultimate sovereignty on their own text at the end of the process that legal experts were able to introduce modifications to the text (some of which proved harmful and changed the spirit of the law as the Constitutional Council had intended it; see Landemore 2015 for details).

19. Researchers' questionnaires indicated a majority in favor of a carbon tax as of the second session, a surprising result given the violently anti-carbon tax positions taken by some publicly in plenaries and working groups.

a carbon tax triggered the Yellow Vest revolt in November 2018). Similarly, when facing the director of the sustainable development and environment of Bouygues corporation in one of the speed-dating sessions between experts and citizens that took place during the third meeting of the Convention, the citizens present at that session were not shy about pointing out the conflict of interests in his recommendations. The expert recommended that in order to renovate houses and make them energy-efficient and carbon-neutral, one needed to conduct the renovation of the entire French real estate inventory simultaneously because of the economies of scale that could be realized compared to a piecemeal renovation distributed over time. He also recommended a Marshall plan to train 200,000 people for modern construction work, a carbon tax, and 10–20 percent cuts on social charges that, in his view, made French labor too expensive in the European market (he mentioned cheap Polish labor as a comparison). A tense conversation followed in which the citizens pushed back, in particular, against the idea of making labor cheaper. What is interesting is that, even as the citizens explicitly pointed out the conflict of interests in the discourse of a Bouygues representative pushing for a vast renovation plan and for cheaper labor, both of which the company would be the first to benefit from, the citizens did take seriously the point about economies of scale and the need for educating the work force to new, ecological construction technologies. They rejected, however, the claim about making labor cheaper.

I'll mention a last example from the fourth session of the Convention on Climate Change. The representative of a non-profit association of companies for the environment came to give advice to the working group "Housing." She was giving good advice on the whole, but at some point she slipped into admonishing mode: "You are calling for a lot of expenses. But if what you propose is going to increase the deficit by 10%, the President will say no. He'll say 'I can't sink France.'" The previously mentioned troublemaker exploded: "It's not true. It's your interpretation. Let the President decide. Who is this lady anyway? Please have her introduce herself. Who is she working for?" Later, another citizen, though he disapproved of the outburst, emphasized his support of the first citizen's pushback against the expert: "Telling us to pay attention to financing it's a little quick—of course we will think about it. We will find solutions, I have no doubt. But don't pressure us." I should say that later on, the first citizen came to the defense of the expert on another issue, proving that these kinds of clashes were not the result of a systematic anti-expert posture on the part of citizens but rather an expression of their strong sense of autonomy and right to make up their minds on their own. Given the same kind of prerogatives and independence, any group of randomly selected citizens is similarly likely to stand up for themselves and resist pressure and capture of all kinds.

The Objection from the Possible Illiberalism of More Majoritarian Institutions

Assuming the objections above can be successfully countered, what about the desirability objection? It is now time to return to the objection already mentioned in the introduction, the fear that promoting a purer democratic regime against electoral democracies risks undoing the minority rights protections built into the liberal core of the latter. For some readers, the undemocratic, or at least counter-majoritarian, aspects of electoral, liberal democracy (aka representative democracy) are intended and desirable features, not problems to be solved.

This view explains why scholars like Aziz Huq and Thomas Ginsburg tend to focus on the "constitutional" aspect of the crisis of democracy today, as opposed to its properly democratic aspect. It also explains their seemingly conservative effort to merely shore up and restore the integrity of existing constitutional arrangements in the United States, rather than open them up to meet rising democratic expectations. Their solutions include classic ideas such as establishing independent election bodies, nonpartisan electoral commissions, guaranteeing the effective supervision of electoral processes and guarding against corruption, or reinforcing legal protections of bureaucratic autonomy. The only authentically democratic solutions they offer are more careful and thorough articulations of very basic democratic rights in the Constitution (such as free speech) and a legislative (but supermajoritarian) "escalator" for the authorization of emergency powers.

While prioritizing a strong constitutional order over the democratization of power seems like a legitimate goal, this prioritization is rooted in questionable empirical premises, themselves developed in the context of a particular and contingent history. In the genealogy of our modern representative governments, liberalism came first and democracy second. The idea that democracy is only viable and desirable within the preexisting and constraining parameters of liberalism is a plausible but ultimately just-so story that cannot be falsified (short of re-running history enough times to show that stable democracies can never be born outside of a framework of liberal institutions). This narrative conveniently fits the version of history that has unfolded in the last two hundred years. But beyond this limited amount of evidence we do not know for certain that democracy without the core tenets of liberalism is bound to turn into mob rule and tyranny of the majority. Indeed, we have some evidence—from Classical Athens—that the opposite might be true. It could well be that "basic" democracy—as Ober calls it in contrast to our hybrid version—has in itself the resources to address at least some of the liberals' worries. Adam Przeworski similarly makes the provocative argument that "there are both logical and empirical reasons to question whether supra-majoritarian institutions, such as bicameralism or presidential veto, or counter-majoritarian institutions, such as constitutional courts or independent central banks, are necessary to support the rule of law" (Przeworski 2019: 5). He approvingly quotes Roberto Gargarella (2003), who lists several mechanisms by which a majority can and would want to constrain itself even in the absence of such institutions. He mentions well-established democracies, including the United Kingdom and Sweden, "which have neither a separation of powers nor judicial review of the constitution, and yet in which majorities constrain themselves from violating rights" (Przeworski 2019: 6, citing McGann 2006). Finally, he refers to the work of Dixit, Grossman, and Gull (2000: 533) who demonstrate that "violations of rights are likely to be more egregious in the presence of supra-majoritarian institutions once a government enjoys supra-majority support" (Przeworski 2019: 6). All of this suggests that democracy may well be capable of enjoying the benefits of the rule of law without at least some of the liberal bells and whistles of the constitutional orders we are familiar with.

To the extent that democracy demonstrably needs those liberal constraints, we should, of course, maintain constitutional limits, separation of power, and checks and balances of various kinds on the democratic political process. Open democracy is in principle compatible with basic constitutionalist views. Notice, however, that open democracy would naturally lead to a much more open-ended and revisable theory of constitutionalism. On such a view, the constitution is the basic social contract of a society, which needs to be periodically revisited and possibly modified and amended as needed, perhaps, as Jefferson wanted, once every generation (or about every twenty-five years).

But it is also entirely possible that, by starting with a liberal rather than a democratic framework, the founders of our modern "democracies" have turned the screw too tightly on the elements of popular rule that they have also tried to incorporate (while compounding that mistake by locking the design and throwing away the key with almost impossible-to-revise constitutional entrenchments). My own suspicion is that we do not fully appreciate what democracy is capable of on its own, so to speak, and it would be worth experimenting (cautiously of course) with more democracy, rather than less.[20] In this respect, I find myself very much inspired by Josiah Ober's recent attempt at drawing a clearer distinction between democracy and liberalism (2017), and bringing out the individual merits of the former, including the fact that, unlike liberalism, democracy is a self-sustaining regime form.

Ober's scholarship has thus begun to challenge the view that the tradition of political liberalism, and consequently representative government as its central emanation, is the only ideology or historic system that can protect at least

---

20. Whereas some people advocate "10% less democracy" (Jones 2020), my sense is that we should go for perhaps 50 percent more.

certain individual rights and freedoms. Pre-liberal, non-representative democracy was not all that unstable or even as terribly "illiberal" on the substance (bracketing of course the question of inclusion of non-citizens) as is often feared. Ober makes the compelling case that what he calls "democracy before liberalism"—that is, fifth and fourth century BC Athens—was not the mob rule or dictatorship of the many, as it is often portrayed. Nor was it as "direct" as the Federalists claimed (Ober 2017).[21] Instead, Ober argues, *demokratia*, as such, was able to generate a number of individual rights and rule entrenchments that bear some resemblance to constitutionally protected liberal rights and even the rule of law, and yet preceded the doctrine of liberalism. In other words, democracy may well have the internal resources, under the right conditions, to generate a number of features we have grown accustomed to thinking only liberalism could equip it with.

One of these important features is, centrally, constitutionalism. A reinvented, open form of democracy in the twenty-first century could thus take the familiar features of a constitutional democracy, whereas some fundamental rights are entrenched and protected from, among other things, direct majoritarian will, without endorsing all the added features we have come to associate with representative democracy per se. For example, one could imagine a constitutional democracy in which property and religious rights were not essential or at least not defined in the way familiar to contemporary liberal democracies. One may disagree on the normative desirability of such a regime on other grounds, but it would be nonetheless perfectly democratic and protective of democracy-enhancing individual rights (see also Ober 2017).

One could make the bolder claim, however, that the protection of at least some individual rights—political rights specifically—need not necessarily be entrusted to counter-majoritarian institutions such as constitutions, supreme courts, and the practice of judicial review. They could instead conceivably be entrusted to democratic institutions with a judicial function, such as the large popular juries of Classical Athens (what we would call "mini-publics" today, applied to judicial matters).[22]

21. I argue this point at greater length in chapter 3.

22. Socrates' death at the hands of a popular jury is always, rightly, pointed out as evidence of the danger of such democratic institutions. But one mistake, however tragic, is not necessarily enough to invalidate an entire system, especially as one can read the whole affair as resulting in large part from a strategic decision by Socrates not to avail himself of the safety mechanisms built into the Athenian design (such as the possibility to defend oneself with good arguments and propose a reasonable alternative sentence). Socrates wanted to prove, at his own expense, that Athenian democracy was flawed (as all systems are), and he succeeded all too well, proving more in the eyes of posterity than was strictly needed.

Empirically there is also some evidence of democracies that, at least on the scale of smaller nation-states, have resisted the closure entailed by familiar representative institutions without ipso facto endangering liberal rights. Switzerland remains an outstanding example of a participatory democracy that is at least as pluralist and liberal as its more exclusively representative competitors in the rest of Europe. Lest a critic immediately bring up the infamous referendum on banning the construction of minarets, let me point out that this decision was quickly judged unconstitutional by the Swiss Supreme Court *and never passed into law*. Proponents of constitutional constraints on democracy should not, however, feel validated because in Switzerland, the Supreme Court does have the final say and its decision could have easily been overturned by another popular vote process. In other words, the decision to invalidate the referendum result on minaret banning can ultimately be traced back, in the remarkable Swiss system, to the people themselves. More recently, in the Chiapas in Mexico and in the Northeastern part of Syria, self-organizing communities at the level of entire regions—sometimes extremely plural in ethnic and religious makeup—have demonstrated the viability, including in extremely challenging circumstances, of seemingly non-representative (or at least non-classically representative), decentralized, and indeed barely constitutional forms of politics, where ordinary citizens rather than professional politicians are in charge of daily political decisions.

These recent theoretical and empirical developments suggest that there may be an opportunity to recover some of the accessibility of older, pre-liberal, or more participatory democracies (such as Classical Athens, the Viking parliamentary regime, or modern-day Switzerland) without necessarily endangering the individual and minority rights we moderns care so deeply about, especially in societies as large and diverse as ours. Exploring this opportunity may ultimately mean revisiting our constitutional commitments and perhaps, in certain cases, even rewriting undemocratic or insufficiently democratic national social contracts from scratch.

The Lack of Accountability (at the Systems Level)

One natural objection to the idea of an open democracy in which the role of non-elected assemblies is made central is the problem of political accountability. I have already touched on that issue in chapter 4, where I addressed the accountability issues of non-electoral forms of democratic representation and where I invoked Classical Athens as providing us with numerous non-electoral mechanisms of accountability. Let me here revisit the question of how to make the institutions of an open democracy accountable in some robust way at the systems level (not just that of the representatives). Even a maximally inclusive and egalitarian democratically representative system still creates a difference between rulers and ruled that will inevitably end up causing trouble.

Indeed, even if the previous sections have been successful in demonstrating the limited dangers of incompetence, capture by the bureaucracy, and illiberal tyranny of the majority for open democracy, we would want to know what internal resources a potentially non-electoral democracy could rely on. What are the accountability mechanisms that open democracy could draw on, even absent electoral mechanisms?

I would argue that at least three of the principles of open democracy—participatory rights, deliberation, and transparency—can by themselves directly function as ways to establish and maintain accountability (in a broad sense) in the system. Deliberation inscribes accountability stricto sensu at the heart of the system, namely the opportunity and requirement to give reasons for political decisions and laws. Participatory rights and transparency serve to disincentivize bad behavior on the part of officials. Let me consider each argument in greater detail.

Deliberation requires that any law or policy be the outcome of an exchange of arguments among free and equals. In theory, this principle strictly limits what representatives can decide and do to what they can properly justify. The deliberation principle thus translates into what is sometimes called "discursive accountability," namely the obligation for decision-making assemblies and representatives to produce credible reasons and arguments as to why they support a given agenda, law, or set of policies and regulations. The pressure of arguments—whose "force," though non-violent, is nonetheless real—means that in a system genuinely governed by deliberative norms and in which deliberation is properly institutionalized, representatives would feel morally and institutionally compelled to provide good reasons for their decisions. To the extent that they failed, as judged for example by an independent citizen's jury, they could then be liable to a variety of sanctions, from public shaming to legal penalties.

The participatory rights institutionalized in open democracy would ensure a different kind of accountability (dissuading bad behavior). Thanks to such rights, representatives (lottocratic ones for example, but this could also apply to elected ones) would have to think hard before suggesting or passing laws that are likely to be rejected by the larger population. Citizens' initiatives—the right of citizens to put a proposal either directly to a referendum or on the agenda of the legislative assembly for discussion and a vote—and rights of referral—the possibility to trigger a referendum on an existing law—would indeed empower sufficiently strongly motivated minorities to fight against majoritarian mistakes or injustices. Let us say a minority group notices intolerable blind spots or flaws in the existing system or in a recently passed policy or law. The participatory rights just described allow them to initiate solutions for the problems, either via a new idea for a law (direct or indirect citizens' initiative) or the repeal of an existing law (right of referral). As a result, it would be in the interest of the legislature (again, whether randomly selected or classically elected) to anticipate, and avoid, such predictable counter-reactions. Policy- and law-makers would internalize the need to consult widely, deliberate extensively and inclusively, and negotiate with all the relevant interests before making any decision. They would also internalize the need to communicate clearly with the larger public throughout their entire thought and decision process.

Transparency, finally, is a principle of open democracy explicitly meant as an accountability mechanism. For all the dangers of transparency—the risk, for example, that the meaningful conversations are taking place outside of official meetings or televised plenaries—the benefits most likely outweigh the costs. This is recognized by all the advocates of open government initiatives worldwide who count on the sanitizing effects of lights and information on policymaking.

In addition to these institutional features of open democracy, one may also count on the individual psychological mechanism that arguably already plays a role in elected assemblies, such as a sense of honor or duty or even the fraternity and solidarity felt for one's fellow citizens. Honor and duty would arguably play even more of a role in non-electoral contexts, where partisanship and the need to win power at any cost are often used as excuses to override virtues seen as outdated and undermine rather than promote feelings of identification and belonging.[23]

For such psychological mechanisms to work, however, they probably need to be reinforced by reputation-based mechanisms of the kind that have proved quite robust in the context of at least some online communities. In open digital communities where participants cannot be vetted at the gate, reputation mechanisms, often based on peer evaluations, ensure a relatively accurate ranking or rating of the competence of participants, at least over the medium- to long-term. Similarly, digital information about the past records of self-selected representatives, including peer evaluations and history of past activities and contributions, could allow other individuals to gauge the reliability of those who self-appoint the task of speaking, giving information about, or even potentially deciding on an issue. In turn it would force, or at least strongly incentivize, self-selected representatives to pay attention to and even actively build their reputational status.[24]

---

23. By contrast, the love and affection among the randomly selected participants of the French Convention on Climate Change was striking, as was the sense of personal responsibility toward each other and the larger public that these feelings, or others, seem to have promoted in most. Ethnographers reporting on the sociability of traffic circles in the Yellow Vest movements describe similar phenomena.

24. This type of reputation-based system is what Wikipedia uses to select its thousands of administrators (1,300 for the main English Wikipedia), who are akin to political representatives for this particular community. Wikipedia administrators' responsibilities include the right to make

Finally, a special ethics committee might be needed to audit the functioning of non-electoral assemblies and the behavior of their members to make sure nothing untoward happens (such as misappropriation or misuse of public funds, systematic lying or spreading of misinformation during debates, intimidation or corruption of other members, abuses of power, moral or sexual harassment). The special ethics committee could be composed like a citizen's jury, at random, or chosen from among former lottocratic or self-selected representatives with a particularly good reputation.

Just as for democratic representation, we are used to thinking of political accountability in the context of electoral democracies, which make us overly sensitive to the lack of electoral mechanisms in open democracy. Yet elections are not a definitional element of political accountability (as argued in chapter 4). They are at most one possible mechanism for it, in other words something that causes the relationship of accountability between rulers and ruled to obtain. In an open democracy where elections would play a less prominent role (perhaps only being used to select the head of the executive and other similar functions), one should thus not expect the relationship of accountability to be causally obtained via the usual mechanisms. But there is no reason to think, either, that it could not be obtained through other ones.

How Many Evenings Would Open Democracy Take?

One way in which the book's proposal will I hope seem realistic is that it refrains from making demands on citizens' time and attention beyond what is strictly necessary in a system characterized by an efficient division of cognitive labor. Open democracy does not celebrate participation as an intrinsic good and does not seek to maximize it for its own sake or the sake of a conception favoring something like "the liberty of the Ancients." In my view, participation is compatible with, not an alternative to, representation, and while moments of direct democracy (such as referendums or mass online voting) are still needed on occasion, they are not expected to be particularly frequent, or more frequent than strictly necessary. In most cases, representation will be needed in some fashion and open democracy is more concerned with making sure access to representative functions is as easy and equally distributed as possible than it is with maximizing participation per se.

---

editorial decisions on behalf of the entire Wikipedia community, including in edit wars between users (when two disagreeing parties keep deleting each others' edits). They gain this right, among others, through an accumulation of trust and respect from the rest of the community. Accountability in this context is ensured not so much by sanctionability or the threat of punishment (although peer criticism or ridicule in such contexts is a form of punishment), but mostly by the positive incentive to gain reputation.

My assumption is that there is nothing about politics that makes it an activity worthier of pursuit than raising a family or writing poetry. It is true that under open democracy citizens would probably have to spend more time overall on politics than they currently do under representative democracy, especially for those of us who would be selected to participate in mini-publics (the number of which, if this scheme were to be implemented at all levels of politics, could be quite large and thus require the involvement of a great many people). But the time investment would be episodic (a few days, weeks, months, or more rarely years) and more meaningful and rewarding. Outside of the participation in mini-publics, participation would not be necessarily more time-consuming than it is currently. Instead of wasting hours in line waiting to vote, for example, or marching for half a day against policies or presidents we do not like, we could instead spend the same amount of time on a crowdsourced platform helping a mini-public come up with relevant information and arguments to make a difference to a legislative text of importance to us. Demonstrations and protests, while still crucial political tools even under open democracy, would presumably need to be mobilized much less often because the causes for discontent would be nipped in the bud much earlier in the process.

I count myself, nonetheless, as a participatory democrat on a broad meaning of participation whereby a lot of activities besides voting count as such, and my model also makes room for the kind of mass participation (specifically citizen-initiated referendums) that advocates of direct democracy privilege at crucial junctures. Yet I believe we should economize on citizens' time and attention, out of respect for their own private pursuits, and also because of the upward and lateral expansion of democracy that my model also recommends. To the extent that open democracy ultimately implies decentralizing decision-making at lower levels, expanding democratic decision-making at supranational levels and extending democratic decision-making into spheres currently not considered political (e.g., the firm), it is essential to consider citizens' time and attention as scarce resources that must be used wisely. This is why I think a model that emphasizes openness and plural forms of democratic representation is a better approach than one that emphasizes frequent, mass, and direct participation of the public as a whole.

From Here to There

Ultimately, the feasibility and attractiveness of an open, possibly non-electoral democracy will vary depending on the point of departure or the kind of system we are trying to democratize. Are we trying to evolve from an existing electoral democracy, like the United States, or to reform a non-democratic regime, like China or even the global international order, in a democratic direction? Are we trying to implement an entirely new governance system, and is it for something as concrete and unwieldy as a state, an international organization, a firm, or something more virtual, such as an online community? The first case, an existing electoral democracy, like the United States, is probably the least plausible testbed for a non-electoral model of open democracy, considering the transition costs and the unknown implications of replacing familiar elected assemblies with, say, mini-publics. But in the second case (a regime like the People's Republic of China or the global international order, which both already lack periodic elections), it might be much easier to evolve from a one-party dictatorship or an absence of democratic representative structures altogether to a democracy of mini-publics. In the third case (a new community), everything is in theory possible when we start from scratch, except that we may want to proceed with extreme caution in the case of states where design mistakes may cost lives, and more boldly in the case of online communities where mistakes cost merely time and money.

If the question is how to transition from our electoral democracies to more open ones, a good place to start seems to be with sortition-based assemblies, which could be initially used as agenda-setting or advisory bodies but which would slowly chip away at the prerogatives of existing legislatures, inviting a greater division of labor over time. Alex Guerrero, who envisages a system of multiple single-issue mini-publics grafted onto existing electoral institutions, suggest that these new bodies "could be used just for a few select kinds of political problems, perhaps only after some general triggering conditions were satisfied (legislative stalemate through the normal political process, special call by referendum vote, and so on), or perhaps only if those problems satisfied certain criteria of being particularly complex or susceptible to capture" (Guerrero 2014: 155). Guerrero sees them as either "part of the permanent political structure" or "as 'one-off' institutions" which could be used either as "an oversight mechanism, charged only with making recommendations regarding legislation" or else "with having some level of veto power over traditional legislative processes" (ibid.).

John Gastil suggests, as a first step, giving such bodies exclusive authority to handle issues that would not threaten existing legislatures, such as issues pertaining to (a) legislative conflicts of interest (legislators' salaries, electoral rules, districting, ethics inquiries, etc.) or (b) issues that permit a majority party to dominate procedurally. If the sortition body proved capable, it could expand from there with limited powers—say, the ability to force votes on a limited number of bills that get stuck in committee or suppressed by the majority party (Gastil and Wright 2019). Such a slow and progressive change would allow the lottocratic assemblies to test their larger systemic effects without endangering the stability of existing political systems.

An example of successful transition is already evidenced in the way Ireland first introduced in 2012 a hybrid citizens' assembly of sixty-six randomly selected citizens and thirty-four professional politicians already in power to deliberate about marriage equality. The experiment, while theoretically impure, was successful in generating trust among the two categories of actors and, most important, buy-in from the political class in what was at the time seen as a radical democratic innovation. Six years later, Ireland has embraced the practice of fully random citizens' assemblies, most recently in its constitutional reform on the topic of abortion, where the assembly of ninety-nine citizens made a recommendation ultimately passed by a nationwide referendum. In France, the Convention on Climate Change has demonstrated that citizens have the potential to be not only agenda-setters but legislators as well.

In non-Western contexts, it might be even easier to transition into open democracy. One can imagine countries like China, where competitive elections do not exist and their adversarial spirit is sometimes described as incompatible with local Confucian values of consensus and harmony, easing their way into a different form of democracy, one institutionalized via randomly selected bodies of citizens at multiple levels of the polity. Provided these bodies have actual decision power over laws and policies and are broadly open to the rest of the population via deliberative and crowdsourcing platforms, as well as citizen initiatives, rights of referral, and appropriately frequent referendums, it would seem to me difficult to question their democratic credentials, even if such countries chose never to implement the principle of competitive elections.

Finally, the potential of open democracy might ultimately be best realized in the context of online communities, where governance problems are pervasive and allow for experimentation at both an unprecedented scale and little cost when the experiments fail (at least compared to the costs of trying out new institutional governance schemes in real life nation-states, where success or failure have life and death implications).[25] Open democracy might provide a good set of guidelines for various digital networks and communities, from social media like Facebook to crypto-currency communities like Bitcoin.

25. At least if one is to trust the people closest to the ground on those issues. See, for example, https://medium.com/@FEhrsam/blockchain-governance-programming-our-future-c3bfe30f2d74.

9

Conclusion

OPEN DEMOCRACY IN A GLOBAL WORLD

On January 20, 2017, Donald Trump was inaugurated as president of the United States. In his speech, he thanked "the people of the world" for the outcome of the election—even though no non-American citizen was allowed to vote—and, shortly after, emphasized, by repeating it twice, that with him came the age of "America first." The speech thus acknowledged a global audience—the fact that to the world an American president is never just an American president, but somehow embodies, as "leader of the free world," the hopes and fears of millions of non-American citizens as well[1]—and made a point of immediately disappointing these global expectations. A Trump presidency would mark the return to a more isolationist, protectionist, and nationalist era, one that would be at odds, one surmises, with, for example, the more universal ideals of democracy, poverty alleviation, and fight against climate change. President Trump would stand first for Americans who elected him, and only second, if at all, for the rest of the world.

A day after Trump's inauguration, on January 21, 2017, millions of people took to the streets of Washington, DC and various other major cities across the United States to peacefully protest this particular American electoral result. More strikingly still, the same thing happened in various capitals around the world as well. Large groups of non-American citizens worldwide protested a

---

1. American presidents matter to the world so much that not only are American elections carefully watched abroad, but some foreign governments may even go to great lengths to affect their results.

president for whom they did not and could not expect to vote, and for whose decisions they were not expecting or expected to bear any responsibility.

It is not just the sheer power of the United States that places this burden of representation on its leader.[2] It is the fact that this power is embedded in democratic norms that seems to generate expectations above and beyond the boundaries of the American demos. There thus seems to be a logic to democracy that is conducive to universal inclusion (Dahl 1979). This logic eats away at the closed borders of a nationally defined demos and cracks them open.

Further opening the scope of democracy to the international and truly global community of human beings need not translate into a world state or government, let alone, at least for the foreable future, a world of open borders.[3] But it does demand of democratic leaders that they accept the task of representing stakeholders, at least on some issues, beyond their own national citizens.

At the same time, phenomena such as the Trump election and Brexit indicate the need for democracies to regain local strength and sovereignty over some globalized forces that weaken them. While some have read these outcomes as irrational and ill-motivated (by xenophobia and racism among other things), another reading is that they are a partly justified and rational backlash against the neoliberal and profoundly undemocratic policies of a hypercapitalist international order. The pandemic of COVID-19 that is raging all over world as I'm putting the final touches to this manuscript further exposed that too much local sovereignty on, among other things, sanitary and health issues has been conceded, since the early 1980s, to international markets and the liberal mantra of free trade, division of labor, and minimization of costs. Expanding the scope of democracy on some things (like capital flow regulation, climate change, etc.) is compatible with relocalizing popular rule on other issues.

In the same way, the chapter also argues for reconsidering the sites of democracy. For one thing, the logic of democracy can, does, and should probably expand laterally, from the political realm into the economic realm of "private governments" (Anderson 2017) or, in other words, modern corporate firms. In a world of international corporations that dwarf the power of states, democratizing the governance of firms and the workplace generally is probably intrinsically just and most certainly instrumentally necessary. At the same time, reimagining democracy for the twenty-first century probably means deterritorializing democracy altogether by exploring the potential of immaterial or virtual communities of interests among digitally connected

---

2. Again, no one is protesting Iranian or Chinese leaders, though they do hold a lot of power over the fate of the world.

3. As advocated by, e.g., Bryan Caplan (Caplan and Weinersmith 2019).

individuals, within nations, across nations, at the micro- and macro-levels, and across the narrowly defined siloes of the political and the economic.

Expanding the scope of democracy outward toward expanded demoi and expanding the site of democracy laterally from the polity to other human organizations might be not just instrumentally necessary steps in the particular context of the globalized capitalist order of the twenty-first century, in order, for example, to make democracy at the national level a functioning reality once again. I would argue that these expansions are, in fact, inscribed in the DNA of democracy. As to the de-territorialization of democracy, it seems both unavoidable in light of recent technological changes and at least partly desirable if we consider that voluntary choice is a sounder normative foundation for certain kinds of rights and obligations than the morally arbitrary fact of "birthright lottery" (Shachar 2009).

Yet I have so far left relatively undiscussed the scale and site of democracy, assuming for the most part the familiar framework of nation-states and governments of geographic territories. In this concluding chapter I explore, tentatively and in ways that inevitably call for a deeper treatment, these two distinct questions, suggesting that a genuinely open democracy would have to be based on revised assumptions about both the scale and site of democracy. Such revised assumptions should lead us to refine our understanding of the basic pillars of democracy, namely inclusion and equality. I thus put forward two additional institutional principles beyond the five I have so far advocated for in this book. When it comes to the scale of democracy, I propose to call the revised principle of inclusion "dynamic inclusiveness." With respect to the expanded site of democracy, I argue that it calls for a principle of equality refined, perhaps unoriginally, as "substantive equality."

This concluding chapter is organized as follows. The first section considers the need to expand the boundaries of the demos outward, beyond the nation-state and toward something like a global democracy, perhaps one rendered possible by digital technologies. At the same time the need to decentralize decision-making to the level of relevantly affected interests suggests that the nation-state level should only retain historic and pragmatic as opposed to logical privilege. Something like a subsidiary principle should apply across the board, to diffuse and decentralize popular rule as needed as well. The second section turns to the expansion of the site of democracy from the narrowly political to the economic. It could be that, in the twenty-first century, the most urgent battle is that of firm governance. Since it is likely that the world institutions needed to keep the worst excesses of global capitalism in check will not emerge in time, a pragmatic focus on the reform of firm governance in order to give more say to more stakeholders seems in order. The third section, finally, recapitulates the ways in which open democracy is a new paradigm of popular rule.

On the Scale of Popular Rule: Toward
Dynamic Inclusiveness

There is much to say today about the ways in which the assumed and historically inherited scale of nation-states might be problematic. First, the nation-state could be too large for popular rule. It is a common trope in political theory that democracy is most appropriate at the smaller scale of cities, cantons, or very small states like Switzerland or, better still, islands like Corsica and Iceland. Partisans of direct forms of democracy similarly often emphasize the need to return to smaller scale, face-to-face communities, such as municipalities (Barber 1984). The most radical participatory democrats even suggest abolishing the state altogether as an oppressive framework irreconcilable with self-rule (Bookchin 2015; Occalan 2015). And, indeed, historically one can plausibly see states as sites of oppression rather than liberation, created by and for the sake of elites and their need to render populations "legible" and controllable essentially for the purpose of tax extraction (Scott 1999, 2017).

These critics of the nation-state as the improper scale for democracy, however, often also have an overly romantic and demanding notion of democracy, as an almost full-time job for citizens. When they acknowledge the need for delegation to higher levels of decision-making, they claim, problematically, that federations of direct assemblies are not "representative" because the elected delegates are strictly bound by their mandates. On the definition used in chapter 3, however, representation has nothing to do with how binding the mandate of a representative is. Representation is defined, instead, as acting on behalf of someone else in a way that is accepted by the relevant audience. In democratic conferederalism schemes, therefore, there are de facto representatives, who happen to be of the "delegate" kind, with strict mandates. A strict mandate, however, not only does not preserve the directness as immediacy of decision-making by all so valued by advocates of democratic confederalism, but it creates problems of its own, such as the impossibility of genuine, open-ended deliberation about problems that arise at scale and may require adapting the preferences of individuals at the local levels, including therefore those of the delegates who represent them at the level of the confederation. Strict mandates do not allow for the transformation of the strict preferences of the direct assemblies and their subordination to the power of "the forceless force of the better argument." Because deliberation, on the view defended in this book, is central to democratic legitimacy, I do not think that "democratic confederalism" is a conceptually sound alternative, at least as currently formulated by its proponents.

There is nonetheless a valid point one can take from the philosophy of democratic confederalism, namely the need for greater decentralization of power, wherever possible, and the thickening of participation rights at levels below those of the nation-state. This need for greater decentralization, however, is compatible with the preservation of existing nation-states, as the historically inherited starting points of greater democratization.

At the same time, however, the changing realities of a globalized and digitally interconnected world press us to scale up our frame of reference beyond the nation-state. Nation-states may no longer reflect the proper or only level at which people have allegiances as well as prove inadequate sites of decision-making in the face of transnational—even global—collective action problems, such as corporate tax evasion, immigration fluxes, terrorism, or environmental threats, including climate change. Immigration fluxes in particular have demonstrated the moral deficiencies of a merely *inter*-national world order, where nation-states remain the primary sites of democratic sovereignty and only some international organizations serve as fallible and insufficient bridges between them. This world order is unable to address the problem of millions of refugees who find themselves stranded by war or poverty, rejected from every nation-state, and often unable to secure basic human rights. As Seyla Benhabib puts it, individuals in this post–World War II order find themselves caught "between hospitality and sovereignty," that is, the conflicting principles of a universal right to emigrate guaranteed by international treatises and the preserved principle of state sovereignty that allows states to close their doors to those in need (Benhabib 2006).

This same world order is unable to efficiently fight the global scourges of north-south inequalities, nuclear proliferation, the rogue behavior of some international corporations, depletion of natural resources, extinction of animal species, climate change, and, most recently, pandemics. The international order built after World War II—though an undeniable achievement in its own right compared to the lawlessness that reigned before—has proven incapable of dealing with truly transnational and global phenomena. As a result, more and more people call for transnational, supranational forms of "cosmopolitan democracy," where the sovereignty over certain decision-making is taken away from states and handed over to larger regional entities, international courts, or other forms of global authorities (Benhabib 2006; Archibugi 2008; Held 1995; Gould 2004; Dryzek and Stevenson 2011; Macdonald 2008).

All such critics question the scale at which we should think of democracy and the reference frame we should use to think of a relevant demos. At a deeper level, such criticisms call into question the very first principle of democracy—one that I have left undiscussed so far and taken for granted—namely, inclusiveness. As Robert Dahl argued long ago, inclusiveness cannot just mean inclusion of all the members of the demos, for the demos itself could be defined in extraordinarily restricted ways (only men, only whites, only property holders, only the members of the Communist party, etc.). Surely, Dahl argued, the demos itself must be defined in ways that recognize all human adults affected by the laws and policies at stake (Dahl 1979: 120–124). There is a sense in which the principle of inclusiveness itself, in an authentic democracy, must be made to include more individuals as human communities become more connected and interdependent, and the effects of laws thus affect or apply to more people.

To the five principles proposed so far in this book I propose to add here a sixth one, which operates on the very definition of the demos itself. I call this principle "dynamic inclusiveness."

The idea is inspired both by an empirical example and a philosophical principle. The example is that of the Icelandic crowdsourcing moment explored in chapter 7. In the crowdsourcing phase of the Icelandic process anyone, including non-Icelanders, was able to have a say in the various drafts of the constitutional proposal. This openness of the process thus allowed an American citizen with property in Iceland a chance to express her concerns about the fate of her property under the new scheme. It also gave, quite importantly as well, all sorts of admiring foreigners the opportunity to write notes of gratitude and encouragement to the constitution-drafters. The other source of inspiration for the principle of dynamic inclusiveness is the "all-affected principle" (Goodin 2007), which claims that all those possibly affected by the outcome of a decision ought to be given a say about it. For all its conceptual problems, the all-affected principle—or its often-favored close cousin the all-subjected principle (defended by, e.g., Abizadeh 2008)—expresses a profound intuition about the proper way to extend rights and obligations under a democratic regime. We do not need to get the formulation of the principle perfectly right to start thinking of ways to open up the community of decision-makers to people beyond it who may be affected by or subjected to its decisions. Like the all-affected principle, the principle of "dynamic inclusiveness" that I propose has essentially centrifugal tendencies. It starts from universal franchise within a given historically, territorially given demos and works by expanding beyond these given geographic boundaries, not by redrawing them in a more exclusionary manner.[4] It may also expand the boundaries beyond the immediate time horizon, taking into consideration the interests of future generations as well. This principle, though centrifugal in spirit, is compatible with the principle of subsidiarity and general claims for greater decentralization of power.

What does such a principle of dynamic inclusiveness mean in practice? It might mean including resident aliens in many if not most of the decisions taken at the national level, since they are equally affected by national laws and policies. It could also mean including immigrants or their democratic

4. Although one could imagine a dystopian future in which all modern communication methods have been irreparably destroyed and the memory and awareness of our shared humanity threw us back into a pre-globalization world. In that case perhaps dynamic inclusiveness could justifiably work in a centripetal way, narrowing the boundaries of the demos rather than expanding them.

representatives in deliberations about immigration policies in the United States or the European Union (as opposed to deliberations involving only their generally not-so-democratic representatives, i.e., the decision-makers of their respective countries).[5]

It would also mean never starting a war, not even a commercial war, without first engaging in deliberation with the democratic representatives of all the people likely involved. At a minimum, such a thought points toward what is sometimes called "transnational representation" (Kinsky and Crum 2020), whereby national parliamentarians make claims on behalf of citizens of other national constituencies. It could also point toward what Philippe Schmitter calls "reciprocal representation" (1997), whereby neighboring nation-states award each other a few seats, excluding voting rights, in their respective parliamentary assemblies. More ambitiously still, it could point toward earlier and visionary proposals by Jeremy Bentham to swap members of parliament across nations or even adopt foreign delegates unilaterally (respectively Bentham 2002 [1789] and 1998 [1822], cited in Niesen 2019). Bentham's proposal, which revolutionarily includes voting rights for foreign delegates, was recently rendered in a modernized version as "transnational democracy" (Blatter 2019).[6]

Obviously taking seriously dynamic inclusiveness points to extremely utopian politics, perhaps ultimately those advocated by cosmopolitan democrats, with a single planetary demos on the horizon. At the limit, dynamic inclusiveness should indeed lead to the global inclusion of all human beings in a polity perhaps equivalent to a world state but perhaps also sufficiently different as not to raise the Kantian specter of global despotism.

On the Site of Popular Rule:
Toward Substantive Equality

In addition to the scale of democracy, there are many reasons to think that we should also revisit our preconceived notions about the proper "site" of democracy. In this book so far, I have only considered the familiar political sites of geographic territories and, within them, state institutions, such as parliaments and, by implication the bureaucracies, independent agencies, and courts that continue their work (though I did not say much about the latter[7]).

---

5. Does open democracy ultimately entail a politics of open borders—a global Shengen-style federation of open democracies? Maybe, but there is no guarantee, and this outcome would need to be a decision stemming from a careful, democratic, and open process sensitive to the transition and distributive costs of such a politics for all involved, as opposed to a decision imposed by even well-meaning libertarian ideologues.

6. I thank Professor David Owen for the Bentham, Blatter, and Niesen suggestions.

7. For an interesting take on the democratic legitimacy of independent agencies, see Paul Tucker 2018.

Some critics, however, object to any kind of narrowly territorial approach to democracy, whether at the infra- or supranational level. Instead they advocate, as a supplement rather than a replacement for territory-based communities, for self-configuring communities of choice, across borders and geography. Models range from the idea of a world federation of cities (Barber 2013, 2017) to the digitally empowered and de-territorialized "ideational e-constituencies" (Peixoto 2009) united by common goals, interests, or identities to "cloud nations" that function as government service platforms.[8] While the first model of a democratic community of cities challenges the Westphalian order of nation-states, the latter model of borderless virtual communities challenges the territorial premise altogether. These communities are meant to occupy "cyberspace" rather than territorial space per se. Two very different examples so far include e-Estonia and Bitnation. One is the virtual complement and digital extension of the physical state of Estonia. E-Estonia offers goods and services to those individuals who, all over the world, may want to join the community in exchange for a monetary contribution to the financing of its infrastructures. As of this moment, e-Estonia includes 10 million individuals, against 1.3 million for Estonia itself. The other example, Bitnation, is breaking entirely with the territorial model to offer "an anarchic post-nation state world of voluntary virtual communities" (Orgad 2018: fn 6).

Whether these cloud nations truly amount to "nations" can be disputed. They are also not particularly democratic in relation to their own demos—e-Estonia is essentially ruled by Estonians, not e-Estonians, and Bitnation aims to be a decentralized, ruler-less market rather than a political community ruled by a democratic government (Tempelhof et al. 2017). But one could imagine self-ruling virtual communities of climate change activists, gun lovers, vegans, or survivors of abuse authentically united by core values and goals. One could even imagine Facebook reinventing itself as a global Citizenbook run by its users following the principles of the open democracy paradigm (Landemore 2021).[9]

De-territorializing democracy also allows us to expand our reflection about the domain of popular rule laterally, so to speak, toward institutions that are not typically considered "political." Many allegedly non-political institutions would probably benefit from such a lateral expansion of the scope of popular rule, including the army, the church, the university, hospitals, schools, and even families. Here, however, I want to focus on the set of institutions that are arguably in

---

8. See the proponents of such a view, and their critics: http://globalcit.eu/cloud-communities -the-dawn-of-global-citizenship/. Last accessed July 24, 2018.

9. And for a meritorious but so far unsuccessful effort at creating such a democratic online platform, see a company called empowr, which has built the technology for it but has yet to gather the critical mass of "citizens"—perhaps in part because its original concept is closer to that of a market or an economy than a genuine political community. Full disclosure: I consulted for this company on governance structure and constitutional processes for a few years.

most immediate need of democratization, if only for the contingent reason that in a globalized world of competing nation-states, some of these organizations have accrued powers that threaten democratic sovereignty at that level. I'm thinking primarily of large multinational corporations, some of which straddle continents and which benefit from impotent state regulations and weak international regulations to engage in frequently unjust, exploitative, and environmentally irresponsible practices.[10] There is also the specifically problematic subcase of tech giants, such as Google, Apple, Facebook, Amazon, and Microsoft. This particular nexus of companies, called GAFAM in European parlance, arguably wield a disproportionate and worrying aggregated power. These corporations are global in nature and state-like in many of their capabilities. Some of them are akin to de facto monopolies, with resulting adverse effects on consumers and communities the world over. Facebook raises issues of its own, in that it not only benefits from the network effect that limits any hope of emerging competition, but as we now know, it is able, as a global media platform, to affect the public sphere of democracies and even elections the world over, raising serious questions about its role as a political agent. All of these giant corporations also problematically profit from farming and commodifying their user communities' attention and online data, in ways that cannot be adequately rationalized as a fair contract between consenting parties.

In relation to this lateral expansion of popular rule to new "sites" of governance, such as the firm, I propose an eighth (and for now final) principle of open democracy: "substantive equality." This principle captures the idea that in order for equality to be meaningful it cannot be merely formal and reduced to a set of formal "political" rights, or even "participation rights," as I have put forward. Such rights are essential but must be backed up by, among others, economic rights and opportunities in order to be substantive, that is, meaningful. Among those rights are typically included socioeconomic rights, or third generation rights meant to be guaranteed by the state. Among the most debated are various schemes for a universal basic income, whether offered at the level of closed nation-states or on a global scale (e.g., Van Parijs and Vanderborght 2018).[11]

Such rights should also be complemented by the workplace rights to have a say in economic organizations. These rights should be guaranteed by firms themselves (with backup coercion threats from the nation-state or international organizations as ultimate enforcers). I leave beyond the purview of this book the question of whether economic organizations in general, including

---

10. See here for example the reflexion I started engaging in on this topic, together with my co-author Isabelle Ferreras (in Landemore and Ferreras 2016), or her own theory of "firms as political entities" (Ferreras 2017). See also Piketty 2019, where he explores the idea of reforming the governance of firms in a democratic direction.

11. At the global scale a universal basic income could perhaps be facilitated by blockchain technology through the creation of a deflationary crypto-currency (see Ford 2018).

those of a smaller size or a different legal nature (private partnerships), should be democratized to focus instead on the most egregious cases of unjust economic organizations, especially those posing a threat to democracy. Democratizing firm governance would arguably be the most efficient way to make equality "substantive" in a context where redistributive policies at the national level prove insufficient and the ideal of a universal basic income remains, for now, out of reach.

This conclusion is not the place to develop in full a new argument for the justice and necessity of democratizing the firm, even as there will be no shortage of objections to everything I have said thus far.[12] Addressing them, however, is a project for another book. My aim here is simply to sketch the directions in which open democracy is likely to take us.

Conclusion

This book has offered a paradigm of democracy different from the liberal-republican construct we have known as "representative democracy" since the eighteenth century. This new paradigm puts ordinary citizens, rather than elected elites, at the center of political institutions.

In open democracy, popular rule no longer only means, as it has meant from the eighteenth century onward, "consenting" to power. It means, for the ordinary citizen, having access to power (though not necessarily office), whether as a simple citizen able to affect the agenda of the legislative assembly through an initiative or vote in a referendum where options were shaped by her views; or, more directly, by being chosen to participate in a randomly selected assembly charged with setting the agenda or making the law; or through vote delegation allowing her to vote on behalf of others who trust her on certain issues.

What would open democracy look like in practice? There is presumably no single best way to implement open democracy. Iceland itself is only a partial and flawed model. Nonetheless, a central institutional feature of open democracy across all contexts would be what I have called the "open mini-public."

This mini-public is an all-purpose, randomly selected body open to the input of the larger public via citizen initiatives and rights of referral as well as a permanent online crowdsourcing and deliberative platform, and ultimately connected to a demos-wide referendum on central issues (including, ideally, via the same online platform used for crowdsourcing and deliberation, this time used for electronic voting). The idea of the open mini-public is to empower ordinary citizens in a way that renders deliberation feasible while maximizing wider access (in part to increase the likelihood of good deliberative outcomes, whether they are actual decisions or recommendations to be

12. Some of them are addressed in Landemore and Ferreras 2016.

voted on). At the same time, citizens' initiatives and rights of referral ensure that the agenda set by the representative mini-public can still be decisively influenced by the larger public. The existence of a crowdsourcing and deliberative platform—what others have called an "online civic commons" (Gastil and Richards 2017)—functions as both a comment board and a virtual and interactive "gallery" (as in the galleries overlooking parliaments around the world, whereby ordinary citizens can come, witness, and influence the debates of their representatives). This latter design feature is meant to allow willing members of the larger public to peek into the deliberations of the mini-public and contribute ideas, information, and arguments as well as engage in deliberation with each other and with the members of the mini-public at almost any point in time up to the point of decision-making. Finally, the possibility of a referendum on at least the most salient issues connects the open mini-public to the larger public in a way that is mindful of citizens' time (we wouldn't want to ask all citizens to vote on every issue all the time) while preserving an essential connection between the entirety of the demos and the open mini-public.

The open mini-public seems to me the central institutional feature of open democracy, in contrast with the leitmotiv of the elected assembly only intermittently directly connected to the public that remains at the heart of representative democracy, including in recent reconceptualizations (e.g. Pettit 2016). Ideally, this general-purpose mini-public would form the center of a network of other mini-publics, some of them single-issue, others generalist, operating at various sub-levels of the polity. Combined, they would form a web of connected mini-publics all staffed with randomly selected citizens.

It is important to distinguish between a set of institutional guidelines, which I offer as a lens through which to approach institutional reforms, and the reforms themselves. I am not making very detailed specific recommendations about how to implement open democracy (except for the open mini-public just sketched). Nor am I able, in this book, to fully sketch the road "from here to there." On the latter point, my instincts as a reformer—thinking about the conditions under which one can get from representative to open democracy— are much more conservative than my instincts as a political theorist—thinking in terms of conceptual frameworks. Nonetheless, using institutional reform with open democracy as a normative guideline would, in my view, change the way reformists, activists, and political leaders envisage the scope of necessary changes and the role of ordinary citizens in democratic politics. It would change, I believe, the way ordinary citizens themselves see their role in a democracy worthy of this name. Short of implementing open democracy per se, any opening up, rather than further closure, of our existing institutions would be, in my view and all other things equal otherwise, an improvement.

Ultimately, one might ask, what are the concrete benefits of the open democracy model? They are at least threefold.

First, open democracy is a more faithful instantiation of the ideal of popular rule. It simply approximates more closely the democratic ideal of people's power. Open democracy, even as it may end up in some of its more conservative implementations retaining some familiar features of electoral democracy, is nonetheless meant to offer a fundamentally different lens through which to see the role of citizens in the polity. As a normative guideline for institutional reforms, it aims to include and empower citizens rather obtain their consent while keeping them at bay.

Second, because open democracy is more widely inclusive of citizens, it is—in theory at least—also more likely to tap their "democratic reason" or "collective wisdom" (Landemore 2012, 2013a; Landemore and Elster 2012). In other words, open democracy is not simply more genuinely democratic; it is, *as a result of its openness*, likely to perform better as well (in the sense of tracking more accurately the common good of the relevant community, such as the welfare, health, and happiness of its citizens among other things).

Third, open democracy is also likely to be more stable and durable than electoral democracy. Because it is less subject to the latter's oligarchic biases, open democracy is simply more likely to resist closure, loss of legitimacy, slow decay (Runciman 2018) or, possibly, collapse.

It is now time to conclude this book and finally deliver on a promise made at the beginning. To capture the spirit of democracy as a set of collective decision procedures, I have used in past work the imagery of a group of friends lost in a maze (a collective version of Descartes's thought experiment of being lost in a forest in the *Discourse on Method*); a jury of ordinary citizens (inspired by the film *Twelve Angry Men*); and a nomadic tribe exploring the savannah (a simple version of what I take politics to be at least partly about). The metaphor of the jury—a theoretically random sample of ordinary citizens—captured quite neatly what I had in mind for the context of a representative democracy where size constraints necessitate delegating the decision to a subset of the larger group.

But even a popular jury seems, in retrospect, too exclusive, too closed to the outside world and the larger public. Between the publication of my previous book and the writing of this one, reality taught me that inclusiveness can be understood in more expansive ways than I was prepared to conceptualize.

Open democracy is thus best conceptualized as an open doorframe leading to an ungated space. The frame is there because politics always involves representation and, indeed, a necessary framing of issues and questions, which brings them into focus. Mediations are thus needed in ways that are rarely optional, except, perhaps, in the smallest of democracies (private partnerships, departmental meetings, very small villages). But there is no door hanging on that frame; entry is left open, with no possibility of closure. The door frame leads to an equally open space—reminiscent of the Pnyx or Thingvellir—the locus of popular power or rule, which is accessible to all.

REFERENCES

Abizadeh, Arash. 2008. "Democracy and Border Coercion: No Right to Unilaterally Control Your Own Borders." *Political Theory* 36(1): 37–65.

Abizadeh, Arash. 2020. "Representation, Bicameralism, Political Equality, and Sortition: Reconstituting the Senate as a Randomly Selected Citizen Assembly." *Perspectives on Politics.* Published online first, https://doi.org/10.1017/S1537592719004626.

Abramson, Jeffrey B. 2000. *We, the Jury: The Jury System and the Ideal of Democracy.* Cambridge, MA: Harvard University Press.

Achen, Christopher, and Larry Bartels. 2016. *Democracy for Realists: Why Elections Do Not Produce Responsive Government.* Princeton, NJ: Princeton University Press.

Ackerman, Bruce, and James Fishkin. 2005. *Deliberation Day.* New Haven, CT: Yale University Press.

Adams, John. [1776] 1856. *Thoughts on Government.* Reprinted in *The Works of John Adams*, edited by Charles Francis Adams. Boston: Little, Brown & Co. 1856.

Aitamurto, Tanja. 2012. *Crowdsourcing for Democracy: New Era in Policy-Making.* Committee for the Future, Parliament of Finland. Available online at http://iis-db.stanford.edu/pubs/23963/Crowdsourcing_for_DemocracyF_www.pdf.

Aitamurto, Tanja, and Hélène Landemore. 2016. "Crowdsourced Deliberation: The Case of an Off-Traffic Law Reform in Finland." *Policy & Internet* 8(2): 174–196.

Aitamurto, Tanjaa, Hélène Landemore, and Jorge Saldivar Galli. 2017. "Unmasking the Crowd: Participants' Motivation Factors, Expectations, and Profile in a Crowdsourced Law Reform." *Information, Communication, and Society* 20(8): 1239–1260.

Alexander, Amy C., and Christian Welzel. 2017. "The Myth of Deconsolidation: Rising Liberalism and the Populist Reaction." *Journal of Democracy.* ILE Working Paper Series, No. 10, University of Hamburg, Institute of Law and Economics (ILE), Hamburg. http://hdl.handle.net/10419/170694

Anderson, Elizabeth. 2017. *Private Government: How Employers Rule Our Lives (and Why We Don't Talk about It).* Princeton, NJ: Princeton University Press.

Annany, Mike. 2020. "Presence of Absence: Exploring the Democratic Significance of Silence." In H. Landemore, R. Reich, and L. Bernholz, eds., *Digital Technology and Democratic Theory.* Chicago: University of Chicago Press.

Archibugi, Daniele. 2008. *The Global Commonwealth of Citizens: Towards Cosmopolitan Democracy.* Princeton, NJ: Princeton University Press.

Árnason, Ágúst Thór. 2011. "A Review of the Icelandic Constitution—Popular Sovereignty or Political Confusion." *Tijdschrift voor Constitutioneel Recht* 3, 342–351.

Bachrach, Peter, and Morton S. Baratz. 1962. "Two Faces of Power." *American Political Science Review* 56(4): 947–952.

Bächtiger, André, and Simon Beste. 2017. "Deliberative Citizens, (Non)Deliberative Politicians: A Rejoinder." *Daedalus* 146(3): 106–118.

Bai, Tongdong. 2020. *Against Political Equality: The Confucian Case*. Princeton, NJ : Princeton University Press.

Balinski, Michel, and Rita Laraki. 2010. *Majority Judgment*. Cambridge, MA: MIT Press.

Barber, Benjamin. 1984. *Strong Democracy: Participatory Politics for a New Age*. Berkeley: University of California Press.

Barber, Benjamin. 2013. *If Mayors Ruled the World: Dysfunctional Nations, Rising Cities*. New Haven, CT: Yale University Press.

Barber, Benjamin. 2017. *Cool Cities: Urban Sovereignty and the Fix for Global Warming*. New Haven, CT: Yale University Press.

Bell, Daniel. 2013. *The China Model. Political Meritocracy and the Limits of Democracy*. Princeton, NJ: Princeton University Press.

Benhabib, Seyla. 2006. *Another Cosmopolitanism*. Oxford: Oxford University Press.

Bentham, Jeremy [1822] 1998. "Codification Proposal Addressed by Jeremy Bentham to All Nations Professing Liberal Opinions." In Jeremy Bentham, *Legislator of the World*, edited by P. Schofield. Oxford: Oxford University Press.

Bentham, Jeremy [1789] 2002. "Projet of a Constitutional Code for France." In P. Schofield, C. Pease-Watkin, and C. Blamires, eds., *Jeremy Bentham, Rights, Representation and Reform*. Oxford: Oxford University Press, 227–262.

Bergsson, Baldvin, and Paul Blokker. 2014. "The Constitutional Experiment in Iceland (September 4, 2013)." In Ellen Bos and Kálmán Pócza, eds., *Verfassunggebung in konsolidierten Demokratien: Neubeginn oder Verfall eines Systems?*. Baden-Baden, Germany: Nomos Verlag.

Bermeo, Nancy. 2016. "On Democratic Backsliding." *Journal of Democracy* 27(1): 5–19.

Bernholz, Lucy, Hélène Landemore, and Rob Reich. 2020. *Digital Technology and Democratic Theory*. Chicago: Chicago University Press.

Besley, Timothy, Rohini Pande, and Vijayendra Rao. 2005. "Participatory Democracy in Action: Survey Evidence from South India." *Journal of the European Economic Association* 3(2–3): 648–657.

Blatter, Joachim. 2019. "Let me vote in your country, and I'll let you vote in mine. A proposal for transnational democracy." Blog post. Available at http://globalcit.eu/let-me-vote-in-your-country-and-ill-let-you-vote-in-mine-a-proposal-for-transnational-democracy/. Last accessed April 18, 2020.

Blum, Christian, and Christina Isabel Zuber. 2016. "Liquid Democracy: Potentials, Problems, and Perspectives." *Journal of Political Philosophy* 24(2): 162–182.

Bohman, James. 2004. "Expanding Dialogue: The Internet, the Public Sphere and Prospects for Transnational Democracy." *Sociological Review* 52(1): 131–155.

Bohman, James. 2006. "Democracy, Solidarity, and Global Exclusion." *Philosophy and Social Criticism* 32(7): 809–817.

Boldi, Paolo, Francesco Bonchi, Carlos Castillo, and Sebastiano Vigna. 2011. "Viscous Democracy for Social Networks." *Communications of the ACM* 54(6): 129–137.

Bookchin, Murray. 2015. *The Next Revolution: Popular Assemblies and the Promise of Direct Democracy*. New York: Verso.

Bouricius, Terril. 2013. "Democracy Through Multi-Body Sortition: Athenian Lessons for the Modern Day." *Journal of Public Deliberation* 9(1):1–19. Article 11. Available online at https://www.publicdeliberation.net/jpd/vol9/iss1/art11.

Brennan, Jason. 2016. *Against Democracy*. Princeton, NJ: Princeton University Press.

Brennan, Jason, and Hélène Landemore. Forthcoming. *Debating Democracy*. Oxford: Oxford University Press.

Brown, Nathan. 2016. "Islam and Constitutionalism in the Arab World: The Puzzling Course of Islamic Inflation." In Aslı Bali and Hanna Lerner, eds., *Constitution Writing, Religion, and Democracy*. Cambridge: Cambridge University Press.

Buchanan, A. 2003. *Justice, Legitimacy, and Self-Determination: International Relations and the Rule of Law.* Oxford: Oxford University Press.

Buchanan, James. 1999. *The Collected Works of James M. Buchanan*, Vol. 3. "The Calculus of Consent: Logical Foundations of Constitutional Democracy," with a Foreword by Robert D. Tollison. Indianapolis, IN: Liberty Fund.

Buge, Eric, and Camille Morio. 2019. "Le Grand débat national, apports et limites pour la participation citoyenne." *Revue du droit public* 5: 1205–1238.

Burnheim, John 1985. *Is Democracy Possible? The Alternative to Electoral Politics.* Berkeley: University of California Press.

Cagé, Julia. 2020. *The Price of Democracy.* Cambridge, MA: Harvard University Press.

Cammack, Daniela. 2018. "The Democratic Significance of the Classical Athenian Courts." In *Decline: Decadence, Decay, and Decline in History and Society.* Budapest: Central European University Press.

Cammack, Daniela. 2020. "Deliberation and Discussion in Classical Athens." *Journal of Political Philosophy.* Online first.

Caplan, Bryan, and Zach Weinersmith. 2019. *Open Borders: The Science and Ethics of Immigration.* London: St Martin's Press.

Carey, John M. 2009. "Does It Matter How a Constitution Is Created?" In Z. Barany and R. G. Moser, eds., *Is Democracy Exportable?* New York: Cambridge University Press, 155–177.

Carey, John M., Richard G. Niemi, and Lynda W. Powell. 1998. "The Effect of Term Limits on State Legislatures." *Legislative Studies Quarterly* 23(2): 271–300.

Carey, John M., Richard G. Niemi, Lynda W. Powell, and Gary F. Moncrief. 2006. "The Effects of Term Limits on State Legislatures: A New Survey of the 50 States." *Legislative Studies Quarterly* 31(1):105–134.

Carillo, David, ed. 2018. *The Icelandic Federalist Papers.* Berkeley: Institute of Govermental Studies Press.

Carson, Lyn, and Brian Martin.1999. *Random Selection in Politics.* Westport, CT: Praeger.

Castiglione, Dario, and Mark E. Warren. 2006. "Rethinking Democratic Representation: Eight Theoretical Issues." Paper prepared for delivery to "Rethinking Democratic Representation," Centre for the Study of Democratic Institutions, University of British Columbia, May 18–19.

Chakravarti, Sonali. 2019. *Radical Enfranchisement in the Jury Room and Public Life.* Chicago: Chicago University Press.

Chambers, Simone. 2004. "Behind Closed Doors: Publicity, Secrecy, and the Quality of Deliberation." *Journal of Political Philosophy* 12: 389–410.

Chambers, Simone. 2017. "The Epistemic Ideal of Reason-Giving in Deliberative Democracy. A Reply to Landemore." *Social Epistemology Review and Reply Collective* 6(10): 59–64.

Chan, J. 2013. "Political Meritocracy and Meritorious Rule." In D. Bell and C. Li, eds., *The East Asian Challenge for Democracy: Political Meritocracy in Comparative Perspective.* Cambridge: Cambridge University Press, 31–54.

Cheneval, Francis, and A. el-Wakil. 2018. "The Institutional Design of Referendums: Bottom-Up and Binding." *Swiss Political Science Review* 24 (3): 294–304.

Christiano, Thomas. 1996. *The Rule of the Many.* Boulder, CO: Westview Press.

Christiano, Thomas. 2004a. "Authority." In E. Zalta, ed., *The Stanford Encyclopedia of Philosophy.* Available online at http://plato.stanford.edu/entries/authority/.

Christiano, Thomas. 2004b. "The Authority of Democracy." *Journal of Political Philosophy* 12(3): 266–290.

Chwalisz, Claudia. 2017. *The People's Verdict: Adding Informed Citizen Voices to Public Decision-Making.* Washington, DC: Policy Network/Rowman & Littlefield International.

Cohen, Elizabeth. 2018. *The Political Value of Time. Citizenship: Duration, and Democratic Justice.* Cambridge: Cambridge University Press.

Cohen, Joshua. 1989. "Deliberation and Democratic Legitimacy." In A. Hamlin and P. Pettit, eds., *The Good Polity.* New York: Basil Blackwell, 17–34.

Cohen, Joshua. 2011. *Rousseau: A Free Community of Equals.* Oxford: Oxford University Press.

Coleman, Stephen. 2005. "New Mediation and Direct Representation: Reconceptualizing Representation in the Digital Age." *New Media & Society* 7(2): 177–198.

Coleman, Stephen, and Peter M. Shane, eds. 2012. *Connecting Democracy.* Cambridge, MA: MIT Press.

Crouch, Colin. 2004. *Post-Democracy.* Cambridge: Polity Press.

Curato, Nicole, John S. Dryzek, Selen A. Ercan, Carolyn M. Hendriks, and Simon Niemeyer. 2017. "Twelve Key Findings in Deliberative Democracy Research." *Daedalus* 146(3): 14–38.

Dahl, Robert. 1970. *After the Revolution.* New Haven, CT: Yale University Press.

Dahl, Robert. 1971. *Polyarchy.* New Haven, CT: Yale University Press.

Dahl, Robert. 1979. "Procedural Democracy." In Peter Laslett and Jim Fishkin, eds., *Philosophy, Politics and Society* (fifth series). New Haven, CT: Yale University Press, 97–133.

Dahl, Robert. 1985. *A Preface to Economic Democracy.* Berkeley: University of California Press.

Dahl, Robert. 1989. *Democracy and Its Critics.* New Haven, CT: Yale University Press.

Dahlgren, Peter. 2005. "The Internet, Public Spheres, and Political Communication: Dispersion and Deliberation." *Political Communication* 22:147–162.

Dal Bó, Ernesto, Pedro Dal Bó, and Jason Snyder. 2009. "Political Dynasties." *Review of Economic Studies* 76(1): 115–142.

DeCanio, Samuel. 2014. "Democracy, the Market, and the Logic of Social Choice." *American Journal of Political Science* 58(3): 637–652.

De Djin, Annelien. 2019. "Republicanism and Democracy. The Tyranny of Majority in Eighteenth-century Political Debate." In Y. Elazar and G. Rousselière, eds., *Republicanism and the Future of Democracy.* Cambridge: Cambridge University Press, 59–74.

Della Porta, Donatella. 2013. *Can Democracy Be Saved?: Participation, Deliberation, and Social Movements.* Cambridge: Polity Press.

Deutsch, Karl. 1976. *Die Schweiz als ein Paradigmatischer Fall Politischer Integration.* Bern: Haupt.

Dewey, John. [1927] 1954. *The Public and Its Problems.* Athens, OH: Swallow Press.

Dewey, John. 1993. *Political Writings*, edited by I. Shapiro. Indianapolis, IN: Hackett, 121–124.

Diamond, Larry. 2008. *The Spirit of Democracy: The Struggle to Build Free Societies Throughout the World.* New York: Times Books.

Diamond, Larry. 2016. "Global Democracy Is Spiraling Down. Here's What That Looks Like—And What President-Elect Trump Should Do." Stanford, CA: Institute for International Studies. Available online at https://medium.com/@FSIStanford/global-democracy-is-spiraling-down -7b2206643ad4#.jgafd4rkt, December 13.

Dixit, Avinash, Gene M. Grossman, and Faruk Gul. 2000. "The Dynamics of Political Compromise." *Journal of Political Economy* 108: 531–568.

Dowlen, Oliver. 2008. *The Political Potential of Sortition: A Study of the Random Selection of Citizens for Public Office.* Charlottesville, VA: Imprint Academic.

Dryzek, John S. 2009. "Democratization as Deliberative Capacity Building." *Comparative Political Studies* 42(11): 1379–1402. Available online at https://doi.org/10.1177/0010414009332129.

Dryzek, John S., André Bächtiger, Simone Chambers, Joshua Cohen, James N. Druckman, Andrea Felicetti, James S. Fishkin, David M. Farrell, Archon Fung, Amy Gutmann, Hélène Landemore, Jane Mansbridge, Sofie Marien, Michael A. Neblo, Simon Niemeyer, Maija Setälä, Rune Slothuus, Jane Suiter, Dennis Thompson, and Mark E. Warren. 2019. "The Crisis of Democracy and the Science of Deliberation." *Science* 363(6432): 1144–1146.

Dryzek, John S., and Simon Niemeyer. 2008. "Discursive Representation." *American Political Science Review* 102(4): 481–493.

Dryzeck, John, and Hayley Stevenson. 2011. "Global Democracy and Earth System Governance." *Ecological Economics* 70(11): 1865–1874.

Du Bois, W.E.B. 1999. *Darkwater: Voices from within the Veil*. Mineola, NY: Dover Publications.

Dunn, John. 2019. *Setting the People Free: The Story of Democracy*, second edition. Princeton, NJ: Princeton University Press.

Dworkin, Ronald. 1986. *Law's Empire*. Cambridge, MA: Harvard University Press.

Elazar, Y., and G. Rouselière, eds. 1999. *Republicanism and the Future of Democracy*. Cambridge: Cambridge University Press.

Elkins, Zachary, Tom Ginsburg, and James Melton. 2012. "A Review of Iceland's Draft Constitution." Available online at https://webspace.utexas.edu/elkinszs/web/CCP%20Iceland%20Report.pdf.

Elster, Jon. 1993. "Constitution-Making in Eastern Europe: Rebuilding the Boat in the Open Sea." *Public Administration* 71: 169–217.

Elster, Jon. 1995. "Forces and Mechanisms in the Constitution-Making Process." *Duke Law Journal* 45: 364–396.

Elster, Jon. 1999. "Accountability in Athenian Politics." In A. Przeworski, S. C. Stokes, and B. Manin, eds., *Democracy, Accountability, and Representation*. Cambridge: Cambridge University Press, 253–278.

Elster, Jon. 2012. "The Optimal Design of a Constituent Assembly." In H. Landemore and J. Elster, *Collective Wisdom: Principles and Mechanisms*. Cambridge: Cambrige University Press, 148–172.

Elster, Jon. 2020. "Some Notes on 'Populism.'" *Philosophy and Social Criticism* 1–10.

el-Wakil, Alice. 2020. "Government with the People: The Value of Facultative Referendums in Democratic Systems." PhD dissertation, University of Zurich.

Empatia (consortium). 2018. "Enabling Multichannel Participation through Adapations." Final Report. Available at https://empatia-project.eu/wp-content/uploads/2018/07/EMPATIA_Final_Progress_Report_D6.2-6July2018.pdf.

Erbentraut, Philipp. 2017. "Politics without Parties? Moisei Ostrogorski and the Crisis of Party Politics." Application for a John F. Kennedu Memorial Fellowship (Harvard University). Available online at http://www.fb03.uni-frankfurt.de/71953258/Politics-without-parties_rev.pdf?

Estlund, David. 2008. *Democratic Authority: A Philosophical Framework*. Princeton, NJ: Princeton University Press.

Estlund, David. 2020. *Utopophobia: On the Limits (If Any) of Political Philosophy*. Princeton, NJ: Princeton University Press.

Farrar, Cynthia, James S. Fishkin, Donald P. Green, Christian List, Robert C. Luskin, and Elizabeth Levy Paluck. 2010. "Disaggregating Deliberation's Effects: An Experiment within a Deliberative Poll." *British Journal of Political Science* 40(2): 333–347.

Farrell, David M., and Jane Suiter. 2019. *Reimagining Democracy: Lessons in Deliberative Democracy from the Irish Front Lines*. Ithaca, NY: Cornell University Press.

Farrell, David M., Jane Suiter, and Clodagh Harris. 2018. "'Systematizing' Constitutional Deliberation: The 2016–18 Citizens' Assembly in Ireland." *Irish Political Studies* 34(1).

Fearon, James D. 1999. "Electoral Accountability and the Control of Politicians: Selecting Good Types Versus Sanctioning Poor Performance." In A. Przeworski, S. C. Stokes, and B. Manin, eds., *Democracy, Accountability, and Representation*. Cambridge: Cambridge University Press, 55–97.

Ferejohn, John. 1999. "Accountability and Authority: Toward a Theory of Political Accountability." In A. Przeworski, S. C. Stokes, and B. Manin, eds., *Democracy, Accountability, and Representation*. Cambridge: Cambridge University Press, 131–153.

Ferejohn, John, and Francis Rosenbluth. 2009. "Electoral Representation and the Aristocratic Thesis." In I. Shapiro, S. C. Stokes, E. J. Wood, and A. S. Kirshner, eds., *Political Representation*. Cambridge: Cambridge University Press, 271–303.

Ferreras, Isabelle. 2017. *The Firm as Political Entity*. Cambridge: Cambridge University Press.

Fillmore-Patrick, Hannah. 2013. "The Iceland Experiment (2009–2013): A Participatory Approach to Constitutional Reform." DPC Policy Note New Series 2.

Fischer, Frank. 2016. "Participatory Governance: From Theory to Practice." In Susan Fainstein and James DeFilippis, eds., *Readings in Planning Theory*. Oxford: Wiley.

Fishkin, James S. 2014. "Hagnýtt rökræðulýðræði (Deliberative Democracy and the 'Crowd-sourced Constitution': The Experiment Must Continue)." In J. Ólafsson, ed., *Tilraunir með Lýðræði—Ísland í Kreppu og Endurreisn (Experiments in Democracy—Iceland in Crisis and Recovery)*. Reykjavík: University of Iceland Press and Bifröst University.

Fishkin, Jim. 2009. *When the People Speak: Deliberative Democracy and Public Consultation*. Oxford: Oxford University Press.

Fishkin, Jim. 2018. *Democracy When the People Are Thinking: Revitalizing Our Politics Through Public Deliberation*. Oxford: Oxford University Press.

Flichy, Patrice. 2007. *The Internet Imaginaire*. Cambridge, MA: MIT Press.

Foa, Roberto, and Yashka Mounk. 2016. "The Democratic Disconnect." *Journal of Democracy* 27(3): 5–17.

Ford, Bryan. 2002. "Delegative Democracy." Unpublished paper. Available online at http://www.brynosaurus.com/deleg/deleg.pdf. Last accessed September 21, 2018.

Ford, Bryan. 2014. "Delegative Democracy Revisited." Blog post available online at https://bford.github.io/2014/11/16/deleg.html. Last accessed September 23, 2018.

Ford, Bryan. 2018. "Democratic Value and Money for Decentralized Digital Society." Working paper presented at the Stanford Workshop on Digital Technology and Democratic Theory, June 27, 2018.

Fralin, Richard. 1978. *Rousseau and Representation: A Study of the Development of His Concept of Political Institutions*. New York: Columbia University Press.

Freedom House. 2000. *Democracy's Century: A Survery of Global Political Change in the 20th Century*. New York: Freedom House.

Freitag, Markus, and Carolin Rapp. 2013. "Intolerance Toward Immigrants in Switzerland: Diminished Threat Through Social Contacts?" *Swiss Political Science Review* 9(4): 425–446.

Fuller, Roslyn. 2015. *Beasts and God: How Democracy Changed Its Meaning and Lost Its Purpose*. London: Zed Books

Galbraith, Kate, and Asher Price. 2013. *The Great Texas Wind Rush. How George Bush, Ann Richards, and a Bunch of Tinkerers Helped the Oil and Gas State Win the Race to Wind Power*. Austin: University of Texas Press.

Galston, William A. 2018. *Antipluralism: The Populist Threat to Liberal Democracy*. New Haven, CT: Yale University Press.

Gangadharan, Seeta P. 2020. "Digital Exclusion: A Politics of Refusal." In H. Landemore, R. Reich, and L. Bernholz, eds., *Digital Technology and Democratic Theory*. Chicago: University of Chicago Press.

Gargarella, Roberto. 2003. "The Majoritarian Reading of the Rule of Law." In Jose Maria Maravall and Adam Przeworski, eds., *Democracy and the Rule of Law*. New York: Cambridge University Press, 147–167.

Gastil, John, Katherine R. Knoblock, Justin Reedy, Mark Henkels, and Katherine Cramer. 2018. "Assessing the Electoral Impact of the 2010 Oregon's Citizens' Initiative Review." *American Politics Research* 46(3): 534–563.

Gastil, John, and Robert C. Richards. 2017. "Embracing Digital Democracy: A Call for Building an Online Civic Commons." *PS: Political Science & Politics* 50(3): 758–763.

Gastil, John, and Erik Olin Wright. 2019. *Legislature by Lot: Transformative Designs for Deliberative Governance.* London: Verso.

Gaus, Gerald. 2016. *The Tyranny of the Ideal: Justice in a Diverse Society.* Princeton, NJ: Princeton University Press.

Gilens, Martin, and Benjamin Page. 2014. "Testing Theories of American Politics: Elites, Interest Groups, and Average Citizens." *Perspectives on Politics* 12(3): 564–581.

Ginsburg, Tom, and Zachary Elkins. 2014. "Stjórnarskrárgerð á tímum gagnsæis: Ísland ísamanburði" (Drafting constitutions in an era of transparency: Iceland in comparative perspective). In J. Ólafsson, ed., *Tilraunir með Lýðræði—Ísland í Kreppu og Endurreisn (Experiments in Democracy—Iceland in Crisis and Recovery).* Reykjavík: University of Iceland Press and Bifröst University.

Ginsburg, Tom, Zachary Elkins, and Justin Blount. 2009. "Does the Process of Constitution-Making Matter?" *Annual Review of Law and Social Science* 5: 201–223.

Ginsburg, Tom, and Aziz Z. Huq. 2018. *How to Save a Constitutional Democracy.* Chicago: University of Chicago Press.

Goldin, Claudia, and Lawrence F. Katz. 2007. "The Race Between Education and Technology: The Evolution of U.S. Educational Wage Differentials, 1890 to 2005." NBER Working Paper No. 12984.

Goodin, Robert. 2007. "Enfranchising All Affected Interests, and Its Alternatives." *Philosophy & Public Affairs* 35(1): 40–68.

Goodin, Robert. 2008. *Innovating Democracy: Democratic Theory and Practice After the Deliberative Turn.* Oxford: Oxford University Press.

Goodin, Robert, and Kai Spiekermann. 2018. *An Epistemic Theory of Democracy.* Oxford: Oxford University Press.

Goodin, Robert E., and John S. Dryzek. 2006. "Deliberative Impacts: The Macro-Political Uptake of Mini-Publics." *Politics & Society* 34(2): 219–244.

Goodin, Robert E., and Chiara Lepora. 2015. "Guaranteed Rotation in Office: A 'New' Model of Democracy." *Political Quarterly* 86(3): 364–371.

Gould, Carole. 2004. *Globalizing Democracy and Human Rights.* Cambridge: Cambridge University Press.

Green, Jeffrey E. 2010. *The Eyes of the People: Democracy in an Age of Spectatorship.* Oxford: Oxford University Press.

Green-Armytage, J. 2015. "Direct Voting and Proxy Voting." *Constitutional Political Economy* 26(2): 190–220.

Greene, Amanda. 2016. "Consent and Political Legitimacy." In D. Sobel, P. Vallentyne, and S. Wall, (eds.), *Oxford Studies in Political Philosophy* 2, 71–97.

Guerrero, Alex. 2014. "Against Elections: The Lottocratic Alternative." *Philosophy and Public Affairs* 42(2): 135–178.

Guinier, Lani. 2008. "Beyond Electocracy: Rethinking the Political Representative as Powerful Stranger." *Modern Law Review* 71(1): 1–35.

Gurin, J. 2014. "Open Governments, Open Data: A New Lever for Transparency, Citizen Engagement, and Economic Growth." *SAIS Review of International Affairs* 34(1): 71–82.

Gutmann, Amy, and Dennis Thompson. 1996. *Democracy and Disagreement.* Cambridge, MA: Belknap Press.

Gylfason, Thorvaldur. 2013. "Democracy on Ice: A Post-Mortem of the Icelandic Constitution." *Open Democracy*, June 19. Available online at http://www.opendemocracy.net/can-europe-make-it/thorvaldur-gylfason/democracy-on-ice-post-mortem-of-icelandic-constitution.

Gylfason, Thorvaldur. 2016. "Chain of Legitimacy: Constitution Making in Iceland." CESifo Working Paper Series 6018, CESifo Group Munich.

Habermas, Jürgen. 1996. *Between Facts and Norms.* Translated by William Rehg. Cambridge, MA: MIT Press.

Habermas, Jürgen. 2006. "Political Communication in Media Society: Does Democracy Still Enjoy an Epistemic Dimension? The Impact of Normative Theory on Empirical Research." *Communication Theory* 16(4): 411–426.

Hamilton, Alexander, James Madison, and John Jay. 2003. *The Federalist* (edited by Terence Ball). Cambridge: Cambridge University Press.

Hansen, Mogens Herman. 1974. *The Sovereignty of the People's Court in Athens.* Odense: Odense Universitetsforlag.

Hansen, Mogens Herman. 1989. "Demos, Ekklesia and Dikasterion. A Reply to Martin Ostwald and Josiah Ober." *The Athenian Ecclesia II: A Collection of Articles 1983–9*, pp. 213–218.

Hansen, Mogens Herman. 1991. *The Athenian Democracy in the Age of Demosthenes: Structures, Principles and Ideology.* Oxford and Cambridge: Blackwell.

Hansen, Mogens Herman. 2010. "The Concept of *Demos, Ekklesia*, and *Dikasterion* in Classical Athens." *Greek, Roman, and Byzantine Studies* 50: 499–536.

Hayward, Jack, ed. 1996. *The Crisis of Representation in Europe.* Abingdon, Oxon: Routledge, 1996.

Held, David. 1995. *Democracy and the Global Order.* Cambridge: Polity Press.

Helgadóttir, Ragnhildur. 2014. "Which Citizens?—Participation in the Drafting of the Icelandic Constitutional Draft of 2011." Blog of the *International Journal of Constitutional Law.* . Available online at http://www.iconnectblog.com/2014/10/which-citizens-participation-in-the-drafting-of-the-icelandic-constitutional-draft-of-2011/

Heller, Nathaniel. 2011. "Is Open Data a Good Idea for the Open Government Partnership?" Available online at http://www.globalintegrity.org/2011/09/open-data-for-ogp/. Last accessed October 8, 2017.

Hennig, Bret. 2017. *The End of Politicians. Time for a Real Democracy.* Unbound Digital.

Hindman, Matthew. 2010. *The Myth of Digital Democracy.* Princeton, NJ: Princeton University Press.

Hobbes, Thomas. 1996. *Leviathan.* Revised student edition. Cambridge: Cambridge University Press.

Hoffman, Hasso. 1974. *Repräsentation. Studien zur Wort- and Begriffgeschichte von der Antike bis in 19. Jahrhundert.* Berlin: Duncker & Humblot.

Hong, Lu, and Scott E. Page. 2004. "Groups of Diverse Problem Solvers Can Outperform Groups of High-Ability Problem Solvers." *Proceedings of the National Academy of Sciences of the United States of America* 101(46): 16, 385–389.

Hudson, Alexander. 2018. "When Does Public Participation Make a Difference? Evidence from Iceland's Crowdsourced Constitution." *Policy & Internet* 10(2): 185–217. doi:10.1002/poi3.167.

Immergut, Helen. 1992. "Institutions, Veto Points, and Policy Results: A Comparative Analysis of Health Care." *Journal of Public Policy* 10(4): 391–416.

Ingham, Sean. 2019. *Rule by Multiple Majorities: A New Theory of Popular Control.* Cambridge: Cambridge University Press.

Jóhannesson, Guoni T. H. 2011. Tjaldað til einnar nætur: Uppruni bráðabirgðarstjórnarskrárinnar (Preparing for the Short-Term: The Origin of the Interim Constitution). *Icelandic Review of Politics and Administration* 7(1): 61–72.

Johns, Melissa Marie, and Valentina Saltane. 2016. "Citizen Engagement in Rulemaking—Evidence on Regulatory Practices in 185 Countries." Policy Research working paper no. WPS 7840. Washington, DC: World Bank Group.

Jones, Garett. 2020. *10% Less Democracy: Why You Should Trust Elites a Little More and the Masses a Little Less.* Stanford, CA: Stanford University Press.

Jordan, S. R. 2011. "Accountability in Two Non-Western Contexts." In M. J. Dubnick and H. G. Frederickson, eds., *Accountable Governance: Problems and Promises.* Armonk, NY: M. E. Sharpe, 241–254.

Kanra, Bora. 2009. *Islam, Democracy, and Dialogue in Turkey: Deliberating in Divided Societies.* Aldershot, UK: Ashgate.

Kantorowitz, Ernest H. 1998 [1957]. *The King's Two Bodies: A Study in Mediaeval Political Theology.* Princeton, NJ: Princeton University Press.

Karlsson, Gunnar. 2000. *The History of Iceland.* Minneapolis: University of Minnesota Press.

Keane, John. 2009. *The Life and Death of Democracy.* New York: Simon & Schuster.

Khanna, Parag. 2017. *Technocracy in America: The Rise of the Info-State.* Scotts Valley, CA: CreateSpace.

Kinsky, Lucy, and Ben Crum. 2020. "Transnational Representation in EU National Parliaments: Concept, Case Study, Research Agenda." *Political Studies* 68(2): 370–388.

Klein, Mark. 2011. "How to Harvest Collective Wisdom on Complex Problems: An Introduction to the MIT Deliberatorium." Center for Collective Intelligence Working Paper, available online at http://cci.mit.edu/docs/working_papers_2012_2013/kleinwp2013.pdf.

Kloppenberg, James T. 2016. *Toward Democracy: The Struggle for Self-Rule in European and American Thought.* Oxford: Oxford University Press.

Knight, Jack, and James Johnson. 1994. "Aggregation and Deliberation: On the Possibility of Democratic Legitimacy." *Political Theory* 22(2): 277.

Knight, Jack, and Melissa Schwartzberg, eds. 2019. *Nomos LXI. Political Legitimacy.* New York: NYU Press.

Kok, Alexander. 2011. "Icelandic National Forum 2010." *Participedia.* Available online at http://participedia.net/en/cases/icelandic-national-forum-2010.

Kousser, Thad. 2005. *Term Limits and the Dismantling of State Legislative Professionalism.* Cambridge: Cambridge University Press.

Krahé, Maximilian. 2019. "The Modern Predicament: Capitalism, Democracy, and the Extended Division of Labour." PhD dissertation, Yale University.

Kuehn, Daniel. 2017. "Diversity, Ability, and Democracy: A Note on Thompson's Challenge to Hong and Page." *Critical Review: A Journal of Politics and Society* 29(1): 72–87.

Kuyper, Jonathan W. 2016. "Systemic Representation: Democracy, Deliberation, and Nonelectoral Representatives." *American Political Science Review* 110(2): 308–324.

Lafont, Cristina. 2015. "Deliberation, Participation, and Democratic Legitimacy: Should Deliberative Mini-publics Shape Public Policy?." *Journal of Political Philosophy* 23(1): 40–63.

Lafont, Cristina. 2020. *Democracy Without Shortcuts.* Oxford: Oxford University Press.

Landauer, Matthew. 2019. *Dangerous Counsel: Accountability and Advice in Ancient Greece.* Chicago: University of Chicago Press.

Landemore, Hélène. 2012. "Democratic Reason: The Mechanisms of Collective Wisdom in Politics." In H. Landemore and J. Elster, *Collective Wisdom: Principles and Mechanisms.* Cambridge: Cambridge University Press, 251–289.

Landemore, Hélène. 2013a. *Democratic Reason: Politics, Collective Intelligence, and the Rule of the Many.* Princeton, NJ: Princeton University Press.

Landemore, Hélène. 2013b. "Deliberation, Cognitive Diversity, and Democratic Inclusiveness: An Epistemic Argument for the Random Selection of Representatives." *Synthese* 190: 1209–1231.

Landemore, Hélène. 2014a. "On Minimal Deliberation, Partisan Activism, and Teaching People How to Disagree." *Critical Review: A Journal of Politics and Society* 25: 210–225.

Landemore, Hélène. 2014b. "Yes We Can (Make It Up On Volume): Reply to Critics." *Critical Review* 6 (1–2): 184–237.

Landemore, Hélène. 2014c. "Democracy as Heuristic: The Ecological Rationality of Political Equality." *Good Society* 23(2): 160.

Landemore, Hélène. 2015. "Inclusive Constitution-Making: The Icelandic Experiment." *Journal of Political Philosophy* 23(2): 166–191.

Landemore, Hélène. 2016. "What Is a Good Constitution? Assessing the Icelandic Constitutional Proposal." In T. Ginsburg and A. Huq, eds., *Assessing Constitutional Performance.* Cambridge: Cambridge University Press, 71–98.

Landemore, Hélène. 2017a. "Beyond the Fact of Disagreement? The Epistemic Turn in Deliberative Democracy." *Social Epistemology* 31(3): 277–295.

Landemore, Hélène. 2017b. "Inclusive Constitution-Making and Religious Rights: Lessons from the Icelandic Experiment." *Journal of Politics* 79(3): 762–779.

Landemore, Hélène. 2017c. "Deliberative Democracy as Open, Not (Just) Representative Democracy." *Daedalus* 146(3): 51–63.

Landemore, Hélène. 2018. "What Does It Mean to Take Diversity Seriously? On Open-Mindedness as a Civic Virtue." *Georgetown Journal of Law and Public Policy* 16: 795–805.

Landemore, Hélène. 2020a. "Que représente la Convention Citoyenne sur le climat?" *Le Monde*, February 10. Available online at https://www.lemonde.fr/idees/article/2020/02/10/la-convention-citoyenne-pour-le-climat-pourrait-prefigurer-une-nouvelle-forme-de-democratie_6029098_3232.html.

Landemore, Hélène. 2020b. "When Public Participation Matters: The 2010–2013 Icelandic Constitutional Process." *International Journal of Constitutional Law.*

Landemore, Hélène. 2021. "Open Democracy and Digital Technologies." In L. Bernholz, H. Landemore, and R. Reich, eds., *Digital Technology and Democratic Theory.* Chicago: University of Chicago Press.

Landemore, Hélène, and Jon Elster, eds. 2012. *Collective Wisdom. Principles and Mechanisms.* Cambridge: Cambridge University Press.

Landemore, Hélène, and Isabelle Ferreras. 2016. "In Defense of Workplace Democracy: Towards a Justification of the Firm-State Analogy." *Political Theory* 44(1): 53–81.

Landemore, Hélène, Bernard Manin, and Nadia Urbinati. 2008. "Is Representative Democracy Really Democratic?" *Books & Ideas.* Available online at http://www.booksandideas.net/Is-representative-democracy-really-democratic.

Landemore, Hélène, and Scott E. Page. 2015. "Deliberation and Disagreement: Problem Solving, Prediction, and Positive Dissensus." *Philosophy, Politics, and Economics* 14(3): 229–254.

Lane, Melissa. 2016. *Birth of Politics: Eight Greek and Roman Political Ideas and Why They Matter.* Princeton, NJ: Princeton University Press.

Langlamet, Helene. 2018. "Can Digital Technologies Create a Stronger Model for Democratic Participation? The Case of Crowdlaw." Proceedings of the 51st Hawaii International Conference on System Sciences, 2039–2319.

Lee, Youngjae. 2018. "The Criminal Jury, Moral Judgments, and Political Representation." *University of Illinois Law Review* 1256–1290.

Leib, Ethan J. 2004. *Deliberative Democracy in America: A Proposal for a Popular Branch.* University Park: Pennsylvania State University Press.

Leib, Ethan J., and David L. Ponet. 2012. "Citizen Representation and the American Jury." In P. Lenard and R. Simeon, eds., *Imperfect Democracies: The Democratic Deficit in Canada and the United States.* Vancouver: University of British Columbia Press, 269–290.

Lessig, Lawrence. 2012. *One Way Forward: The Outsider's Guide to Fixing the Republic.* Byliner Inc.

Levitsky, Steve,n and Daniel Ziblatt. 2018. *How Democracies Die.* New York: Crown.

Levy, Ron. 2013. "'Deliberative Voting': Realising Constitutional Referendum Democracy." *Public Law* 555.

Lijphart, Arend. 1984. *Democracies: Patterns of Majoritarian and Consensus Government in Twenty-One Counries.* New Haven, CT: Yale University Press.

Lipset, Seymour M. 1960. *Political Man: The Social Bases of Politics.* New York: Doubleday.

List, Christian, Robert C. Luskin, James S. Fishkin, and Iain McLean. 2013. "Deliberation, Single-Peakedness, and the Possibility of Meaningful Democracy." *Journal of Politics* 75(1): 80–95.

Lukes, Steven. 1974. *Power: A Radical View*. New York: Palgrave Macmillan.

Luskin, Robert C., Ian O'Flynn, James S. Fishkin, and David Russell. 2014. "Deliberating across Deep Divides." *Political Studies* 62(1): 117.

Maboudi, Tofigh, and Ghazal P. Nadi. 2016. "Crowdsourcing the Egyptian Constitution: Social Media, Elites, and the Populace." *Political Research Quarterly* 69(4): 716–731. Available online at https://doi.org/10.1177/1065912916658550.

Macdonald, Terry. 2008. *Global Stakeholder Democracy*. Oxford: Oxford University Press.

Magnusson, Finnur. 2013. "How to Write a Constitution in the 21st Century. Presentation at the Conference on Right to Information and Transparency." CDDRL Stanford University, March 11.

Maier, Peter. 2013. *Ruling the Void: The Hollowing-Out of Western Democracy*. New York: Verso.

Manin, Bernard. 1987. "On Legitimacy and Political Deliberation." Translated from the French by E. Stein and J. Mansbridge. *Political Theory* 15(3): 338–368.

Manin, Bernard. 1997. *The Principles of Representative Government*. Cambridge: Cambridge University Press.

Mankiw, Gregory. 2013. "Defending the One Percent." *Journal of Economic Perspectives* 27(3): 21–34.

Mansbridge, Jane. 2003. "Rethinking Representation." *American Political Science Review* 97(4): 515–528.

Mansbridge, Jane. 2009. "A Selection Model of Representation." *Journal of Political Philosophy* 17(4): 369–398.

Mansbridge, Jane. 2010. "Deliberative Polling as the Gold Standard." *Good Society* 19(1): 55–62.

Mansbridge, Jane. 2012. "On the Importance of Getting Things Done." The 2011 James Madison Lecture.

Mansbridge, Jane. 2014. "What Is Political Science For?" *Perspective on Politics* 12(1): 8–17.

Mansbridge, Jane. 2019. "Accountability in the Constituent-Representative Relationship." In J. Gastil and E. O. Wright, eds., *Legislature by Lot: Transformative Designs for Deliberative Governance*, London: Verso, pp. xxx.

Mansbridge, Jane. 2020. "Representation Failure." In Melissa Schwartzberg and Daniel Viehoff, eds., *NOMOS LXIII: Democratic Failure*. New York: New York University Press.

Matsusaka, John G. 2005. "Direct Democracy Works." *Journal of Economic Perspectives* 19(2): 185–206.

Matsusaka, John G. 2020. *Let the People Rule. How Direct Democracy Can Meet the Populist Challenge*. Princeton, NJ: Princeton University Press.

McCarthy, Nolan, Keith T. Poole, and Howard Rosenthal. 2006. *Polarized America: The Dance of Ideology and Unequal Riches*. Cambridge, MA: MIT Press.

McCormick, John. 2011. *Machiavellian Democracy*. Cambridge: Cambridge University Press.

McCormick, John. 2019. "The New Ochlophobia? Populism, Majority Rule, and Prospects for Democratic Republicanism." In Y. Elazar and G. Rousselière, eds., *Republicanism and the Future of Democracy*. Cambridge: Cambridge University Press, 130–151.

McCormick, John. Forthcoming. In G. Ballacci and R. Goodman, eds., *Populism, Demagoguery, and Rhetoric in Historical Perspective*.

McGann, Anthony. 2006. *The Logic of Democracy: Reconciling Equality, Deliberation, and Minority Protection*. Ann Arbor: University of Michigan Press.

Meuwese, Anne. 2013. "Popular Constitution-Making: The Case of Iceland." In D. Galligan and M. Versteeg, eds., *The Social and Political Foundations of Constitutions*. New York: Cambridge University Press, 469–496.

Mill, John Stuart. 1915 [1848]. *Principles of Political Economy with Some of Their Applications to Social Philosophy* 752, 9th edition. London: J.W. Ashley.

Miller, James. 1984. *Rousseau: Dreamer of Democracy*. New Haven, CT: Yale University Press.

Miller, James C. 1969. "A Program for Direct and Proxy Voting in the Legislative Process." *Public Choice* 7–7(1): 107–13.

Miller, Susan, Jill Nicholson-Crotty, and Sean Nicholson-Crotty. 2011. "Reexamining the Institutional Effects of Term Limits in U.S. State Legislatures." *Legislative Studies Quarterly* 36(1): 71–97.

Moeckli, Daniel. 2018. "Referendums: Tyranny of the Majority?" In Francis Cheneval and Alice el-Wakil, "Do Referendums Enhance or Threaten Democracy?" *Swiss Political Science Review* 24(3): 335–341.

Moehler, Devra C. 2006. "Participation and Support for the Constitution in Uganda." *Journal of Modern African Studies* 44(2): 275–308.

Moncrieffe, J. M. 1998. "Reconceptualizing Political Accountability." *International Political Science Review* 19(4): 387–406.

Montanaro, Laura. 2012. "The Democratic Legitimacy of Self-Appointed Representatives." *Journal of Politics* 74(4): 1094–1107.

Mooney, Christopher. 2007. "Lobbyists and Interest Groups." In K. Kurtz, B. Cain, and B. Niemi, eds. *Institutional Change in American Politics: The Case of Term Limits.* Ann Arbor: University of Michigan Press.

Morris-Jones, W. H. 1954. "In Defense of Apathy." *Political Studies* 11: 25–37.

Mounk, Yashka. 2018. *The People versus Democracy: Why Our Freedom Is in Danger and How to Save It.* Cambridge, MA: Harvard University Press.

Mutz, Diana. 2006. *Hearing the Other Side: Deliberative versus Participatory Democracy.* Cambridge: Cambridge University Press.

Nelson, Eric. 2014. *The Royalist Revolution: Monarchy and the American Founding.* Cambridge, MA: Harvard University Press.

Newsom, Gavin. 2014. *Citizenville: How to Take the Town Square Digital and Reinvent Government.* New York: Penguin.

Niesen, Peter. 2019. "Reinventing the Wheel? Reciprocal Representation in Bentham and Blatter." Blog post available at http://globalcit.eu/let-me-vote-in-your-country-and-ill-let-you-vote-in-mine-a-proposal-for-transnational-democracy/11/. Last accessed January 17, 2020.

Norbäck, Per. 2012. *The Little Horse from Athens.* Amazon Kindle.

Norris, Pippa. 2011. *Democratic Deficit: Critical Citizens Revisited.* Cambridge: Cambridge University Press.

Norris, Pippa. 2017. *Why American Elections Are Flawed (and How to Fix Them).* Ithaca, NY: Cornell University Press.

Noveck, Beth. 2012. "Open Data—The Democratic Imperative." Blog post. https://crookedtimber.org/2012/07/05/open-data-the-democratic-imperative/. Last accessed April 17, 2020.

Noveck, Beth. 2018. "Crowdlaw: Collective Intelligence and Lawmaking." *Analyse & Kritik* 40(2): 359–380.

Ober, Josiah. 1996 [1989]. "Review Article: The Nature of Athenian Democracy." *Classical Philology* 84(4): 322–334.

Ober, Josiah. 1997. *Mass and Elites in Ancient Athens: Rhetoric, Ideology, and the Power of the People.* Princeton, NJ: Princeton University Press.

Ober, Josiah. 2008. *Democracy and Knowledge: Innovation and Learning in Classical Athens.* Princeton, NJ: Princeton University Press.

Ober, Josiah. 2017. *Demopolis. Democracy Before Liberalism in Theory and Practice.* Cambridge: Cambridge University Press.

Ober, Josiah. 2018. *Democracy Before Liberalism.* Princeton, NJ: Princeton University Press.

Occalan, Abdullah. 2015. *Democratic Confederalism.* Honolulu: Transmedia Publishing.

Oddsdóttir, Katrín. 2014. "Iceland: The Birth of the World's First Crowd-Sourced Constitution?." *Cambridge Journal of International and Comparative Law* 1207.

OECD (Organisation for Economic Co-operation and Development). 2009. *Focus on Citizens: Public Engagement for Better Policy and Services*. OECD Studies on Public Engagement. Paris: OECD Publishing.

OECD. 2020. *Catching the Deliberative Wave: Innovative Citizen Participation and New Democratic Institutions*. Paris: OECD Publishing.

O'Flynn, Ian. 2007. "Divided Societies and Deliberative Democracy." *British Journal of Political Science* 37(4): 731–751.

O'Leary, Kevin. 2006. *Saving Democracy: A Plan for Real Democracy in America*. Stanford, CA: Stanford University Press.

Orgad, Liav. 2018. "Cloud Communities: The Dawn of Global Citizenship?." In R. Bauböck, ed., *Debating Transformations of National Citizenship*. IMISCOE Research Series. New York: Springer: 251–260.

Ostrogorski, Moisei. 1903. *La démocratie et l'organisation des partis*. Paris: Calmann-Lévy.

Page, Scott E. 2007. *The Difference: How the Power of Diversity Creates Better Groups, Firms, Schools, and Societies*. Princeton, NJ: Princeton University Press.

Page, Scott E. 2015. "Diversity Trumps Ability and the Proper Use of Mathematics." *Notices of the AMS* 62(1): 9–10.

Papadopoulos, Yannis. 1998. *La Démocratie Directe*. Paris: Economica.

Papadopoulos, Yannis. 2013. *Democracy in Crisis?: Politics, Governance, and Policy*. London: Palgrave Macmillan.

Partlett, William. 2012. "The Dangers of Popular Constitution-Making." *Brooklyn Journal of International Law* 38(1): 193–238.

Peixoto, Tiago. 2009. "Territorial Representation and Ideational e-Constituencies." Blog post. Democracy Spot. Available online at https://democracyspot.net/2009/09/10/territorial-representation-and-ideational-e-constituencies/.

Peter, Fabienne. 2009. *Democratic Legitimacy*. New York: Routledge.

Peter, Fabienne. 2017. "Political Legitimacy." In E. Zalta, ed., *The Stanford Encyclopedia of Philosophy*. Available online at https://plato.stanford.edu/archives/sum2017/entries/legitimacy/.

Peters, B. 1993. *Die Integration moderner Gesellschaften*. Frankfurt am Main: Suhrkamp.

Peters, B. 2008. "On Public Deliberation and Public Culture." In H. Wessler, ed., *Public Deliberation and Public Culture: The Writings of Bernhard Peters, 1993–2005*. New York: Palgrave Macmillan.

Pettit, Philip. 2010. "Representation, Responsive and Indicative." *Constellations* 17(3): 426–434.

Pettit, Philip. 2012. *On the People's Terms. A Republican Theory and Model of Democracy*. Cambridge: Cambridge University Press.

Philp, M. 2009. "Delimiting Democratic Accountability." *Political Studies* 57(1): 28–53.

Piketty, Thomas. 2013. *Capital in the Twenty-First Century*. Cambridge, MA: Harvard University Press.

Piketty, Thomas. 2019. *Capital and Ideology*. Paris: Le Seuil.

Pitkin, Hannah. 1989 [1967]. *The Concept of Representation*. Berkeley: University of California Press.

Pitkin, Hannah. 2004. "Representation and Democracy: Uneasy Alliance." *Scandinavian Political Studies* 27(3): 335–342.

Plotke, David. 1997. "Representation Is Democracy." *Constellations* 4(1): 19–34.

Pogrebinschi, Thamy. 2013. "The Squared Circle of Participatory Democracy: Scaling Up Deliberation to the National Level." *Critical Policy Studies* 7(3): 219–241.

Pollitt, Christopher. 2011. "Performance Blight and the Tyranny of Light? Accountability in Advanced Performance Measurement Regimes." In M. J. Dubnick and H. George Frederickson, eds., *Accountable Governance: Problems and Promises*. New York and London: M.E. Sharpe, 81–97.

Popper, Karl. 2013 [1945]. *The Open Society and Its Enemies*. Princeton, NJ: Princeton University Press.

Poster, Mark. 1997. "Cyberdemocracy: The Internet and the Public Sphere." In David Holmes, ed., *Virtual Politics, Identity and Community in Cyberspace*. London: Sage, 212–228.

Powell, Richard J. 2007. "Executive-Legislative Relationships." In Karl Kurtz, Bruce Cain, and Richard G. Niemi, eds., *Institutional Change in American Politics: The Case of Term Limits*. Ann Arbor: University of Michigan Press.

Przeworski, Adam. 2019. *The Crises of Democracy*. Cambridge: Cambridge University Press.

Quirk, Paul J. 2014. "Making It Up on Volume: Are Larger Groups Really Smarter?" *Critical Review* 26(1–2): 129–150.

Qvortrup, M. 2000. "Are Referendums Controlled and Pro-hegemonic?" *Political Studies* 48(4): 821–826.

Rachman, Gideon. 2016. "The Global Democratic Recession: Democracy Is in Retreat Around the World—for Now." *Financial Times*, August 8.

Rae, Lang. 1969. "Decision-Rules and Individual Values." *American Political Science Review* 63(1): 40–56.

Ragin, Charles C. 2008. "Measurement Versus Calibration: A Set-Theoretic Approach." *The Oxford Handbook of Political Methodology*. Oxford: Oxford University Press.

Rawls, John. 1993. *Political Liberalism*. New York: Columbia University Press.

Rawls, John. 2001. *Justice as Fairness: A Restatement*. Cambridge, MA: Belknap Press of Harvard University Press.

Rehfeld, Andrew. 2005. *The Concept of Constituency: Political Representation, Democratic Legitimacy, and Institutional Design*. Cambridge: Cambridge University Press.

Rehfeld, Andrew. 2006. "Towards a General Theory of Political Representation." *Journal of Politics* 68(1): 1–21.

Rehfeld, Andrew. 2009. "Representation Rethought: On Trustees, Delegates, and Gyroscopes in the Study of Political Representation and Democracy." *American Political Science Review* 103(2): 214–230.

Reutemann, Tim, 2018. *Liquid Reign*. Independently published.

Rheingold, Howard. 1994. *The Virtual Community. Homesteading on the Electronic Frontier*. New York: Harper Perennial.

Richardson, Lilliard E., David Valentine, and Shannon Daily Stokes. 2005. "Assessing the Impact of Term Limits in Missouri." *State & Local Government Review* 37(3):177–192.

Risse, Mathias. 2004. "Arguing for Majority Rule." *Journal of Political Philosophy* 12(1): 41–64.

Rodrik, Dani. 2007. "The Inescapable Trilemma of the World Economy." Available online at http://rodrik.typepad.com/dani_rodriks_weblog/2007/06/the-inescapable.html.

Rogers, Melvin and Jack Turner. 2020. *African American Political Thought*. Chicago: University of Chicago Press.

Rosanvallon, Pierre. 2008. *Counter-Democracy: Politics in an Age of Distrust*. Cambridge: Cambridge University Press.

Rosanvallon, Pierre. 2011a. *Democratic Legitimacy: Impartiality, Reflexivity, Proximity*. Princeton, NJ: Princeton University Press.

Rosanvallon, Pierre. 2011b. "The Metamorphoses of Democratic Legitimacy: Impartiality, Reflexivitiy, Proximity." *Constellation* 18(2): 539–549.

Rose, Julie. 2016. *Free Time*. Princeton, NJ: Princeton University Press.

Rosenberg, Gerald N. 1991. *The Hollow Hope: Can Courts Bring About Social Change?* Chicago: University of Chicago Press.

Rosenblatt, Helena. 2018. *The Lost History of Liberalism: From Ancient Rome to the Twenty-First Century*. Princeton, NJ: Princeton University Press.

Rosenbluth, Frances and Ian Shapiro. 2018. *Responsible Parties: Saving Democracy from Itself*. New Haven, CT: Yale University Press.

Rousseau, Jean-Jacques. 1964. *Oeuvres Complètes* (tome III). Paris: La Pléiade.

Rousseau, Jean-Jacques. 1997. *The Social Contract and Other Later Political Writings.* Edited by V. Gourevitch. Cambridge: Cambridge University Press.

Rummens, Stefan. 2012. "Staging Deliberation: The Role of Representative Institutions in the Deliberative Democratic Process." *Journal of Political Philosophy* 20(1): 223–244.

Rummens, Stefan. 2016. "Legitimacy Without Visibility: On the Role of Mini-Publics in the Democratic System." In Min Reuchamps and Jane Suiter, eds., *Constitutional Deliberative Democracy in Europe*, Colchester: ECPR Press Available online at file:///Users/helenelandemorejelaca/Downloads/Reuchamps%20and%20Suiter_final%20cover.pdf.

Runciman, David. 2013. *The Confidence Trap: A History of Democracy in Crisis from World War I to the Present.* Princeton, NJ: Princeton University Press.

Runciman, David. 2018. *How Democracy Ends.* New York: Basic Books.

Saati, Abrak. 2015. "The Participation Myth: Outcomes of Participatory Constitution Building Processes on Democracy." Research Report. Department of Political Science, Umeå University. Available online at http://umu.diva-portal.org/smash/get/diva2:809188/FULLTEXT01 .pdf. Accessed April 10, 2017.

Saez, Emmanuel, and Gabriel Zucman. 2014. "Wealth Inequality in the United States since 1913: Evidence from Capitalized Income Tax Data." NBER Working Paper No. 20625, issued in October.

Sanyal, Paromita, and Vijayendra Rao. 2018. *Oral Democracy: Deliberation in Indian Village Assemblies.* Cambridge: Cambridge University Press.

Saunders, Ben. 2008. "The Equality of Lotteries." *Philosophy* 83(3): 359–372.

Saward, Michael. 2008. "Representation and Democracy: Revisions and Possibilities." *Sociology Compass* 2(3): 1000–1013.Sayke. 2014. "Liquid Democracy." Blog post. Available online at https://web.archive.org/web/20040616144517/http://www.twistedmatrix.com/wiki /python/LiquidDemocracy. Last accessed April 29, 2020.

Saward, Michael. 2010. *The Representative Claim.* Oxford: Oxford University Press.

Scharpf, Fritz. 2003. "Problem-Solving Effectiveness and Democratic Accountability in the EU." MPIfG Working Paper. Max-Planck-Institut für Gesellschaftsforschung. Available online at https://www.econstor.eu/handle/10419/41664.

Schmidt, Vivien A. 2013. "Democracy and Legitimacy in the European Union Revisited: Input, Output, and 'Throughput.'" *Political Studies* 61: 2–22.

Schmitter, Philippe. 1997. "Exploring the Problematic Triumph of Liberal Democracy and Concluding with a Modest Proposal for Improving Its International Impact." In A. Hadenius, ed. *Democracy's Victory and Crisis.* Cambridge: Cambridge University Press.

Schmitter, Philippe C. 2019. "The Vices and Virtues of 'Populisms.'" *Sociologica* 13(1): 75–81.

Schumpeter, Joseph. 1975 [1942]. *Capitalism, Socialism, and Democracy.* New York: Harper and Brothers.

Schwaliz, Claudia. 2019. "A New Wave of Deliberative Democracy." Blog Post, November 26. Available online at https://carnegieeurope.eu/2019/11/26/new-wave-of-deliberative-democracy -pub-80422. Last accessed February 14, 2020.

Schwartzberg, Melissa. 2014. *Counting the Many. The Origins and Limits of Supermajority Rule.* Cambridge: Cambridge University Press.

Scott, James. 1999. *Seeing Like a State: How Certain Schemes to Improve the Human Condition Have Failed.* New Haven, CT: Yale University Press.

Scott, James. 2017. *Against the Grain.* New Haven, CT: Yale University Press.

Shachar, Ayelet. 2009. *The Birthright Lottery: Citizenship and Global Inequality.* Cambridge: Harvard University Press.

Shapiro, Ian. 2016. *Politics Against Domination.* Cambridge, MA: Harvard University Press.

Shapiro, Ian. 2017. "Collusion in Restraint of Democracy: Against Political Deliberation." *Daedalus* 146(3): 64–76.

Shapiro Ian, Susan C. Stokes, Elizabeth Jean Wood, and Alexander S. Kirshner. 2009. *Political Representation*. Cambridge: Cambridge University Press.

Simmons, A. John. 2001. *Justification and Legitimacy: Essays on Rights and Obligations*. Cambridge: Cambridge University Press.

Singer, Daniel J. 2018. "Diversity, Not Randomness, Trumps Ability." *Philosophy of Science* 86(1): 178–191.

Sintomer, Yves. 2018. *From Radical to Deliberative Democracy: Random Selection in Politics from Athens to the Present*. Cambridge: Cambridge University Press.

Siri, Santiago. 2015. "Democracy Earth Foundation." Retrieved from http://democracy.earth/.

Sjoberg, Fredrik M., Jonathan Mellon, Tiago C. Peixoto, Johannes Hemker, and Lily L. Tsai. 2019. "Voice and Punishment: A Global Survey Experiment on Tax Morale." Policy Research Working Paper 8855. World Bank.

Skalski, Jérôme. 2012. *La Révolution des Casseroles: Chroniques d'une nouvelle constitution pour l'Islande*. Paris: Contre Allée.

Slobodian, Quinn. 2018. *Globalists: The End of Empire and the Birth of Neoliberalism*. Cambridge, MA: Harvard University Press.

Smith, Graham. 2009. *Democratic Innovations: Designing Institutions for Citizen Participation*. Cambridge: Cambridge University Press.

Smith, Melancton. 1987. Speech at the 1788 New York Convention, reprinted in Philip B. Kurland, *The Founders' Constitution*, ch. 13, Ralph Lerner and Philip B. Kurland, eds. Chicago: University of Chicago Press.

Spada, Paolo, Mark Klein, Raffaele Calabretta, Luca Iandoli, and Ivana Quinto. 2016. "A First Step toward Scaling-up Deliberation: Optimizing Large Group E-Deliberation using Argument Maps." Working paper.

Spada, Paolo, Jonathan Mellon, Tiago Peixoto, and Fredrik M. Sjoberg. 2016. "Effects of the Internet on Participation: Study of a Public Policy Referendum in Brazil." *Journal of Information Technology & Politics* 13(3): 187–207.

Stone, Peter. 2011. *The Luck of the Draw*. Oxford: Oxford University Press.

Storing, Herbert J., ed. 1981. *What the Anti-Federalists Were For: The Political Thought of the Opponents of the Constitution*. Chicago: University of Chicago Press.

Suiter, Jane. 2018. "Deliberation in Action—Ireland's Abortion Referendum." *Political Insight* 9(3): 30–32.

Suteu, Silvia. 2015. "Constitutional Conventions in the Digital Era: Lessons from Iceland and Ireland 38 BC." *International and Comparative Literature Review* 251.

Sutherland, Keith. 2008. *A Peoples' Parliament*. Charlottesville, VA: Imprint Academic.

Swierczek, Björn. 2011. "5 Years of Liquid Democracy in Germany." *Liquid Democracy Journal* 1. Available online at http://www.liquid-democracy-journal.org/issue/1/The_Liquid _Democracy_Journal-Issue001-02-Five_years_of_Liquid_Democracy_in_Germany.html.

Tempelhof, Susanne Tarkowski, Eliott Teissonniere, James Fennell Tempelhof, and Dana Edwards. 2017. *BITNATION, Pangea Jurisdiction and Pangea Arbitration Token (PAT): The Internet of Sovereignty*. Bitnation: Planet Earth. Available at https://eliott.teissonniere.org /assets/files/bitnation.pdf.

Terwel, B. W., F. Harinck, N. Ellemers, and D. D. Daamen. 2010. "Voice in Political Decision-Making: The Effect of Group Voice on Perceived Trustworthiness of Decision Makers and Subsequent Acceptance of Decisions." *Journal of Experimental Psychology: Applied* 16(2): 173.

Thompson, Abigail. 2014. "Does Diversity Trump Ability? An Example of the Misuse of Mathematics in the Social Sciences." *Notices of the American Mathematical Society* 61(9): 1024–1030.

Torfason, Hjörtur. 2009. Influential Constitutional Justice: Some Icelandic Perspectives. World Conference on Constitutional Justice, Cape Town, January 23–24.

Tormey, Simon. 2015. *The End of Representative Politics*. Cambridge: Polity Press.

Touchton, Michael, Brian Wampler, and Tiago C. Peixoto. 2019. "Of Governance and Revenue: Participatory Institutions and Tax Compliance in Brazil." Policy Research Working Paper 8797. World Bank.

Trechsel, Alexander H. 2010. "Reflexive Accountability and Direct Democracy." *West European Politics* 33(5): 1050–1064.

Trechsel, Alexander H. 2012. "Reflexive Accountability and Direct Democracy." In D. Curtin, Peter Mair, and Yannis Papadopoulos, eds., *Accountability and European Governance*. London: Routledge, ch. 7.

Treisman, Daniel. 2018. "Is Democracy in Danger? A Quick Look at the Data." Paper presented at the Conference on Democratic Backsliding and Electoral Authoritarianism. Yale University, April.

Tuck, Richard. 2016. *The Sleeping Sovereign: The Invention of Modern Democracy*. Cambridge: Cambridge University Press.

Tucker, Paul. 2018. *Unelected Power: The Quest for Legitimacy in Central Banking and the Regulatory State*. Princeton, NJ: Princeton University Press.

Tüfekçi, Zeynep. 2017. *Twitter and Tear Gas: The Power and Fragility of Networked Protest*. New Haven, CT: Yale University Press.

Tullock, Gordon. 1967. *Toward a Mathematics of Politics*. Ann Arbor: University of Michigan Press.

Tushnet, Mark. 2013. "Constitution-Making: An Introduction." *Texas Law Review* 91: 1983–2013.

Urbinati, Nadia. 2006. *Representative Democracy: Principles and Genealogy*. Chicago: University of Chicago Press.

Urbinati, Nadia. 2014. *Democracy Disfigured*. Cambridge, MA: Harvard University Press.

Urbinati, Nadia and Mark Warren. 2008. "The Concept of Representation in Contemporary Democratic Theory." *Annual Review of Political Science* 11: 387–412.

Valsangiacomo, Chiara. 2020. "Liquid Democracy: Outline and Defense of a New, Minimal Conceptualization." Working Paper.

Valtysson, Bjarki. 2014. "Democracy in Disguise: The Use of Social Media in Reviewing the Icelandic Constitution." *Media, Culture, and Society* 36(1): 3–19.

Vandamme, Pierre-Etienne. 2018. "Des référendums plus délibératifs? Les atouts du vote justifié." *Participations* 20: 29–52.

Van der Vossen, Bas. 2018. *In Defense of Openness: Why Global Freedom Is the Humane Solution to Global Poverty*. Princeton, NJ: Princeton University Press.

Van Parijs, Philip and Yannick Vanderborght. 2018. *Basic Income: A Radical Proposal for a Free Society and a Sane Economy*. Cambridge, MA: Harvard University Press.

Van Reybrouck, David. 2016. *Against Elections: The Case for Democracy*. London: Bodley Head.

Vasilev, George. 2015. *Solidarity across Divides: Promoting the Moral Point of View*. Edinburgh: Edinburgh University Press.

Vedel, Thierry. 2003. "L'idée de démocratie électronique. Origines, visions, questions." In Pascal Perrineau, ed., *Le désenchantement démocratique*, La Tour d'Aigues: Editions de l'Aube, 243–266 ("The Idea of Virtual Democracy. Origins, Visions, Questions" in *Democratic Disenchantment*).

Velikanov, Cyril. 2012. "Mass Online Deliberation: Requirements, Metrics, Tools and Procedures." Working paper.

Venice Commission (European Commission for Democracy Through Law). 2013. "On the Draft New Constitution of Iceland." Opinion Nber 702. Available at https://www.althingi.is/pdf /Feneyjanefnd_skyrsla_e_11_03_2013.pdf.

Vieira, Monica Brito and David Runciman. 2008. *Representation*. Cambridge, UK: Polity.

Voeten, Erik. 2017. "Are People Really Turning Away from Democracy?" *Journal of Democracy*. Online debate available at https://www.journalofdemocracy.org/online-exchange-%E2%80%9Cdemocratic-deconsolidation%E2%80%9D.

Waldron, Jeremy. 1999. *Law and Disagreement*. Oxford: Oxford University Press.

Warren, Mark E. 2008. "Citizen Representatives." In M. E. Warren and H. Pearse, eds., *Designing Deliberative Democracy: The British Columbia Citizens Assembly*. Cambridge: Cambridge University Press.

Warren, Mark. 2013. "Citizen Representatives." In Jack H. Nagel and Rogers M. Smith, eds., *Representation: Elections and Beyond*. Philadelphia: University of Pennsylvania Press, 269–294.

Warren, Mark, and Hilary Pearse. 2008. *Designing Deliberative Democracy: The British Columbia Citizens' Assembly*. Cambridge: Cambridge University Press.

Weisberg, Michael, and Ryan Muldoon. 2009. "Epistemic Landscapes and the Division of Cognitive Labor." *Philosophy of Science* 76(2): 225–252.

Werner-Müller, Jan. 2016. *What Is Populism?* Philadelphia: University of Pennsylvania Press.

White, Jonathan, and Lea Ypi. 2016. *The Meaning of Partisanship*. Oxford: Oxford University Press.

Willemsen, Roger. 2014. *Das Hohe Haus: Ein Jahr im Parlament*. Frankfurt am Main: Fischer.

Williams, Melissa, ed. 2020. *Deparochializing Political Theory*. Cambridge: Cambridge University Press.

Winroth, Anders. 2012. *The Conversion of Scandinavia: Vikings, Merchants, and Missionaries in the Remaking of Northern Europe*. New Haven, CT: Yale University Press.

Wolff, Robert Paul. 1970. *In Defense of Anarchism*. New York: Harper & Row.

Yu, Harlan, and David G. Robinson. 2012. "The New Ambiguity of 'Open Government.'" *UCLA Law Review Discourse* 59: 178–208.

Zakaria, Fareed. 2018. "Democracy Is Decaying Worldwide. America Isn't Immune." *Washington Post*, February 22.

INDEX

A NOTE ON THE TYPE

This book has been composed in Adobe Text and Gotham.
Adobe Text, designed by Robert Slimbach for Adobe,
bridges the gap between fifteenth- and sixteenth-century
calligraphic and eighteenth-century Modern styles.
Gotham, inspired by New York street signs, was designed
by Tobias Frere-Jones for Hoefler & Co.